LITERATURE AND THE SOCIAL ORDER IN EIGHTEENTH-CENTURY ENGLAND

WORLD AND WORD SERIES
Edited by Professor Isobel Armstrong,
University of Southampton

ENGLISH HUMANISM:
WYATT TO COWLEY
Joanna Martindale

Literature and the Social Order

IN EIGHTEENTH-CENTURY ENGLAND

STEPHEN COPLEY

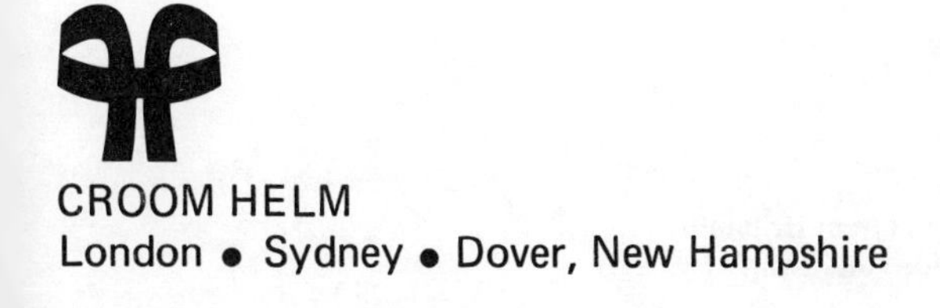

Croom Helm Ltd, Provident House, Burrell Row,
Beckenham, Kent BR3 1AT
Croom Helm Australia Pty Ltd, First Floor,
139 King Street, Sydney, NSW 2001, Australia

British Library Cataloguing in Publication Data

Copley, Stephen
Literature and the social order in
eighteenth-century England. –
(World and word series).
1. Great Britain – Social conditions –
18th century – Sources
I. Title II. Series
941.07 HN385

ISBN 0-7099-0755-9
ISBN 0-7099-3400-9 Pbk

Croom Helm, 51 Washington Street,
Dover, New Hampshire, 03820 USA

Library of Congress Cataloging in Publication Data

Copley, Stephen, 1954-
Literature and the social order in eighteenth-century
England.

(World and word series).
Bibliography: p. 198.
Includes index.
1. English literature – 18th century – History and
criticism – Sources. 2. Literature and society – England –
History – 18th century – Sources. 3. England – Social
conditions 18th century. 4. England – Economic conditions –
18th century. I. Title. II. Series.
PR448.S64C66 1984 820'.9'005 84-14940
ISBN 0-7099-0755-9
ISBN 0-7099-3400-9 Pbk

**Printed and bound in Great Britain by
Biddles Ltd, Guildford and King's Lynn**

CONTENTS

SERIES EDITOR'S PREFACE

The *World and Word* series, as its title implies, is based on the assumption that literary texts cannot be studied in isolation. The series presents to students, mainly of English literature, documents and materials which will enable them to have first-hand experience of some of the writing which forms the context of the literature they read. The aim is to put students in possession of material to which they cannot normally gain access so that they may arrive at an independent understanding of the inter-relationships of literary texts with other writing.

There are to be twelve volumes, covering topics from the Middle Ages to the twentieth century. Each volume concentrates on a specific area of thought in a particular period, selecting from religious, philosophical or scientific works, literary theory or political or social material, according to its chosen topic. The extracts included are substantial in order to enable students themselves to arrive at an understanding of the significance of the material they read and to make responsible historical connections with some precision and independence. The task of compilation itself, of course, predetermines to a great extent the kind of connections and relationships which can be made in a particular period. We all bring our own categories to the work of interpretation. However, each compiler makes clear the grounds on which the choice of material is made, and thus the series encourages the valuable understanding that there can be no single, authoritative account of the relationships between world and word.

Each volume is annotated and indexed and includes a short bibliography and suggestions for further reading. The *World and Word* series can be used in different teaching contexts, in the student's independent work, in seminar discussion, and on lecture courses.

Isobel Armstrong, University of Southampton

LITERATURE AND THE SOCIAL ORDER
IN EIGHTEENTH-CENTURY ENGLAND

INTRODUCTION

The passages in this anthology are taken from periodicals, pamphlets, general and philosophical works and more specialised economic treatises published between 1700 and 1776. They are broadly concerned with economics and related questions of social policy, and form part of an extensive literature on these subjects addressed largely to the 'polite' general reader. I have arranged them in various sections, covering the workings of the economy, the composition of the social establishment, the problems posed by the poor and the control of crime. These divisions are fairly arbitrary: many of the passages include general discussions of the nature of society, and most involve consideration of problems in two or three of my categories at once. As far as possible I have indicated this in cross-references throughout the book, and have suggested alternative connections that might be made between passages in the introductions to each section.

The works from which the passages are taken are published in a period of apparent political and social stability after the turmoil of the seventeenth century and before the rapid industrial development and consequent social upheaval of the early nineteenth century. As Christopher Hill has pointed out,[1] the 1688 Revolution determines the political structure of Britain for the next hundred years. The Revolution Settlement represents a victory for the great land-owning and merchant classes in society, which then form an unchallenged establishment, monopolising political and economic power and dominating the social life of the country throughout the eighteenth century. During that period, however, economic changes take place which affect the whole fabric of British society. In the late seventeenth century Britain's economy is predominantly rural and agricultural and its social structure still owes much to the legacy of feudal social organisation. By 1776 (the publication date of *The Wealth of Nations*, the latest work represented here) the country is established as a major commercial and imperial power, with a rapidly developing capitalist economy and most of the characteristic institutions of the nineteenth century bourgeois state.

The anthology is not intended to provide material for an empirical historical account of these changes. Instead I hope that it will give some idea of the ideological terms in which they are perceived, endorsed or contested by contemporaries, and provide a set of discursive contexts in which the imaginative literature of the period can be read. The changing nature of Britain's economy is discussed directly in a number of passages in the anthology. In other passages, the economic changes can be seen underlying debates about, for instance, the nature of social authority or the role and duties of the poor. In this introduction I want to examine the economic debates; later, in the introduction to each section, I will outline some of the ways in which the debates on other social issues can be related to this central discussion.

The ideological content of the debates which run through the anthology can be identified by considering each individual passage as a text, and using the techniques of literary analysis to examine the construction of the arguments it employs. A detailed analysis of an extract on these lines can reveal a considerable amount about the ideological construction of the work from which the extract is taken. One initial point about reading the passages is worth making. The arguments of any text are conceived in the discourses available at the time of writing. Each of these defines the subjects it will treat in distinctive ways, formulating and giving prominence to particular problems and effectively excluding others from consideration. In doing so each develops a characteristic vocabulary, establishes a particular order of priorities in its discussion and implies particular ideological valuations of the subjects it has defined. If we can identify the characteristics of a discourse we can begin to understand the texts constructed within it. Of course this involves certain problems. Discourses are not static or self-contained; although they are distinctive they are continually modified by the contexts in which they are found, and these modifications must be taken into account in any discussion of them. At the same time, elements of different discourses are often overlaid in the same text, and these must be differentiated before the text can be adequately described. Once this is done, it becomes possible to examine the text, not only following the literal argument it proposes, but also analysing the associations of the vocabulary it employs and the place of omissions, disjunctures, and elisions and ambiguities of meaning within it. This is where the tools of literary analysis are particularly useful: the ideological content of an argument resides in large part in these features of the text, which are essential to its construction and which often imply value judgements not openly admitted by the author. An analysis of the sort I have outlined makes them accessible to examination and critique.

The State and the Economy

Approaching the economic debates in the anthology in the way I have suggested, we can see that there is a striking change over the period in the forms of discourse available for the discussion of social and economic affairs. The works from which the extracts are taken stand at the end of a tradition of humanist writing about society, and mark the emergence of new forms of economic analysis of its working. Three broad discourses can be identified in the passages, one comprising versions of the tradition of civic humanism, one of Mandevillian economic analysis, and one of embryonic political economy. Each has distinctive preoccupations. In the humanist tradition, discussion of political and economic affairs is conducted in explicitly moral terms. The workings of the economy are considered in the course of larger debates about social ethics, the nature of the state and the conduct of state policy. In contrast, the new discourses of economic analysis offer to supply a 'scientific' analysis of the workings of the economy and of its place in society. In developing this analysis they gradually abandon the moral terms of humanism, and define the technical analytical terms on which the later study of economics depends.

The relation between these discourses is obviously complex. To a large extent, the new economic writings develop their distinctive terminology by redefining familiar humanist terms, and ridding them of their usual moral connotations. This can be seen very clearly throughout the anthology in debates on the place of luxury in society. As I will try to show later, the word 'luxury' has definite moral connotations in humanist writing, which are qualified and minimised when it is used in the economic writing. Our understanding of many of the passages depends on 'placing' the word in one discourse or the other, or – more problematically – admitting that it has an ambiguous status, drawing on connotations from both discourses. In the rest of this introduction I want to use details from the anthology to identify some of the characteristics of the discourses I have mentioned, and then outline the complex relation between discourses in a couple of passages.

Civic Humanism

The discourse of civic humanism develops in Renaissance and seventeenth century readings of classical republican texts. It rests on the assumption that the state is ideally governed according to certain ethical principles and that it depends for its well-being and continued existence on the virtues of the population. Texts within the discourse are marked by their preoccupation with the healthy existence or dissolution of the state, often discussed in terms of the metaphor of the healthy or diseased body-politic, and by their definition of the virtues that will preserve and the vices that will destroy it. In them, discussions of state policy and of the 'manners and principles' of the people are inseparable. In both areas a recognisable vocabulary of civic virtues (liberty, valour, frugality, military prowess) is set against a vocabulary of vices that will destroy the state (luxury, effeminacy, cowardice, corruption) and the texts offer exemplary advice to the members of the ruling establishment on the conduct of state policy and on the cultivation of the civic virtues of the population.

The presence of this tradition can be felt in virtually every passage in the anthology. In some its terms are consciously adhered to, in others they are equally consciously qualified or disputed. Justifications of the social order and accounts of the problems posed by criminals and the poor, for instance, constantly betray their origins in the humanist discussion of the nature of civic virtue, while the new discourses of economic analysis of the period define themselves by their departures from the recognised terms of the tradition.

The discourse of humanism appears in the anthology in two main versions, one aristocratic and one bourgeois. Aspects of the first can be seen in the passages from Shaftesbury and Bolingbroke, and of the second in those from Defoe, the periodicals and later political economy. The preoccupations that underlie both are at their clearest in John Brown's *An Estimate of the Manners and Principles of the Times* (passages 3.2 a and b). Brown's discussion is framed in ethical terms. Having laid out the laudable values of liberty, humanity and justice, in the first extract he considers contemporary manners as they 'affect the *Duration* of the *public State*'. Two points are particularly interesting in his discussion: its exclusive nature and the sources of social corruption he identifies. For the first, he is interested only in the manners and morality of the ruling classes – 'of those who *lead*, not of those who *are lead*; of those who *govern*, not of those who *are governed*; of those, in short, who *make* Laws or *execute* them'. The morality of the 'common People' is assumed to be of no consequence, even if he admits that, in moral terms, these people are 'in general much more irreproachable than their Superiors in Station'. Instead he treats them as the passive objects of government and control by their superiors, writing that 'an ungoverned Multitude . . . depends on some superior *Intelligence* to give it both *Impulse* and *Direction*'. This representation of class relations in the social hierarchy is echoed in many of the other passages and underlies many of the assessments of social morality and of the place of the poor to be found in them.

The other interesting feature of this passage is that Brown identifies the ruling 'Character of the Manner of our Times' as 'that of a "*vain*, *luxurious*, and *selfish* EFFEMINACY"', and (in passage 3.2b) traces its origin to the effects of 'our exorbitant Trade and Wealth'. This assessment of the effects of trade is typical of the attitudes adopted in a number of the other passages. It highlights an important feature of many civic humanist texts of the period. In its 'traditional' form, the discourse of humanism lacks a vocabulary to endorse the operations of trade and to account for the workings of a market economy in society: the former being regarded only as a source of social corruption, and the latter being seen to operate by standards far removed from any laudable criteria of civic virtue.

The 'aristocratic' reading of humanism emphasises this antipathy to trade, and the hierarchic exclusivity of the humanist discourse. Both features can be seen in the work of Anthony Ashley Cooper, Third Earl of Shaftesbury. Writing within the humanist tradition in *Characteristicks of Men, Manners, Opinions, Times*, Shaftesbury describes society as an ideal hierarchy regulated by a morally concerned paternalist aristocracy. For him the hierarchic social order is an organic part of the natural order of the world, and he makes the assumption throughout that the 'gentlemen' who constitute the ruling establishment in society are marked out by innate moral qualities which differentiate them from the rest of its members, and which qualify them for their place at its head. Social relations are characterised as reciprocal moral relations, comprising benevolence and indulgence on the part of the aristocracy and (largely presumed) subordination and deference on the part of their inferiors.

Something of Shaftesbury's position can be seen in passage 5.2, in his discussion of the need for 'a virtuous Administration' of society. Here he describes the social order by analogy with the organisation of '*private Familys*'. 'The Magistrate', at the head of society, is in the position of 'the Master of the Family', and Shaftesbury presents him as the only active agent in the whole. It is only by his regulation that the population is 'rais'd from Barbarity . . . civiliz'd by Laws, and made virtuous'; and it is his '*Example* which chiefly influences Mankind, and forms the Character and Disposition of a People'. Shaftesbury's exclusive concern in the passage is to offer exemplary advice to this magistrate on the regulation of the rest of society.

This concentration on the morality of the ruling class informs the other text from Shaftesbury (passage 1.1) where it emerges in a typical representation of the 'economy' of society. As I have mentioned, the discourse of aristocratic humanism lacks a vocabulary for analysing economic relations in society. In so far as economic issues arise they are treated as moral problems involving the right distribution and use of wealth that is taken to be already available, rather than as problems involving the relation between the production and consumption of that wealth. In this passage, Shaftesbury begins by considering the way 'Nature' orders the state of '*Brutes*, and other Creatures, who have not the Use of Reason or Reflection', and then compares '*Mankind*', writing 'it happens with *Mankind*, that whilst some are by necessity confin'd to Labour, others are provided with abundance of all things, by the Pains and Labour of Inferiors'. The hierarchic division between producers and consumers in society is taken as a providential fact of nature ('it happens with *Mankind* . . .'). This sense is reinforced by the ambiguity of 'by necessity', meaning either 'by economic necessity' or 'necessarily', and the passage continues as a discussion of the moral dangers of 'settled Idleness, Supineness, and Inactivity' among the 'superiour and easy sort'.

Shaftesbury's formulations of humanism provide a moral vocabulary of aristocratic paternalism that is adopted very widely in the eighteenth century, where it often emerges in 'Country' or Tory critiques of contemporary commercial society. In the 1720s and 1730s for example it is largely appropriated by writers in Bolingbroke's Country opposition circle, and forms a basis for their attacks on Walpole's administration and the Court and City interests it is taken to represent. In the *Letters on the Spirit of Patriotism* (passage 1.9), for example, Bolingbroke describes an exclusive class of men with innate abilities 'who engross almost the whole reason of the species, who are born to instruct, to guide and to preserve; who are destined to be the tutors and guardians of human kind', and then, with pointed reference to the state of contemporary society, dwells on the consequences when these men desert their divinely appointed duties in the social hierarchy. Similar formulations of aristocratic humanism will be found in the anthology in Berkeley, in John Brown himself, and in Goldsmith.

From early on in the century, an alternative version of the humanist tradition is developed by advocates of the newly emergent bourgeois society. In the works of Defoe, Addison, Steele and their contemporaries the value of an aristocratic governing élite in society remains unquestioned, but traditional humanism is redefined to accommodate commerce in its vocabulary of civic virtues, and the definition of the establishment is widened to celebrate the place and values of the middle class citizen.

Something of the first can be seen in Defoe's *Review*, Vol. VIII, No. 16 (passage 2.2). Defoe appropriates and reinterprets the traditional metaphor of the mutually dependent parts of the body politic to include trade, writing that 'for the Landed Men to rail at Trade, is like the Members Mutinying against the Belly – 'Tis from Trade as the Magazine, that Land receives its Value and Life'. The second redefinition is a constant preoccupation of the periodical writers. In *The Spectator*, No. 69 (passage 2.3), for instance, Addison writes 'there are not more useful Members in a Commonwealth than Merchants. They knit Mankind together in a mutual Intercourse of good Offices, distribute the Gifts of Nature, find Work for the Poor, add Wealth to the Rich and Magnificence to the Great.' Addison scrupulously observes the established order of society: the merchants are presented as servants of the 'Commonwealth' whose activities confirm the relative positions of its other members. However the terms in which they are described give them far more importance than this, implicitly associating them with the virtues of the statesman, the diplomat and the aristocrat. The reference to their ability to 'distribute' 'Gifts' and 'find Work for the Poor', for instance, carries overtones of charitable largesse appropriate to the activities of the aristocratic patron of the poor. In a similar vein, in *The Freeholder*, No. 1 (passage 1.5), he provides an 'apolitical' definition of the unified establishment of British freeholders, writing of 'a Freeholder in our Government being of the Nature of a Citizen of Rome in that famous Commonwealth', and so justifying the place and dignity of the middle class citizen alongside all the conventional (and conventionally opposed) subdivisions of established society – the 'Voter' or the 'Knight of the Shire', the 'Wit' or the 'Fox-Hunter', the 'Alderman' or the 'Courtier'.

Mandevillian Economics

In the writings of the early and mid-century, discussion of the economic workings of society is usually couched in the terms of Mandevillian economic analysis. Mandeville's *The Fable of the Bees* (passages 3.3a, b and c and 4.3a and b) represents a specific attack on Shaftesbury, and a larger attack on the basis of the tradition in which he writes – the assumption that the workings of society can be described in directly moral terms. In a doggerel poem, *The Grumbling Hive*, and a series of explanatory notes and supplementary articles to it, Mandeville expands his initial motto, 'private vices, public benefits', to 'demonstrate' that it is not the moral virtues but the 'vices' (and particularly the vices of consumption) of individuals that sustain civilised society. The *Fable* appears initially as a provocative satiric parody of the conventional moral orthodoxies of contemporary social debate. However, in the course of the book the satiric foundations on which it is based are developed as the foundation for a normative analysis of the economic workings of society. In this guise they are adopted rapidly and widely in the first half of the century, and provide a rationale in economic terms for the hierarchic order of contemporary society.

According to Mandeville the search for a moral sanction for this order is self-defeating. The whole social structure is motivated and maintained by the self-interested vices of fallen man and no class can claim the moral prerogative to power within it. The only division in society is between producers and consumers. Mandeville's accounts of the emergence of this division are worth dwelling on. Passage 4.3b, for instance, begins with a general statement about the fate of fallen man: 'The whole Earth being Curs'd, and no Bread to be had but what we eat in the sweat of our Brows, vast Toil must be undergone before Man can provide himself with Necessaries for his Sustenance.' 'Man' here is a single category embracing all men – the 'we' who 'eat in the sweat of our Brows'. As the passage continues the assumption is made that in civilised society the category 'man' will necessarily divide into the separate categories of 'producer' and 'consumer': 'It is impossible that a Society can long subsist, and suffer many of its Members to live in Idleness, and enjoy all the Ease and Pleasure they can invent, without having at the same time great Multitudes of People that to make good this Defect will condescend to be quite the reverse, and by use and patience inure their Bodies to work for others and themselves besides.' This hierarchic social division is presented as part of the 'mutual compact' of society. The sentence in which it is described reads as a sardonic parody of the humanist assumption that society relies on the moral leadership of those at its head. Here, society 'suffers' their existence, which represents a 'Defect', and is only compensated for by those below them who 'condescend' to work and in doing so themselves reveal the Christian virtue of 'patience'.

Despite this inversion, the *Fable* is by no means a levelling tract. For Mandeville the 'vices' of the rich consumers are socially useful because they stimulate the economy by creating the demand which keeps the poor at work: the same 'vices' inform the conduct of the poor and must be controlled by subsistence wages only because they interfere with their economic function as labourers. Social relations in the hierarchy are defined not as moral but as economic relations in the market, and the social hierarchy itself is redefined as a hierarchy of wealth, not of innate moral capacity.

Luxury in Society

Mandeville's argument rests on a provocative assessment of the place of luxury in society. 'Luxury' is a term of central importance in many of the texts in this anthology. In the discourse of humanism it is a moral term describing a range of vices of extravagance and indulgence – in Johnson's *Dictionary* it is defined as, amongst other things, 'voluptuousness', 'addictedness to pleasure', 'lust', 'lewdness' and 'luxuriance'. As John Sekora has pointed out;[2] in that discourse 'luxury' is the prime source of corruption for the individual and for the state. In the *Fable* and in the later discourse of political economy the word is progressively redefined as a term of economic analysis without condemnatory moral connotations. The process can be seen in various passages here.

In passage 3.1 Bishop Berkeley provides a clear example of the use of the word, in the moral discourse of humanism. He writes 'Frugality of Manners is the Nourishment and Strength of Bodies politic. It is that by which they grow and subsist, until they are corrupted by Luxury; the natural Cause of their Decay and Ruin.' Signs of luxury include 'the wearing of Gold and Silver', 'Vanity of Apparel' 'Gaming . . . Operas . . . Masquerades' and, in a blood-curdling quotation from Isaiah, evidence of sexual 'wantonness'. Its effects are economically destructive, for it prevents national 'retrenchment' and keeps taxes high. More importantly, it destroys the moral basis of society 'ennervate[s] and dispirit[s] the bravest People' 'debase[s] the Virtue and good Sense of our Gentry of both Sexes' and 'draweth after it a Train of Evils which cruelly infest the Public; Faction, Ambition, Envy, Avarice'. Further 'it is evident, that . . . Luxury (which like the other Fashions, never faileth to descend) hath infected all Ranks of People', and Berkeley therefore advocates the passing of 'sumptuary Laws' to control its spread.

Mandeville contests the 'receiv'd Notion, that Luxury is as destructive to the Wealth of the whole Body Politic, as it is to that of every individual Person who is guilty of it', and begins the process of redefinition of the word that I have mentioned. In passage 3.3b he defines it as 'every thing . . . that is not immediately necessary to make Man subsist as he is a living Creature'. This 'rigorous' definition effectively invalidates the word as a term of moral discrimination and establishes 'luxury' simply as a category of economic expenditure: 'If once we depart from calling every thing Luxury that is not absolutely necessary to keep a Man alive, that then there is no Luxury at all.' The only distinction he admits of in his discussion is the social one between the economically useful luxury of the rich and its unproductive counterpart in the poor. The way in which he establishes this distinction is typical of his arguments in the book as a whole. The passage is formulated as an ironic reflection by a distanced satiric commentator: 'what is call'd superfluous to some degree of People, will be thought requisite to those of higher Quality; and neither the World nor the Skill of Man can produce any thing so curious or extravagant, but some most Gracious Sovereign or other, if it either eases or diverts him, will reckon it among the Necessaries of Life; not meaning every Body's Life, but that of his Sacred Person.' By the time of 'Remark Y' (passage 3.3c) the satiric formulation of the 'Gracious Sovereign's' view of luxury has been incorporated in a series of authoritative 'Maxims' about social policy. Mandeville writes that 'it is manifest that I could never have imagined, that Luxury was to be made general through every part of a Kingdom', and insists 'I have laid down as Maxims never to be departed from, that the Poor should be kept strictly to Work, and that it was Prudence to relieve their Wants, but Folly to cure them.'

The relation between humanist and Mandevillian economic rationales of the social hierarchy is problematic. As we have seen they appear to be antithetical in a number of ways. In Mandeville's account, those at the head of society have no special abilities or pedigree to justify their place, which is an adventitious consequence of their wealth. Far from being society's moral guardians, they are the furthest removed from any of the criteria of social morality which might inform it. In ideological terms, the two versions of the hierarchy are often taken to represent opposed interests in society – the first justifying the existence of a traditional aristocratic social order which is threatened by the new monied order rationalised in the second. This is very much the position adopted by Bolingbroke and the Country opposition to Walpole, already mentioned. For these writers Mandeville stands as 'the philosopher of the new order', and their arguments are echoed in Tory writings throughout the period. However the interests of 'old' and 'new' social orders by no means represent polar oppositions in society. In many ways the two are closely mutually dependent and represent complementary elements in a complex establishment. As can be seen from Defoe and the periodical writers (passages 1.2-1.8 and 2.1-2.4) the way to advancement for the new monied interests is by alliance with, and incorporation into, the traditional order based on land. Equally the 'traditional' order has considerable investments, literal and ideological, in the new economy, which largely goes to confirm its position and power in society. Mandeville's analysis of an economy run entirely in the interests of the ruling establishment is often incorporated and accepted in writings defending the traditional social order which officially and strenuously dissociate themselves from it.

Fielding's *Enquiry* (passage 5.4)

The most extended example of the conflict between humanist and Mandevillian accounts of the hierarchy occurs in the passages from Fielding's *An Enquiry into the Causes of the Late Increase in Robbers*. The text is firmly anchored in the discourse of humanism. The problems posed by robbers are presented in the context of a discussion of the nature of the constitution, which reveals all the traditional humanist preoccupations with the health and moral well-being of the body politic. In Fielding's definition, 'the Constitution' is 'the Result of the Disposition of the several Parts' of which it is composed. It includes 'the Customs, Manners, and Habits of the People' and can be described by analogy with the natural body: 'here, as in the Natural Body, the Disorder of any one Part will, in its Consequence, affect the whole.' Fielding's vocabulary draws on the metaphor of the healthy or diseased organic body throughout: 'Constitution' itself can refer to the physical constitution, and 'Disposition' can mean either 'relative position' or 'mood, humour' (referring to the medical theory of the humours). In this context 'Disorder' means either 'lack of order' or (drawing on the body metaphor) 'medical disorder'. Each has different connotations when it is applied to society, and the argument of the *Enquiry* draws on both.

The particular 'Disorder' with which Fielding is concerned is the familiar one of luxury. In his assessment of its effects in society he moves between the moral/organic terms of the humanist discourse and a Mandevillian economic analysis that seems incompatible with them. According to his argument the introduction of trade has subverted the established order of society and 'totally changed the Manners, Customs, and Habits of the People, more especially of the lower Sort'. In particular it has tainted them with luxury. However he admits that although 'the

Philosopher perhaps, will think this a bad Exchange . . . the Politician finds many Emoluments to compensate all the moral Evils introduced by Trade, by which the Grandeur and Power of the Nation is carried to a Pitch that it could never otherwise have reached; Arts and Sciences are improved, and human Life is embellished with every Ornament, and furnished with every Comfort which it is capable of tasting.' Further he insists that trade and luxury are necessarily linked: 'as Riches are the *certain* Consequences of Trade, so is Luxury the no less *certain* Consequence of Riches.'

The conflicting judgements of 'the Philosopher' and 'the Politician' then run in parallel through the rest of Fielding's argument. To some extent the conflict between them is resolved by his concentration on the luxury of the lower classes. This represents a considerable shift in emphasis from 'traditional' humanist writing on luxury. In the passages of Shaftesbury and Berkeley quoted earlier, for example, the particular danger of luxury is that it will corrupt the morals of those at the head of society, 'the superiour and easy Sort' who should be its guardians. Here that effect is disregarded. The role of 'the Great' in society is defined in Mandevillian terms which make any moral criteria irrelevant. Fielding writes 'In Diversions, as in many other Particulars, the upper Part of Life is distinguished from the Lower. Let the Great therefore answer for the Employment of their Time, to themselves, or to their spiritual Governors. The Society will receive some temporal Advantage from their Luxury. The more Toys which Children of all Ages consume, the brisker will be the Circulation of Money, and the greater the Increase of Trade'.

Here, the moral dangers of luxury are of little importance. It is no longer presented as a moral 'Disorder' infecting the body politic, which must be cured to preserve its health. Instead it is seen as being economically appropriate to 'the Great', whose function in life is to consume luxury goods. The threat it presents is defined more narrowly as one of 'Disorder' in the social hierarchy. This only arises when luxury spreads to the lower classes and interferes with their work. In this context, Fielding advocates a series of pragmatic measures to control it, insisting that 'the Business of the Politician is only to prevent the Contagion from spreading to the useful Part of Mankind.' When he calls on moral prescriptions to reinforce his pragmatic defence of the social *status quo* they produce sharp disjunctures in his argument, as is apparent near the end of passage 5.4b: 'To be born for no other Purpose than to consume the fruits of the Earth is the Privilege (if it may be really called a Privilege) of very few. The greater Part of Mankind must sweat hard to produce them, or Society will no longer answer the Purposes for which it was ordained. *Six Days shalt thou labour*, was the positive Command of God in his own Republick.' The social hierarchy is seen as being providentially organised (it is 'ordained' and people are 'born for' purposes within it). However Fielding is strained in his attempt to accommodate 'the Great' within the providential design. Their economic 'Privilege' can only be accounted for by denying that it represents privilege at all, and they are the one section of society whose conduct expressly contradicts the 'positive Command of God' to the citizens of 'his own Republick'.

The conflicts in Fielding's account of the social hierarchy are echoed in many of the other passages. They can be traced very clearly in a single sentence from Goldsmith's *Citizen of the World*, Letter CI (passage 1.10). Goldsmith writes 'In every society some men are born to teach, and others to receive instruction; some to work, and others to enjoy in idleness the fruits of their industry; some to govern, and others to obey.' The three clauses seem to stand in parallel and to describe aspects of the same organic hierarchy in society. In the outer clauses the hierarchy is given implicit moral endorsement; those with an elevated position within it justify that position by being active and 'teaching' or 'governing' those below them, who are passive. In the middle clause the economic relation between those who 'work' and those who are 'idle' seems to be parallel to the other two. However, to preserve the parallel Goldsmith has to invert the hierarchy so that the active (and moral?) agents are now those at the bottom of society who work to support those whose 'idleness' has no moral sanction.

Political Economy

In the 1740s, particularly in Scotland, political economy begins to emerge as an important new discipline of social thought. The texts of political economy, represented here by passages from Hume, Tucker, Steuart and Adam Smith, are in every sense transitional. They mark the end of the humanist tradition and the beginnings of the discipline of scientific economics that develops more fully in the early nineteenth century. In them the traditional concerns of civic humanism are modified and to some extent displaced by an analysis of the workings of the market economy and of its place in society. In the course of this analysis a new order of priorities is gradually established in political discourse. According to this, man's economic activities in the market are taken to be the natural basis of his social existence, and the formations of society are presented as being dependent on the operations of the market. The economic analysis of society offered in this political economy owes a considerable amount to Mandeville. The ideological content of the passages I have included can be seen in part in the extensions and modifications of his arguments that appear in them, and in the attempts to incorporate those arguments within the framework of a humanist discussion of social policy.

As I have mentioned, Mandeville describes an economy that is motivated by the self-interested 'vices' of man. His argument is extended in each of these passages. In different ways each passage redefines Mandeville's 'vices' as natural human passions or propensities, and then argues that the market is the natural setting in which those passions can express themselves to the mutual good of all concerned. In each, this poses the problem of the relation between the market economy and the state within which it develops: to what extent can or should the former be regulated by the latter, and how should that regulation be exercised?

One response can be seen in the passages from Tucker and Steuart, both of whom explicitly advocate a division in society between those who are involved in the economy and those in the state who regulate it from above. In passage 3.6a Tucker writes of 'the natural Disposition of Mankind to *Commerce*', which derives from '*Self-Love* [which] is known to be the great Mover in human Nature'. He then goes on to discuss the ways in which the 'Legislature' can organise and make use of that 'Disposition', assuming that the 'Legislature' itself is outside and above the human nature it controls.

Similarly, at the opening of the Introduction to Book II of the *Principles of Political Oeconomy* (passage 3.8) Steuart writes that 'the principle of self-interest will serve as a general key to this inquiry; and it may, in one sense, be considered as the ruling principle of my subject, and may therefore be traced throughout the whole'. However he immediately makes a distinction between those who are motivated by this 'principle' and 'the statesman', who makes use of it 'in order to engage a free people to concur in the plans he lays down for their government': 'I beg I may not here be understood to mean, that self-interest should conduct the statesman: by no means. Self-interest, when considered with regard to him, is public spirit; and it can only be called self-interest when it is applied to those who are to be governed by it.' He expands the distinction throughout the passage, insisting for instance that 'public spirit, in my way of treating this subject, is as superfluous in the governed, as it ought to be all-powerful in the statesman . . . Were the principle of public spirit carried farther; were a people to become quite disinterested; there would be no possibility of governing them.' The divorce between the market and the state outlined here is essential to Steuart's argument. In the context of the market, 'self-interest' can be described as a natural 'ruling principle' informing human actions. In the context of the state, it is presented entirely as a mechanism of social control: the operation of 'self-interest' is precisely what makes a 'free' people governable, and it is manipulated to that end by 'the statesman'.

The passages from Hume and Smith are particularly interesting for their representations of the relation between the state and the market, and for their accounts of the controls that operate in each. At first sight the works of these two writers seem to differ considerably from those already discussed. In their separate ways, all the earlier English works justify the existence of a rigidly hierarchic and in many respects static social order. In comparison, these Scottish writers seem to propound the values of a relatively egalitarian society. Both of them, for instance, break with the general consensus of English writing that the wages of the labouring classes should be kept at subsistence level, and argue for a high wage economy. However, the values of hierarchic social division remain firmly inscribed in the texts of their political economy. They can be recognised largely in their definitions of the natural human proclivities that underlie the workings of the market.

The two passages from Hume's *Essays* show some of the consequences of his accommodation of an account of the market within the discourse of classical humanism. Passage 3.5 continues the redefinition of luxury, discussed earlier. Hume disagrees with Mandeville's proposition that 'vice' is generally advantageous to the state, but accepts in a more sophisticated analysis than Mandeville offers, that certain aspects of the vice of luxury can be seen to have social advantages. He identifies two forms of luxury. The first, 'innocent luxury', is defined as 'a refinement in the arts and conveniences of life', and he argues that, far from being incompatible with 'liberty', this form of 'luxury' promotes it. It 'nourishes commerce and industry', and, in a development of the bourgeois humanism mentioned earlier, 'draw[s] authority and consideration to that middling rank of men, who are the best and firmest basis of public liberty'. The other form, 'vicious luxury', has advantages in providing a remedy for other vices 'such as indolence, selfishness, [and] inattention to others'. He concedes that 'by banishing *vicious* luxury, without curing sloth and an indifference to others, you only diminish industry in the state, and add nothing to men's charity or their generosity', and concludes 'let us, therefore, rest contented with asserting, that two opposite vices in a state may be more advantageous than either of them alone; but let us never pronounce vice in itself advantageous.'

A similar definition of the place of luxury in society appears in passage 3.4. Here Hume argues that in 'a fortified camp' in which the population were motivated by 'so martial a genius, and such a passion for public good, as to make every one willing to undergo the greatest hardships for the sake of the public' luxury would indeed have deleterious effects. 'But as these principles are too disinterested and too difficult to support', it has a necessary place in the economy of a modern society. Hume's discussion here represents a considerable departure from the English writings on luxury discussed earlier. Instead of describing a society in which the luxury of rich consumers is supplied by the subsistence of poor producers, he envisages an economy in which luxury expenditure is generally prevalent, and all the members of society act both as producers and consumers. 'Luxury' here means both 'luxury goods' and 'the taste for luxury'. In the latter sense it is one of the 'passions' which stimulate 'labour' in society. Hume's representation of these 'passions' is interesting. In the last part of the passage he writes 'Every thing in the world is purchased by labour; and our passions are the only causes of labour.' The 'passions' are here treated as general human characteristics – they are described as '*our* passions'. As the passage continues, however, a distinction rather like that noticed in the passage from Steuart creeps in, between those who are affected by the 'passions' and those who manipulate them. Hume writes 'It is a violent method, and in most cases impracticable, to oblige the labourer to toil, in order to raise from the land more than subsists himself and family. Furnish him with manufactures and commodities, and he will do it of himself. Afterwards you will find it easy to seize some part of his superfluous labour, and employ it in the public service, without giving him his wonted return.'

Two points are interesting here. Firstly, the labourer's 'passions' are controlled not by 'the statesman', as in Steuart's account, but by an undefined 'you' introduced in the last sentence. The 'passions' of all the members of society are apparently subject to the same control: 'the case is the same with regard to the other members of the state.' However, Hume leaves open the question of where in society the 'you' who exercises this control is located. Secondly, he suggests that in this control 'the natural bent of the mind' is 'complied with'. There is an implicit suggestion throughout, however, that 'the passions' themselves are in large part socially constructed, and introduced into men's minds in order to govern them. In the last paragraph he writes that 'it is requisite to govern men by other passions, and animate them with a spirit of avarice and industry, art and luxury.' The claim that those who govern society 'animate' its members suggests that they have an active role in forming 'the natural bent of the mind', rather than merely making sure that it is 'complied with'. Throughout, Hume assumes a hierarchic division in society and a difference in nature between those who govern and those who are governed, similar to that noticed in the humanist texts discussed earlier. However, in his account this division is implicit rather than acknowledged, and is in part concealed by his claim that the economic and social orders develop in response to general human needs and propensities.

The new order of priorities in political economy is at its clearest in passage 3.9a from Adam Smith's *Inquiry into the Nature and Causes of the Wealth of Nations*. Here Smith describes the nature and working of the market economy and its place in society. He takes the cause of economic prosperity and progress to be 'the great multiplication of the productions of all the different arts, in consequence of the division of labour, which occasions, in a well-governed society, that universal opulence which extends itself to the lowest ranks of the people', and traces the division of labour itself to its source in 'human nature'. At the beginning of Chapter II he writes 'This division of labour, from which so many advantages are derived, is not originally the effect of any human wisdom, which forsees and intends that general opulence to which it gives occasion. It is the necessary, though very slow and gradual consequence of a certain propensity in human nature which has in view no such extensive utility; the propensity to truck, barter, and exchange one thing for another.'

Two points are immediately striking in Smith's account: his emphasis on the 'universal opulence' in society engendered by the market and his minimisation of the need for positive regulation in its operations. The first point develops the position already outlined by Hume. For Smith the members of all the 'ranks of society' behave as producers and consumers of surplus goods. In his paradigmatic description of transactions in the market he envisages 'workmen' supplying each other's needs, rather than existing at subsistence level to supply luxuries for others: 'Every workman has a great quantity of his own work to dispose of beyond what he himself has occasion for', and he trades it with other 'workmen'. Similarly, when Smith details the varieties of labour that go into the production of goods in a civilised society, the example he chooses is 'the accommodation of the most common artificer' rather than 'the more extravagant luxury of the great'.

The second point marks the major departure of political economy from the humanist preoccupation with the regulation of society and its economy. Smith mentions that the market must develop 'in a well-governed society', but does not dwell on the nature of that 'government'. In his account, the development of the market is not planned or regulated 'by any human wisdom which forsees and intends the general opulence to which it gives occasion'. It is the 'necessary . . . consequence' of the 'human propensity to truck, barter and exchange one thing for another' operating without intermediate social control. As he defines it, this 'propensity' is based entirely on self-interest: 'It is not from the benevolence of the butcher, the brewer, or the baker, that we expect our dinner, but from their regard to their own interest. We address ourselves, not to their humanity but to their self love, and never talk to them of our own necessities but of their advantage.' The universal operation of this self-interest in society produces a spontaneously self-regulating economy. In turn, the form of society and the character of its members are governed by the 'natural' developments in this economy, which are outside the realm of social regulation. Smith's account is the opposite of the representations of society with which I began, in which hierarchic social division was justified by the differences in the innate capacities of those at different levels in the hierarchy, and by the ability of those at the head of society to regulate the whole. For Smith, the distinctions between different members of society are the result of differences in their roles in the economy: 'The difference of natural talents in different men is, in reality, much less than we are aware of; and the very different genius which appears to distinguish men of different professions, when grown up to maturity, is not upon many occasions so much the cause, as the effect of the division of labour.' The humanist preoccupation with state regulation is displaced by an analytical description of the workings of the economy, and of the social formations it generates. Smith prepares the way for nineteenth century liberal economics, with its emphasis on the free operation of the market, and its advocacy of the political ethics of *laissez-faire*.

A Note on Literature

The 'polite' readers for whom the works represented in this anthology are produced also form the audience for the imaginative literature of the period. Comparisons between literary and non-literary accounts of society written for this audience allow us to identify the special characteristics of the literary texts, 'place' the discourses of imaginative literature in the larger context of discourses available at the time, and analyse the social myths that are reproduced in the literary works.

The most striking point to emerge from these comparisons is the selectivity of the imaginative literature. In various ways the literary representations of society and social behaviour exclude many of the concerns that are central to the non-literary texts. The pattern of these exclusions varies in different works, according to the particular literary forms that are employed, but in almost every case the exclusions themselves are at their clearest in the treatment of economic matters. Particular economic subjects such as trade, manufacturing, labour and the condition of the poor are peculiarly difficult to accommodate within the available forms of literary discourse and within the bounds of literary decorum. More generally, the literary texts seem to lack or exclude an appropriate vocabulary to describe and celebrate the workings of contemporary commercial society.

The exclusions of particular subjects are evident in two main ways; one 'positive' and one 'silent'. The first is particularly clear in the poetry of the period, which is constructed largely on the basis of classical poetic models, and adheres to rules of poetic decorum derived from them. Two such models that figure large in poetic celebrations of society are Pastoral and Georgic, each of which provides ideal fictions in which aspects of the contemporary world can be figured. Pastoral is the more obviously selective of the two, presenting an ideal that excludes 'realistic' representation of the place of labour in society and of the condition of the poor. Georgic provides a more open-ended model, idealising the virtues of a productive life in the country, and providing a possible basis for a larger treatment of industry in the economy as a whole. Indeed some poems such as John Dyer's *The Fleece* (1757) do attempt to employ both models in a celebration of the workings of the agricultural and industrial economy. However such poems are relatively few and far between and suffer in the eyes of contemporary criticism from the inappropriate vulgarity of their subject matter. About Dyer's project, for instance, Dr Johnson writes that 'the meannesss naturally adhering and the irreverence habitually annexed to trade and manufacture, sink him under insuperable oppression.'

'Silent' exclusions become apparent in a cumulative survey of a particular literary form. The novel, for instance, does not attempt a large-scale representation of the economy in the sense that Dyer's poem does or that later 'sociological' novels might be said to do. Either its primary focus of attention is the individual consciousness (as in Richardson) or, if it offers a larger social panorama (as in Fielding) it does so in terms that exclude the economic.

This last example leads us to the general point mentioned earlier. If we trace the social discourses identified in the introduction to the anthology as they appear in the field of literature, we find that the moral vocabulary of humanism is adopted very widely in literary texts, while the new vocabularies of economic analysis find virtually no place in them. The case is particularly clear if we compare the vocabulary of Shaftesburian humanism with that of Mandevillian economics. In the first half of the century the former appears largely in the overtly political context of Country Opposition writings, where it informs both polemical and literary works. Later it survives beyond the point at which it is drawn on in political debate as a specialised 'apolitical' vocabulary of literary representation. At the same time the vocabulary of Mandevillian economics scarcely appears in the realm of literary discourse except where it is parodied or burlesqued.

This polarisation suggests an important change in the configuration of discourses around imaginative literature over the period, which we can lay out in broad schematic terms. In the humanist tradition, discussion of cultural affairs is an essential part of political and social discourse, and literary culture is assumed to have a privileged position in the state. Shaftesbury's *Characteristicks* reflects this fully, being largely devoted to a discussion of the place and influence of polite literary culture in society. For Shaftesbury, this culture is essential for the humane education of the society's rulers, and for the generation of standards of morality that will permeate the social hierarchy. The new discourses of economics exclude any concern with cultural matters. As these discourses come to dominate the field of public and social debate, the cultural domain of literature is implicitly redefined as a specialised area of private response, with a specialised vocabulary of morality and humanity that is divorced from the language of public affairs.

Three examples will perhaps show how literary texts might be read in the light of the material in the anthology and in relation to this schematic outline of developments in the period.

Pope's *Epistles* to Bathurst and Burlington, both entitled *Of the Use of Riches* are among the few literary works of the time that attempt to accommodate a Mandevillian economic analysis of society alongside an orthodox humanist celebration of the moral values that should inform it. The Mandevillian analysis is clear in *Bathurst* (line 169ff.) and *Burlington* (line 169ff.). Beyond the questions that will arise in any close reading of the poem (Is the Mandevillian argument expounded or parodied? Are the Mandevillian and humanist accounts incorporated or juxtaposed?), we can perhaps argue that the inclusion of economic arguments in the poem is itself a polemical gesture aimed at preserving a literature whose domain includes public affairs, against the specialisation of discourses I have outlined.

In the case of Fielding's novels we might argue that the opposite is happening. The pamphlet included in the anthology involves economic arguments that are excluded from the fiction, which celebrates social values in the specialised vocabulary of literary humanity.

Finally, in Goldsmith's *The Deserted Village*, the lament for the destruction of village life wrought by trade draws on many of the issues we have examined, and culminates in a lament for the passing of pastoral, the 'appropriate' literary form to celebrate the values of the life that is destroyed. Our reading of the poem and of its arguments will be conditioned by the changes in the scheme of discourses that I have outlined. Depending on the status of poetry within that scheme, the poem will be read either as a polemical and political statement or as a personal lament and index of private sensibility.

Notes

1. Christopher Hill, *The Century of Revolution* (London, 1961).
2. John Sekora, *Luxury: The Concept in Western Thought, Eden to Smollett* (Baltimore, Maryland, 1977).

Textual Note

As far as possible, I have preserved eighteenth century spelling, punctuation and capitalisation in the passages included in the anthology, without correcting irregularities – which may be worthy of comment in themselves.

1 THE SOCIAL ESTABLISHMENT

Passages 1.1, 1.9 and 1.10 in this section provide accounts of the 'traditional' social order: the other passages discuss the relation between that order and the new middle classes. Passage 1.1, from Shaftesbury's *Characteristicks*, together with passage 5.2 from the same source, describes a natural hierarchy in society and defines the duties of those within it. In passage 1.9 Bolingbroke takes this 'natural' hierarchy as an ideal, and uses it as the basis for a critique of the contemporary establishment. Passage 1.10 presents a later Tory description of the order of society, and this has been discussed in the introduction.

The other passages show the spokesmen for an articulate middle class challenging the social position of the aristocracy and claiming their own right to a place within the establishment. The most brusquely assertive of them are those by Defoe (passages 1.6, 1.7 and 1.8), which dismiss any claims of the gentry to be treated with special respect over and above that afforded to the successful tradesman. The essays from *The Spectator*, *The Guardian* and *The Freeholder* (passages 1.2, 1.3 1.4 and 1.5) are less aggressive in tone, emphasising the unity of purpose of all the members of the establishment, and ensuring that the middle class citizen has a prominent place in any account of that unity. The most elaborate discussion comes in the *Spectator* essays (passages 1.2 and 1.3). The first takes the form of a discussion between the members of the Spectator Club about the mutual dependence of land and trade. The second is a fascinating example of appropriation by the affluent middle class of the life and mythology of the gentry. In his letter on retirement Sir Andrew Freeport adopts all the postures of the paternalist aristocrat and redefines them in his own terms. His account of 'being charitable in my way', for instance, involves 'setting my poor Neighbours to work, and giving them a comfortable Subsistence out of their own Industry', a formulation which combines a description of the charitable largesse of the patron towards his dependants with a description of the relation between the employer and his independent wage labourers.

Passage 1.1
(*from* Anthony Ashley Cooper, Earl of Shaftesbury, 'An Inquiry concerning Virtue, or Merit', Book 2, Part 2, Section 1, *Characteristicks*, 1711)

In *Brutes*, and other Creatures, who have not the Use of Reason or Reflection (at least not after the manner of Mankind) 'tis so order'd in Nature, that by their daily Search after Food, and their Application either towards the Business of their Livelihood, or the Affairs of their Species or Kind, almost their whole time is taken up, and they fail not to find full Imployment for their Passion, according to that degree of Agitation to which they are fitted, and which their Constitution requires. If any one of these Creatures be taken out of his natural laborious State, and plac'd amidst such a Plenty as can profusely administer to all his Appetites and Wants; it may be observ'd, that as his Circumstances grow thus luxuriant, his Temper and Passions have the same Growth. When he comes, at any time, to have the Accommodations of Life at a cheaper and easier rate than was at first intended him by Nature, he is made to pay dear for 'em in another way; by losing his natural good Disposition, and the Orderliness of his Kind or Species.

This needs not to be demonstrated by particular Instances. Whoever has the least knowledge of Natural History, or has been an Observer of the several Breeds of Creatures, and their ways of Life, and Propagation, will easily understand this Difference of Orderliness between the *Wild* and the *Tame* of the same Species. The latter acquire new Habits; and deviate from their original Nature. They lose even the common Instinct and ordinary Ingenuity of their Kind; nor can they ever regain it, whilst they continue in this pamper'd State: But being turn'd to shift abroad, they resume the natural Affection and Sagacity of their Species. They learn to unite in stricter Fellowship; and grow more concern'd for their Offspring. They provide against the Seasons, and make the most of every advantage given by Nature for the Support and Maintenance of their particular Species, against such as are foreign and hostile. And thus as they grow busy and imploy'd, they grow regular and good. Their Petulancy and Vice forsakes them with their Idleness and Ease.

It happens with *Mankind*, that whilst some are by necessity confin'd to Labour, others are provided with abundance of all things, by the Pains and Labour of Inferiours. Now, if among the superiour and easy sort, there be not something of fit and proper Imployment rais'd in the room of what is wanting in common Labour and Toil; if instead of an Application to any sort of Work, such as has a good and honest End in

Society (as Letters, Sciences, Arts, Husbandry, publick Affairs, Oeconomy, or the like) there be a thorow Neglect of all Duty or Imployment; a settled Idleness, Supineness, and Inactivity; this of necessity must occasion a most relax'd and dissolute State: It must produce a total Disorder of the Passions, and break out in the strangest Irregularitys imaginable.

We see the enormous Growth of Luxury in capital Citys, such as have been long the Seat of Empire. We see what Improvements are made in Vice of every kind, where numbers of Men are maintain'd in lazy Opulence, and wanton Plenty. 'Tis otherwise with those who are taken up in honest and due Imployment, and have been well inur'd to it from their Youth. This we may observe in the hardy remote Provincials, the Inhabitants of smaller Towns, and the industrious sort of common People; where 'tis rare to meet with any Instances of those Irregularitys, which are known in Courts and Palaces, and in the rich Foundations of easy and pamper'd Priests.

Passage 1.2

(Richard Steele, *The Spectator*, no. 174, 19 September 1711)
(Meetings of the fictional Spectator Club, referred to here and in passage 1.3, are described at various points in the run of *The Spectator*. Its members are taken as representative spokesmen for the different interests in established society.)

Haec memini & victum frustra contendere Thyrsin
Virg.[1]

There is scarce any thing more common than Animosities between Parties that cannot subsist but by their Agreement: This was well represented in the Sedition of the Members of the human Body in the old *Roman* Fable. It is often the Case of lesser confederate States against a superiour Power, which are hardly held together though their Unanimity is necessary for their common Safety: And this is always the Case of the landed and trading Interest of *Great Britain*; the Trader is fed by the Product of the Land, and the landed Man cannot be cloathed but by the Skill of the Trader; and yet those Interests are ever jarring.

We had last Winter an Instance of this at our Club, in Sir ROGER DE COVERLY and Sir ANDREW FREEPORT, between whom there is generally a constant, though friendly, Opposition of Opinions. It happened that one of the Company, in an historical Discourse, was observing, that

Carthaginian Faith was a proverbial Phrase to intimate Breach of Leagues. Sir ROGER said it could hardly be otherwise: That the *Carthaginians* were the greatest Traders in the World; and as Gain is the chief End of such a People, they never pursue any other: The Means to it are never regarded; they will, if it comes easily, get Money honestly; but if not, they will not scruple to attain it by Fraud or Cosenage: And indeed what is the whole Business of the Trader's Accompt, but to over-reach him who trusts to his Memory? But were that not so, what can there great and noble be expected from him whose Attention is for ever fixed upon ballancing his Books, and watching over his Expences? And at best, let Frugality and Parsimony be the Virtues of the Merchant, how much is his punctual Dealing below a Gentleman's Charity to the Poor, or Hospitality among his Neighbours?

Captain SENTRY observed Sir ANDREW very diligent in hearing Sir ROGER, and had a Mind to turn the Discourse, by taking Notice in general from the highest to the lowest Parts of human Society, there was a secret, tho' unjust Way among Men, of indulging the Seeds of ill Nature and Envy, by comparing their own State of Life to that of another, and grudging the Approach of their Neighbour to their own Happiness; and on the other Side, he who is the less at his Ease repines at the other who, he thinks, has unjustly the Advantage over him. Thus the civil and military List look upon each other with much ill Nature; the Soldier repines at the Courtier's Power, and the Courtier rallies the Soldier's Honour; or to come to lower Instances, the private Men in the Horse and Foot of an Army, the Carmen and Coachmen in the City-streets, mutually look upon each other with ill Will, when they are in Competition for Quarters or the Way in their respective Motions.

It is very well, good Captain, interrupted Sir ANDREW: You may attempt to turn the Discourse, if you think fit, but I must however have a Word or two with Sir ROGER; who, I see, thinks he has paid me off, and been very severe upon the Merchant. I shall not, continued he, at this Time remind Sir Roger of the great and noble Monuments of Charity and publick Spirit which have been erected by Merchants since the Reformation, but at present content my self with what he allows us, Parsimony and Frugality. If it were consistent with the Quality of so antient a Baronet as Sir Roger, to keep an Accompt or measure things by the most infallible Way, that of Numbers, he would prefer our Parsimony to his Hospitality. If to drink so many Hogsheads is to be hospitable, we do not contend for the Fame of that Virtue; but it would be worth while to consider, whether so many Artificers at work ten Days together by my Appointment, or so many Peasants made merry on

Sir ROGER's Charge, are the Men more obliged: I believe the Families of the Artificers will thank me, more than the Housholds of the Peasants shall Sir ROGER. Sir ROGER gives to his Men, but I place mine above the Necessity or Obligation of my Bounty. I am in very little Pain for the *Roman* Proverb upon the *Carthaginian* Traders; the *Romans* were their professed Enemies: I am only sorry no *Carthaginian* Histories have come to our Hands; we might have been taught perhaps by them some Proverbs against the *Roman* Generosity, in fighting for and bestowing other People's Goods. But since Sir Roger has taken Occasion from an old Proverb to be out of Humour with Merchants, it should be no Offence to offer one not quite so old in their Defence. When a Man happens to break in *Holland*, they say of him that *he has not kept true Accompts*. This Phrase, perhaps, among us would appear a soft or humorous way of speaking, but with that exact Nation it bears the highest Reproach; for a Man to be mistaken in the Calculation of his Expence, in his Ability to answer future Demands, or to be impertinently sanguine in putting his Credit to too great Adventure, are all Instances of as much Infamy, as with gayer Nations to be failing in Courage or common Honesty.

Numbers are so much the Measure of every thing that is valuable, that it is not possible to demonstrate the Success of any Action or the Prudence of any Undertaking without them. I say this in Answer to what Sir ROGER is pleased to say, That little that is truly noble can be expected from one who is ever poring on his Cash-book or ballancing his Accompts. When I have my Returns from abroad, I can tell to a Shilling by the Help of Numbers the Profit or Loss by my Adventure; but I ought also to be able to shew that I had Reason for making it, either from my own Experience or that of other People, or from a reasonable Presumption that my Returns will be sufficient to answer any Expence and Hazard; and this is never to be done without the Skill of Numbers. For Instance, if I am to trade to *Turkey*, I ought beforehand to know the Demand of our Manufactures there as well as of their Silks in *England*, and the customary Prices that are given for both in each Country. I ought to have a clear Knowledge of these Matters before-hand, that I may presume upon sufficient Returns to answer the Charge of the Cargo I have fitted out, the Freight and Assurance out and home, the Customs to the Queen, and the Interest of my own Money, and besides all these Expences a reasonable Profit to my self. Now what is there of Scandal in this Skill? What has the Merchant done that he should be so little in the good Graces of Sir ROGER? He throws down no Man's Enclosures, and tramples upon no Man's Corn; he takes nothing from the industrious Labourer; he pays the poor Man for his Work; he communicates his Profit with Mankind; by the Preparation of his Cargo and the Manufacture of his Returns, he furnishes Employment and Subsistence to greater Numbers than the richest Nobleman; and even the Nobleman is oblig'd to him for finding out foreign Markets for the Produce of his Estate, and for making a great Addition to his Rents; and yet 'tis certain that none of all these things could be done by him without the Exercise of his Skill in Numbers.

This is the Oeconomy of the Merchant, and the Conduct of the Gentleman must be the same, unless by scorning to be the Steward, he resolves the Steward shall be the Gentleman. The Gentleman no more than the Merchant is able without the Help of Numbers to account for the Success of any Action or the Prudence of any Adventure. If, for Instance, the Chace is his whole Adventure, his only Returns must be the Stag's Horns in the great Hall, and the Fox's Nose upon the Stable Door. Without Doubt Sir ROGER knows the full Value of these Returns; and if before-hand he had computed the Charges of the Chace, a Gentleman of his Discretion would certainly have hang'd up all his Dogs, he would never have brought back so many fine Horses to the Kennel, he would never have gone so often like a Blast over Fields of Corn. If such too had been the Conduct of all his Ancestors, he might truly have boasted at this Day that the Antiquity of his Family had never been sullied by a Trade; a Merchant had never been permitted with his whole Estate to purchase a Room for his Picture in the Gallery of the COVERLYS, or to claim his Descent from the Maid of Honour. But 'tis very happy for Sir ROGER that the Merchant paid so dear for his Ambition. 'Tis the Misfortune of many other Gentlemen to turn out of the Seats of their Ancestors, to make Way for such new Masters as have been more exact in their Accompts than themselves; and certainly he deserves the Estate a great deal better who has got it by his Industry, than he who has lost it by his Negligence.

Passage 1.3

(Joseph Addison, *The Spectator*, No. 549, 29 November 1712)

Quamvis digressu veteris confusus amici,
Laudo tamen . . .

Juv.[2]

I believe most People begin the World with a Resolution to withdraw from it into a serious kind of Solitude or Retirement, when they have made themselves easie in it. Our Unhappiness is, that we find out some Excuse or other for deferring such our good Resolutions till our intended Retreat is cut off by Death. But among all kinds of People there are none who are so hard to part with the World, as those who are grown old in the heaping up of Riches. Their Minds are so warped with their constant Attention to Gain, that it is very difficult for them to give their Souls another Bent, and convert them towards those Objects, which, though they are proper for every Stage of Life, are so more especially for the last. *Horace* describes an old Usurer as so charmed with the Pleasures of a Country Life, that in order to make a Purchase he called in all his Mony; but what was the event of it? Why in a very few Days after he put it out again. I am engaged in this Series of Thought by a Discourse which I had last Week with my worthy Friend Sir ANDREW FREEPORT, a Man of so much natural Eloquence, good Sense, and Probity of Mind, that I always hear him with a particular Pleasure. As we were sitting together, being the sole remaining Members of our Club, Sir ANDREW gave me an Account of the many busie Scenes of Life in which he had been engaged, and at the same time reckoned up to me abundance of those lucky Hits, which at another time he would have called pieces of good Fortune; but in the Temper of Mind he was then, he termed them Mercies, Favours of Providence, and Blessings upon an honest Industry. Now, says he, you must know, my good Friend, I am so used to consider my self as Creditor and Debtor, that I often state my Accounts after the same manner, with regard to Heaven and my own Soul. In this case, when I look upon the Debtor-side, I find such innumerable Articles, that I want Arithmetick to cast them up; but when I look upon the Creditor-side, I find little more than blank Paper. Now tho' I am very well satisfied that it is not in my power to ballance Accounts with my Maker, I am resolved however to turn all my future Endeavours that way. You must not therefore be surprized, my Friend, if you hear that I am betaking my self to a more thoughtful kind of Life, and if I meet you no more in this Place.

I could not but approve so good a Resolution, notwithstanding the Loss I shall suffer by it. Sir ANDREW has since explained himself to me more at large in the following Letter, which is just come to my Hands.

'*Good Mr* SPECTATOR,

Notwithstanding my Friends at the Club have always rallied me, when I have talked of retiring from Business, and repeated to me one of my own Sayings, *that a Merchant has never enough till he has got a little more*, I can now inform you that there is one in the World who thinks he has enough, and is determined to pass the Remainder of his Life in the Enjoyment of what he has. You know me so well, that I need not tell you, I mean, by the Enjoyment of my Possessions, the making of them useful to the Publick. As the greatest Part of my Estate has been hitherto of an unsteady and volatile Nature, either tost upon Seas or fluctuating in Funds; it is now fixt and settled in Substantial Acres and Tenements. I have removed it from the Uncertainty of Stocks, Winds and Waves, and disposed of it in a considerable Purchase. This will give me great Opportunity of being charitable in my way, that is in setting my poor Neighbours to Work, and giving them a comfortable Subsistence out of their own Industry. My Gardens, my Fishponds, my Arable and Pasture Grounds shall be my several Hospitals, or rather Work-houses, in which I propose to maintain a great many indigent Persons, who are now starving in my Neighbourhood. I have got a fine Spread of improveable Lands, and in my own Thoughts am already plowing up some of them, fencing others; planting Woods, and draining Marshes. In fine, as I have my Share in the Surface of this Island, I am resolved to make it as beautiful a Spot as any in Her Majesty's Dominions; at least there is not an Inch of it which shall not be cultivated to the best Advantage, and do its utmost for its Owner. As in my Mercantile Employment, I so disposed of my Affairs, that from whatever Corner of the Compass the Wind blew, it was bringing home one or other of my Ships; I hope, as a Husband-man, to contrive it so, that not a Shower of Rain, or a Glimpse of Sunshine, shall fall upon my Estate without bettering some part of it, and contributing to the Products of the Season. You know it has been hitherto my Opinion of Life, that it is thrown away when it is not some way useful to others. But when I am riding out by my self, in the fresh Air on the open Heath that lies by my House, I find several other Thoughts growing up in me. I am now of Opinion, that a Man of my Age may find Business enough on himself, by setting his Mind in order, preparing it for another World, and reconciling it to the Thoughts of Death. I must, therefore, acquaint you, that besides those usual Methods of Charity, of which I have spoken, I am at this very Instant finding out a convenient Place where I may build an Alms-house, which I intend to endow very handsomely, for a Dozen superannuated Husbandmen. It will be a great Pleasure to me to say my Prayers twice a Day with Men of my own Years, who all of them, as well as my self, may have their Thoughts taken up how they shall die, rather than how they shall live. I remember an excellent Saying, that I learned at School, *Finis coronat opus*. You know best whether it be in *Virgil* or in *Horace*, it is my business to apply it. If your Affairs will permit you to take the Country Air with me sometimes, you shall find an Apartment fitted up for you, and shall be every Day entertained with Beef or Mutton of my own feeding; Fish out of my own Ponds; and Fruit out of my own Gardens. You shall have free Egress and Regress about my House, without having any Questions asked you, and in a Word such an hearty Welcome as you may expect from

Your most sincere Friend
and humble Servant,
ANDREW FREEPORT'

The Club of which I am a Member being entirely dispersed, I shall consult my Reader next Week, upon a Project relating to the Institution of a new one.

Passage 1.4
(Richard Steele, *The Guardian*, No. 137, 18 August 1713)

sanctus haberi
Justitiaeque tenax, factis dictisque mereris?
Agnosco procerem

Juv.[3]

Horace, *Juvenal*, *Boileau*, and indeed the greatest Writers in almost every Age, have exposed, with all the Strength of Wit and good Sense, the Vanity of a Man's valuing himself upon his Ancestors, and endeavoured to show that true Nobility consists in Virtue, not in Birth. With Submission however to so many great Authorities, I think they have pushed this matter a little too far. We ought in Gratitude to Honour the Posterity of those who have raised either the Interest or Reputation of their Conntry, and by whose Labours we our selves are more Happy, Wise or Virtuous than we should have been without them. Besides, naturally speaking, a Man bids fairer for Greatness of Soul, who is the Descendant of worthy Ancestors, and has good Blood in his Veins, than one who is come of an ignoble and obscure Parentage. For these Reasons I think a Man of Merit, who is derived from an Illustrious Line, is very justly to be regarded more than a Man of equal Merit who has no Claim to Hereditary Honours. Nay, I think those who are indifferent in themselves, and have nothing else to distinguish them but the Virtues of their Forefathers, are to be looked upon with a degree of Veneration even upon that account, and to be more respected than the common Run of Men who are of low and vulgar Extraction.

After having thus ascribed due Honours to Birth and Parentage, I must however take Notice of those who arrogate to themselves more Honours than are due to them on this Account. The first are such who are not enough sensible that Vice and Ignorance taint the Blood, and that an unworthy Behaviour degrades, and disennobles a Man, in the Eye of the World, as much as Birth and Family aggrandize and exalt him.

The second are those who believe a *new* Man of an elevated Merit is not more to be honoured than an insignificant and worthless Man who is descended from a long Line of Patriots and Heroes: Or, in other Words, behold with Contempt a Person who is such a Man as the first Founder of their Family was, upon whose Reputation they value themselves.

But I shall chiefly apply myself to those whose Quality sits uppermost in all their Discourses and Behaviour. An empty Man of a great Family is a Creature that is scarce conversible. You read his Ancestry in his Smile, in his Air, in his Eye-brow. He has indeed nothing but his Nobility to give Employment to his Thoughts. Rank and Precedency are the important Points which he is always discussing within himself. A Gentleman of this Turn begun a Speech in one of King *Charles's* Parliaments: *Sir, I had the Honour to be born at a time* – upon which a rough honest Gentleman took him up short, *I would fain know what that Gentleman means, Is there any one in this House that has not had the Honour to be born as well as himself?* The good Sense which reigns in our Nation has pretty well destroyed this starched Behaviour among Men who have seen the World, and know that every Gentleman will be treated upon a Foot of Equality. But there are many who have had their Education among Women, Dependants or Flatterers, that lose all the Respect, which would otherwise be paid them, by being too assiduous in procuring it.

My Lord *Froth* has been so educated in Punctilio, that he governs himself by a Ceremonial in all the ordinary Occurrences of Life. He Measures out his Bow to the degree of the Person he converses with. I have seen him in every Inclination of the Body, from a familiar Nod to the low Stoop in the Salutation-Sign. I remember five of us, who were acquainted with one another, met together one Morning at his Lodgings, when a Wag of the Company was saying, it wou'd be worth while to observe how he would distinguish us at his first Entrance. Accordingly he no sooner came into the Room, but casting his Eye about, *My Lord such a one*, says he, *your most humble Servant. Sir* Richard *your humble Servant. Your Servant Mr* Ironside. *Mr* Ducker, *how do you do? Hah!* Frank *are you there?*

There is nothing more easie than to discover a Man whose Heart is full of his Family. Weak Minds that have imbibed a strong Tincture of the Nursery, younger Brothers that have been brought up to nothing, Superannuated Retainers to a great House, have generally their Thoughts taken up with little else.

I had some Years ago an Aunt of my own, by Name Mrs *Martha Ironside*, who would never Marry beneath herself, and is supposed to have died a Maid in the Fourscorth Year of her Age. She was the Chronicle of our Family, and past away the greatest part of the last Forty Years of her Life in recounting the Antiquity, Marriages, Exploits and Alliances of the *Ironsides*. Mrs *Martha* conversed generally with a knot of old Virgins, who were likewise of good Families, and had been very cruel at the beginning of the last Century. They were every one of 'em as proud as *Lucifer*, but said their Prayers twice a Day, and in all other respects were the best Women in the World. If they saw a fine Petticoat at Church, they immediately took to Pieces the Pedigree of her that wore it, and would lift up their Eyes to Heaven at the Confidence of the sawcy Minx when they found she was an honest Tradesman's Daughter. It is impossible to describe the pious Indignation that would rise in them at the sight of a Man who lived plentifully on an Estate of his own getting. They were transported with Zeal beyond measure, if they heard of a young Woman's matching into a great Family upon account only of her Beauty, her Merit, or her Mony. In short, there was not a Female within ten Miles of them that was in Possession of a Gold Watch, a Pearl Necklace, or a Piece of *Mechlin* Lace, but they examined her Title to it. My Aunt *Martha* used to chide me very frequently for not sufficiently valuing my self. She would not eat a Bit all Dinner-time, if at an Invitation she found she had been seated below her self: and would frown upon me for an Hour together, if she saw me give place to any Man under a Baronet. As I was once talking to her of a wealthy Citizen whom she had refused in her Youth, she declared to me with great warmth, that she preferred a Man of Quality in his Shirt to the richest Man upon the Change in a Coach and Six. She pretended, that our Family was nearly related by the Mother's Side to half a dozen Peers; but as none of them knew any thing of the matter, we always kept it as a Secret among our selves. A little before her Death she was reciting to me the History of my Fore-fathers; but dwelling a little longer than ordinary upon the Actions of Sir *Gilbert Ironside*, who had a Horse shot under him at *Edghill* Fight, I gave an unfortunate *Pish*, and asked, *What was all this to me?* upon which she retired to her Closet, and fell a Scribling for three Hours together, in which time, as I afterwards found, she struck me out of her Will, and left all she had to my Sister *Margaret*, a wheedling Baggage, that used to be asking Questions about her great Grandfather from Morning to Night. She now lies buried among the Family of the *Ironsides*, with a Stone over her, acquainting the Reader, that she died at the Age of Eighty Years, a Spinster, and that she was descended of the Ancient Family of the *Ironsides* – After which follows the Genealogy drawn up by her own Hand.

Passage 1.5
(Joseph Addison, *The Freeholder*, No. 1, 23 December 1715)

> *Rara temporum felicitas, ubi sentire*
> *quae velis, et quae sentias dicere licet.*
> Tacit.[4]

The Arguments of an Author lose a great deal of their Weight, when we are perswaded that he only writes for Argument's sake, and has no real Concern in the Cause which he espouses. This is the Case of one, who draws his Pen in the Defence of Property, without having any; except, perhaps, in the Copy of a Libel, or a Ballad. One is apt to suspect, that the Passion for Liberty which appears in a Grub-street Patriot, arises only from his Apprehensions of a Gaol; and that, whatever he may pretend, he does not write to secure, but to get something of his own: Should the Government be overturn'd, he has nothing to lose but an old Standish.

I question not but the Reader will conceive a Respect for the Author of this Paper from the Title of it; since, he may be sure, I am so considerable a Man, that I cannot have less than Forty Shillings a Year.

I have rather chosen this Title than any other, because it is what I most glory in, and what most effectually calls to my Mind the Happiness of that Government under which I live. As a *British* Free-holder, I should not scruple taking place of a *French* Marquis; and when I see one of my Countrymen amusing himself in his little Cabbage-Garden, I naturally look upon him as a greater Person than the Owner of the richest Vineyard in *Champagne*.

The House of Commons is the Representative of men in my Condition. I consider myself as one who give my Consent to every law which passes: A Free-holder in our Government being of the Nature of a Citizen of *Rome* in that famous Commonwealth, who, by the Election of a Tribune, had a kind of remote Voice in every Law that was enacted.

So that a Free-holder is but one Remove from a Legislator, and for that Reason ought to stand up in the Defence of those Laws, which are in some degree of his own making. For such is the Nature of our happy Constitution, that the Bulk of the People virtually give their Approbation to every thing they are bound to obey, and prescribe to themselves those Rules by which they are to walk.

At the same time I declare I am a Free-holder, I do not exclude myself from any other Title. A Free-holder may be either a Voter, or a Knight of the Shire; a Wit, or a Fox-hunter; a Scholar, or a Soldier; an Alderman, or a Courtier; a Patriot, or a Stock-Jobber. But I chuse to be distinguish'd by this Denomination, as the Free-holder is the Basis of all other Titles. Dignities may be grafted upon it; but this is the substantial Stock, that conveys to them their Life, Taste and Beauty; and without which they are no more than Blossoms, that would fall away with every Shake of Wind.

And here I cannot but take occasion to congratulate my Country upon the Increase of this happy Tribe of Men, since, by the Wisdom of the present Parliament, I find the Race of Free-holders spreading into the remotest Corners of the Island. I mean that Act which pass'd in the late Session for Encouragement of Loyalty in *Scotland*: By which it is provided, *That all and every Vassal and Vassals in* Scotland *who shall continue peaceable, and in dutiful Allegiance to His Majesty, His Heirs and Successors, holding Lands or Tenements of any Offender* [guilty of High-Treason] *who holds such Lands or Tenements immediately of the Crown, shall be vested and seized, and are hereby enacted and ordained to hold the said Lands or Tenements of His Majesty, His Heirs and Successors, in Fee and Heritage for ever, by such manner of Holding, as any such Offender held such Lands or Tenements of the Crown, &c.*

By this means it will be in the Power of a Highlander to be at all Times a good Tenant, without being a Rebel; and to deserve the Character of a faithful Servant, without thinking himself obliged to follow his Master to the Gallows.

How can we sufficiently extol the Goodness of His present Majesty, who is not willing to have a single Slave in His Dominions! Or enough rejoyce in the Exercise of that Loyalty, which, instead of betraying a Man into the most ignominious Servitude, (as it does in some of our neighbouring Kingdoms) entitles him to the highest Privileges of Freedom and Property! It is now to be hoped, that we shall have few Vassals, but to the Laws of our Country.

When these Men have a taste of Property, they will naturally love that Constitution from which they derive so great a Blessing. There is an unspeakable Pleasure in calling any thing one's own. A Free-hold, tho' it be but in Ice and Snow, will make the Owner pleased in the Possession, and stout in the Defence of it; and is a very proper Reward of our Allegiance to our present King, who (by an unparallel'd Instance of Goodness in a Sovereign, and Infatuation in Subjects) contends for the Freedom of His People against Themselves; and will not suffer many of them to fall into a State of Slavery, which they are bent upon with so much Eagerness and Obstinacy.

A Free-holder of *Great Britain*, is bred with an Aversion to every Thing that tends to bring him under a Subjection to the arbitrary Will of another. Of this we find frequent Instances in all our Histories; where the Persons, whose Characters are the most amiable, and strike us with the highest Veneration, are those who stood up manfully against the Invasions of Civil Liberty, and the complicated Tyranny which Popery imposes upon our Bodies, our Fortunes, and our Minds. What a despicable Figure then must the present Mock-Patriots make in the Eyes of Posterity, who venture to be hang'd, drawn and quartered, for the Ruin of those Civil Rights which their Ancestors rather than part with, chose to be cut to Pieces in the Field of Battle. And what an Opinion will after Ages entertain of their Religion, who bid fair for a Gibbet, by endeavouring to bring in a Superstition, which their Forefathers perished in Flames to keep out.

But how Instructive soever the Folly of these Men may prove to future Times, it will be my Business more immediately to consult the Happiness of the Age in which I live. And since so many profligate Writers have endeavoured to varnish over a bad Cause, I shall do all in my Power to recommend a good One, which indeed requires no more than barely to explain what it is. While many of my gallant Countrymen are employed in pursuing Rebels half discomfited through the Consciousness of their Guilt, I shall labour to improve those Victories to the Good of my Fellow-Subjects; by carrying on our Successes over the Minds of Men, and by reconciling them to the Cause of their King, their Country, and their Religion.

To this End, I shall in the Course of this Paper, (to be published every *Monday* and *Friday*) endeavor to open the Eyes of my Countrymen to their own Interests, to shew them the Privileges of an *English* Free-holder which they enjoy in common with my self, and to make them sensible how these Blessings are secured to us by his Majesty's Title, his Administration, and his Personal Character.

I have only one Request to make to my Readers, that they will peruse these Papers with the same Candour and Impartiality in which they are written; and shall hope for no other Prepossession in favour of them, than what one would think should be natural to every Man, a Desire to be happy, and a good Will towards those, who are the Instruments of making them so.

Passage 1.6
(*from* Daniel Defoe, Letter XXII, *The Complete English Tradesman*, 1726)

Of the Dignity of Trade in England *more than in other Countries*

Sir,
It is said of *England* by way of distinction, and we all value ourselves upon it, that it is a trading country; and King *Charles* II, who was perhaps the Prince of all the Kings that ever reign'd in *England*, that best understood the country and the people that he govern'd, us'd to say, *That the Tradesmen were the only Gentry in* England: His Majesty spoke it merrily, but it had a happy signification in it, such as was peculiar to the best Genius of that Prince, who, tho' he was not the bright governor, was the best acquainted with the world, of all the Princes of his age, if not of all the men in it; and tho' it be a digression give me leave, after having quoted the King, to add three short observations of my own, in favour of *England*, and of the people and trade of it, and yet without the least partiality to our own country.

I. We are not only a trading country, but the greatest trading country in the world.
II. Our climate is the most agreeable climate in the world to live in.
III. Our *Englishmen* are the stoutest and best men (I mean what we call men of their hands) in the world.

These are great things to advance in our own favour, and yet to pretend not to be partial too; and therefore I shall give my reasons, which I think support my opinion, and they shall be as short as the heads themselves, that I may not go too much off from my subject.

1. We are the greatest trading country in the world, because we have the greatest exportation of the growth and product of our land, and of the manufacture and labour of our people; and the greatest importation and consumption of the growth, product, and manufactures of other countries from abroad, of any nation in the world.

2. Our climate is the best and most agreeable, because a man can be more out of doors in *England* than in other countries. This was King

Charles the second's reason for it; and I cannot name it, without doing justice to his Majesty in it.

3. Our men are the *stoutest* and *best*, because strip them naked from the wast upwards, and give them no weapons at all but their Hands and Heels, and turn them into a room, or stage, and lock them in with the like number of other men of any nation, man for man, and they shall beat the best men you shall find in the world.

From this digression, which I hope will not be disagreeable, as it is not very tedious, I come back to my first observation, that *England* is a trading country; and two things I offer from that head.

First, Our tradesmen are not, as in other countries, the meanest of our people.

Secondly, Some of the greatest and best, and most flourishing families among not the gentry only, but even the nobility, have been rais'd from trade, owe their beginning, their wealth, and their estates to trade; and I may add,

Thirdly, Those families are not at all ashamed of their original, and indeed have no occasion to be ashamed of it.

It is true, that in *England* we have a numerous and an illustrious Nobility and Gentry; and it is true also, that not so many of those families have rais'd themselves by the sword as in other nations, though we have not been without men of fame in the field too.

But *Trade* and *Learning* has been the two chief steps, by which our gentlemen have rais'd their relations, and have built their fortunes; and from which they have ascended up to the prodigious height, both in wealth and number, which we see them now risen to.

As so many of our noble and wealthy families are rais'd by, and derive from trade, so it is true, and indeed it cannot well be otherwise, that many of the younger branches of our gentry, and even of the nobility it self, have descended again into the spring from whence they flow'd, and have become tradesmen; and thence it is, that, as I said above, our tradesmen in *England* are not, *as it generally is in other countries*, always of the meanest of our people.

Indeed I might have added here, that trade it self in *England* is not, as it generally is in other countries, the meanest thing the men can turn their hand to; but on the contrary trade is the readiest way for men to raise their fortunes and families; and therefore it is a field for men of figure and of good families to enter upon.

NB By trade we must be understood to include Navigation, and foreign discoveries, because they are generally speaking all promoted and carried on by trade, and even by tradesmen, as well as merchants;

and the tradesmen are at this time as much concern'd in shipping (as Owners) as the merchants, only the latter may be said to be the chief employers of the shipping.

Having thus done a particular piece of justice to ourselves, in the value we put upon trade and tradesmen in *England*, it reflects very much upon the understandings of those refin'd heads, who *pretend to* depreciate that part of the nation, which is so infinitely superiour in number and in wealth to the families who call themselves gentry, and so infinitely more numerous.

As to the wealth of the nation, that undoubtedly lies chiefly among the trading part of the people; and tho' there are a great many families rais'd within few years, in the late war by great employments, and by great actions abroad, to the honour of the *English* Gentry; yet how many more families among the tradesmen have been rais'd to immense estates, even during the same time, by the attending circumstances of the war? such as the cloathing, the paying, the victualling and furnishing, *&c.* both army and navy? And by whom have the prodigious taxes been paid, the loans supplied, and money advanced upon all occasions? By whom are the Banks and Companies carried on? And on whom are the Customs and Excises levied? Has not the trade and tradesmen born the burthen of the war? And do they not still pay four millions a year interest for the publick debts? On whom are the funds levied, and by whom the publick credit supported? Is not trade the inexhausted fund of all funds, and upon which all the rest depend?

As in the trade, so in proportion are the tradesmen; and how wealthy are tradesmen in almost all the several parts of *England*, as well as in *London*? How ordinary is it to see a tradesman go off of the stage, even but from mere shop-keeping, with, from ten to forty thousand pounds estate, to divide among his family? when, on the contrary, take the gentry in *England* from one end to the other, except a few here and there, what with excessive high living, which is of late grown so much into a disease, and the other ordinary circumstances of families, we find few families of the lower gentry, that is to say, from six or seven hundred a year downwards, but they are in debt and in necessitous circumstances, and a great many of greater estates also.

On the other hand, let any one who is acquainted with *England*, look but abroad into the several countries, especially near *London*, or within fifty miles of it: How are the antient families worn out by time and family misfortunes, and the estates possess'd by a new race of tradesmen, grown up into families of gentry, and establish'd by the immense wealth, gain'd, as I may say, behind the counter; that is, in the shop, the warehouse, and the compting-house? How are the sons of tradesmen rank'd among the prime of the gentry? How are the daughters of tradesmen at this time adorn'd with the ducal coronets, and seen riding in the coaches of the best of the nobility? Nay, many of our trading gentlemen at this time refuse to be Ennobled, scorn being knighted, and content themselves with being known to be rated among the richest Commoners in the nation: And it must be acknowledg'd, that whatever they be as to court-breeding, and to manners, they, generally speaking, come behind none of the gentry in knowledge in the world.

At this very day we see the son of Sir *Thomas Scawen* match'd into the ducal family of *Bedford*, and the son of Sir *James Bateman* into the princely house of *Marlborough*, both whose ancestors, within the memory of the writers of these sheets, were tradesmen in *London*; the first Sir *William Scawen's* apprentice, and the latter's grandfather a P——— upon, or near, *London-Bridge*.

How many noble seats, superior to the palaces of sovereign Princes (in some countries) do we see erected within few miles of this city by tradesmen, or the sons of tradesmen, while the seats and castles of the ancient gentry, like their families, look *worn out*, and fallen into *decay*! witness the noble house of Sir *John Eyles*, himself a Merchant, at *Giddy-hall* near *Rumford*; Sir *Gregory Page* on *Black-heath*, the son of a *Brewer*; Sir *Nathaniel Mead* near *Weal-green*, his father a *Linen-Draper*, with many others, too long to repeat; and to crown all, the Lord *Castlemain*'s at *Wanstead*, his father Sir *Josiah Child* originally a Tradesman.

It was a smart, but just repartee of a *London* Tradesman, when a gentleman *who had a good estate too*, rudely reproach'd him in company and bad him hold his tongue, for he was no gentleman; *No, Sir,* says he, *but I can buy a gentleman*, and therefore I claim a liberty to speak among gentlemen.

Again, in how superior a port or figure (as we now call it) do our tradesmen live to what the middling gentry either do or can support? An ordinary Tradesman now, not in the city only, but in the country, shall spend more money by the year, than a gentleman of four or five hundred pounds a Year can do; and shall encrease and lay up every year too; whereas the gentleman shall at the best stand stock still, just where he began, nay, perhaps decline; and as for the lower gentry, from an hundred pounds a year to three hundred, or thereabouts, *though they are often as proud and high in their appearance as the other*; as to them, I say, a *Shoemaker* in *London* shall keep a better house, spend more money, cloath his family better, and yet grow rich too: It is evident where the difference lies, *an Estate's a pond*, but *a Trade's a Spring*; The first, if it keeps full, and the water wholesom, by the ordinarry supplies and dreins from the neighbouring grounds, 'tis well, and 'tis all that is expected; but the other is an inexhausted current, which not only fills the pond, and keeps it full, but is continually running over, and fills all the lower ponds and places about it.

This being the case in *England*, and our trade being so vastly great, it is no wonder that the tradesmen in *England* fill the lists of our nobility and gentry; no wonder that the gentlemen of the best familes marry tradesmen's daughters, and put their younger sons apprentices to tradesmen; and how often do these younger sons come to buy the elder sons' estates, and restore the family, when the elder, and head of the house, proving rakish and extravagant, has wasted his patrimony, and is obliged to make out the blessing of *Israel*'s family, where the younger son bought the birth-right, and the elder was doomed to serve him?

Trade is so far *here* from being inconsistent with a Gentleman, that *in short* trade in *England* makes Gentlemen, and has peopled this nation with Gentlemen; for after a generation or two the tradesmen's children, or at least their grand-children, come to be as good Gentlemen, Statesmen, Parliament-men, Privy-Counsellors, Judges, Bishops, and Noblemen, as those of the highest birth and the most ancient families; and nothing too high for them: Thus the late Earl of *Haversham* was originally a Merchant, the late Secretary *Craggs* was the son of a *Barber*; the present Lord *Castlemain*'s father was a Tradesman; the great grandfather of the present Duke of *Bedford* the same, and so of several others: Nor do we find any defect either in the genius or capacities of the posterity of tradesmen, arising from any remains of mechanick blood, which 'tis pretended should influence them; but all the gallantry of spirit, greatness of soul, and all the generous principles that can be found in any of the ancient families, whose blood is the most untainted, as they call it, with the low mixtures of a mechanick race, are found in these; and, as is said before, they generally go beyond them in knowledge of the world, which is the best education.

We see the tradesmen of *England*, as they grow wealthy, coming every day to the Herald's office, to search for the Coats of Arms of their ancestors, in order to paint them upon their coaches, and engrave them upon their plate, embroider them upon the pediments of their new houses; and how often do we see them trace the registers of their families up to the prime nobility, or the most ancient gentry of the kingdom?

Passage 1.7
(*from* Daniel Defoe, *The Compleat English Gentleman*, Introduction, nd)

That I may begin with the same brevity that I purpose to go on with, I shall onely observ here by way of introduccion that there are two sorts or classes of men who I am to be understood to speak of under the denomination of gentlemen:

1. The born Gentleman,
2. The bred Gentleman.

The complete gentleman I am to speak of will take them in both; and neither of them, singly and abstractedly considred, will stand alone in the class of a compleat gentleman without some thing that may be said to comprehend both.

The born gentleman is a valuable man if bred up as a gentleman ought to be, that is, educated in learning and manners suitable to his birth. This I must insist on as a preliminary, that I may not be censur'd and condemn'd unread, and bring upon me a clamour from the numerous party of old women (whether male or female), idolators who worship escutcheons and trophyes, and rate men and families by the *blazonry* of their houses, exclusiv of learning or virtue, and of all personal merit.

On the other hand, the son of a mean person furnish'd from Heaven with an originall fund of wealth, wit, sence, courage, virtue, and good humour, and set apart by a liberall education for the service of his country; that distinguishes himself by the greatest and best actions; is made acceptable and agreeable to all men by a life of glory and true fame; that hath the naturall beauties of his mind embellish'd and set off with a vast fund of learning and accquir'd knowleg; that has a clear head, a generous heart, a polite behaviour and, in a word, shews himself to be an accomplish'd gentleman in every requisite article, that of birth and blood excepted; I must be allowd to admit such a person into the rank of a gentleman, and to suggest that he being the first of his race may possibly raise a *roof tree* (as the antients call it) of a noble house and of a succession of gentlemen as effectually as if he had his pedigree to show from the Conqueror's army or from a centurion in the legions that landed with Julius Caesar.

Out of the race of either of these, the compleat gentleman I am to describe is to be deriv'd. How to reconcile the antient line to this and bring them, however degenerate, to embrace the modern line, tho' exalted by the brightest virtue and the most valuable accomplishments of a man of honour, is the difficult case before me.

I am resolv'd however to giv antiquity its due homage; I shall worship the image call'd antient lineage as much as possible without idolatry; I shall giv it all the reverence and respect that it can pretend to claim, search for all the glories of birth and blood, and place them in full proportion: no lustre of antient gentry shall be ecclypst by me, onely with this exception, that I must intreat the gentlemen who are to value themselves chiefly upon that advantage, that they will *stoop so low* as to admit that vertue, learning, a liberal educacion, and a degree of naturall and acquir'd knowledge, are necessary to finish the born gentleman; and that without them the entitul'd heir will be but the shaddow of a gentleman, the opaac, dark body of a planet, which can not shine for want of the sun communicating its beams, and for want of being plac'd in a due position to reciev and reflect those beams when they are communicated and reciev'd.

In condicioning for so small an advance in the favour of true merit, and insisting upon its being, as I said, asolutely necessary, I think we differ upon so small a point, that I can not doubt of reconciling it all in the end of this discourse and bringing the blood and the merit together; so we shall soon produce the best and most glorious peice of God's creation, a complete gentleman; which is the deserv'd subject of the whole work.

I shall begin with the born gentleman. I shall do him all the honour due to his distinguisht quallity and birth; I shall giv him the preference upon all occasions; I shall allow him to be superior because he is prior or seignior in blood, expecting nothing of him in return but this trifle onely, that he *but equall* in merit, not tying him down, no, not to that claim of his quallity that he should *excell* his inferiors in virtue as he does in degree.

Passage 1.8
(*from* Daniel Defoe, *A Tour thro' the whole Island of Great Britain*, 1724-7)

Having thus spoken of the City and adjacent Buildings of *London*, and of the Particulars which I find chiefly omitted by other Writers, I have not Room here to enter into all the Articles needful to a full Description: However, I shall touch a little at the Things most deserving a Stranger's Observation.

Supposing now, the whole Body of this vast Building to be considered as one City, *London*, and not concerning myself or the Reader with the

Distinction of its several Jurisdictions; we shall then observe it only as divided into Three, *viz.* the City, the Court, and the Out-Parts.

The City is the Center of its Commerce and Wealth.

The Court of its Gallantry and Splendor.

The Out-Parts of its Numbers and Mechanicks; and in all these, no City in the World can equal it.

Between the Court and City, there is a constant Communication of Business to that degree, that nothing in the World can come up to it.

As the City is the Center of Business; there is the *Customhouse*, an Article, which, as it brings in an immense Revenue to the Publick, so it cannot be removed from its Place, all the vast Import and Export of Goods being, of Necessity, made there; nor can the Merchants be removed, the River not admitting the Ships to come any farther.

Here, also, is the *Excise* Office, the *Navy* Office, the *Bank*, and almost all the Offices where those vast Funds are fixed, in which so great a Part of the Nation are concerned, and on the Security of which so many Millions are advanced.

Here are the *South Sea* Company, the *East India* Company, the *Bank*, the *African* Company, *&c.* whose Stocks support that prodigious Paper Commerce, called *Stock-Jobbing*; a Trade, which once bewitched the Nation almost to its Ruin, and which, tho' reduced very much, and recover'd from that terrible Infatuation which once overspread the whole Body of the People, all the Men of Substance in *England* are more or less concerned in it, and the Property of which is so very often alienated, that even the Tax upon the Transfers of Stock, tho' but Five Shillings for each Transfer, brings many Thousand Pounds a Year to the Government; and some have said, that there is not less than a Hundred Millions of Stock transferred forward or backward from one Hand to another every Year, and this is one thing which makes such a constant Daily Intercourse between the Court Part of the Town, and the City; and this is given as one of the principal Causes of the prodigious Conflux of the Nobility and Gentry from all Parts of *England* to *London*, more than ever was known in former Years, *viz.* That many Thousands of Families are so deeply concerned in those Stocks, and find it so absolutely necessary to be at Hand to take the Advantage of buying and selling, as the sudden Rise or Fall of the Price directs, and the Loss they often sustain by their Ignorance of Things when absent, and the Knavery of Brokers and others, whom, in their Absence, they are bound to trust, that they find themselves obliged to come up and live constantly here, or at least, most Part of the Year.

This is the Reason why, notwithstanding the Encrease of new Buildings, and the Addition of new Cities, as they may be called, every Year to the old, yet a House is no sooner built, but 'tis tenanted and inhabited, and every Part is crouded with People, and that not only in the Town, but in all the Towns and Villages round, as shall be taken Notice of in its Place.

But let the Citizens and Inhabitants of *London* know, and it may be worth the Reflection of some of the Landlords, and Builders especially, that if Peace continues, and the publick Affairs continue in honest and upright Management, there is a Time coming, at least the Nation hopes for it, when the publick Debts being reduced and paid off, the Funds or Taxes on which they are establish'd, may cease, and so Fifty or Sixty Millions of the Stocks, which are now the solid Bottom of the *South-Sea Company*, *East-India Company*, *Bank*, *&c.* will cease, and be no more; by which the Reason of this Conflux of People being removed, they will of Course, and by the Nature of the Thing, return again to their Country Seats, to avoid the expensive living at *London*, as they did come up hither to share the extravagant Gain of their former Business here.

What will be the Condition of this overgrown City in such a Case, I must leave to Time; but all those who know the temporary Constitution of our Funds, know this, 1. That even, if they are to spin out their own Length, all those Funds which were given for Thirty-two Years, have already run out one Third, and some of them almost half the Time, and that the rest will soon be gone: 2. That as in Two Years more, the Government which receives Six *per Cent.* and pays but Five, and will then pay but Four *per Cent.* Interest, will be able every Year to be paying off and lessening the publick Debt, 'till, in Time, 'tis to be hoped, all our Taxes may cease, and the ordinary Revenue may, as it always used to do, again supply the ordinary Expence of the Government.

Then, I say, will be a Time to expect the vast Concourse of People to *London*, will separate again and disperse as naturally, as they have now crouded hither: What will be the Fate then of all the fine Buildings in the Out Parts, in such a Case, let any one judge.

There has formerly been a great Emulation between the Court End of Town, and the City; and it was once seriously proposed in a certain Reign, how the Court should humble the City; nor was it so impracticable a Thing at that Time, had the wicked Scheme been carried on: Indeed it was carried farther than consisted with the Prudence of a good Government, or of a wise People; for the Court envy'd the City's Greatness, and the Citizens were ever jealous of the Court's Designs: The most fatal Steps the Court took to humble the City, and which, as

I say, did not consist with the Prudence of a good Government, were, 1. The shutting up the Exchequer, and, 2. The bringing a *Quo Warranto* against their Charter; but these Things can but be touch'd at here; the City has outliv'd it all, and both the Attempts turn'd to the Discredit of the Court Party, who pushed them on: But the City, I say, has gained the Ascendant, and is now made so necessary to the Court (as before it was thought rather a Grievance) that now we see the Court itself the Daily Instrument to encourage and increase the Opulence of the City, and the City again, by its real Grandeur, made not a Glory only, but an Assistance and Support to the Court, on the greatest and most sudden Emergencies.

Nor can a Breach be now made on any Terms, but the City will have the Advantage; for while the Stocks, and Bank, and trading Companies remain in the City, the Center of the Money as well as of the Credit and Trade of the Kingdom, will be there.

Nor are these Capital Offices only necessarily kept in the City, but several Offices belonging to the publick *Oeconomy* of the Administration, such as the *Post Office*, the *Navy*, the *Victualling*, and the *Pay Offices*, including the *Ordnance Office*, which is kept in the *Tower*. In a Word, the Offices may, indeed, be said to be equally divided.

The City has all those above-mentioned, and the Court has the *Admiralty*, the Exchequer, and the *Secretaries of State's Offices*, with those of the *Pay-Masters of the Army*, *&c*.

Besides these, the *Council*, the *Parliament*, and the *Courts of Justice*, are all kept at the same Part of the Town; but as all Suits among the Citizens are, by Virtue of their Privileges, to be try'd within the Liberty of the City, so the Term is obliged to be (as it were) adjourned from *Westminster-Hall* to *Guild-Hall*, to try Causes there; also Criminal Cases are in like Manner tried Monthly at the *Old Baily*, where a special Commission is granted for the Purpose to the Judges; but the Lord Mayor always presides, and has the Chair.

The Equality, however, being thus preserved, and a perfect good Understanding between the Court and City having so long flourished, this Union contributes greatly to the flourishing Circumstances of both, and the publick Credit is greatly raised by it; for it was never known, that the City, on any Occasion, was so Assistant to the Government, as it has been since this general good Agreement. No Sum is so great, but the *Bank* has been able to raise. Here the *Exchequer* Bills are at all Times circulated, Money advanced upon the Funds as soon as laid, and that at moderate Interest, not encroaching on the Government, or extorting large Interest to eat up the Nation, and disappoint the Sovereign, and defeat his best Designs, as in King *William*'s Time was too much the Practice.

By this great Article of publick Credit, all the King's Business is done with Chearfulness, Provisions are now bought to victual the Fleets without Difficulty, and at reasonable Rates. The several Yards where the Ships are built and fitted out, are currently paid: The Magazines of Military and Naval Stores kept full: In a Word, by this very Article of publick Credit, of which the Parliament is the foundation (and the City, are the Architectures or Builders) all those great Things are now done with Ease, which, in the former Reigns, went on heavily, and were brought about with the utmost Difficulty.

Passage 1.9
(*from* Henry St John, Viscount Bolingbroke, *Letters on the Spirit of Patriotism*, 1749)

My Lord, 1736

You have engaged me on a subject which interrupts the series of those letters I was writing to you; but it is one, which I confess, I have very much at heart. I shall, therefore, explain myself fully, nor blush to reason on principles that are out of fashion among men, who intend nothing, by serving the public, but to feed their avarice, their vanity, and their luxury, without the sense of any duty they owe to God or man.

It seems to me, that in order to maintain the moral system of the world at a certain point, far below that of ideal perfection, (for we are made capable of conceiving what we are incapable of attaining) but however sufficient upon the whole to constitute a state easy and happy, or at the worst tolerable: I say, it seems to me, that the Author of nature has thought fit to mingle, from time to time, among the societies of men, a few, and but a few of those, on whom he is graciously pleased to bestow a larger proportion of the ethereal spirit, than is given in the ordinary course of his providence to the sons of men. These are they who engross almost the whole reason of the species; who are born to instruct, to guide, and to preserve; who are designed to be the tutors and the guardians of human kind. When they prove such, they exhibit to us examples of the highest virtue, and the truest piety: and they deserve to have their festivals kept, instead of that pack of *Anachorites* and *Enthusiasts*, with whose names the calendar is crowded and disgraced. When these men apply their talents to other purposes, when they strive to be great and despise being good, they commit a most sacrilegious breach of trust; they pervert the means, they defeat, as far as lies in them, the designs of providence, and disturb, in some sort, the system of infinite wisdom. To misapply these talents is the most diffused, and, therefore, the greatest of crimes in its nature and consequences; but to keep them unexerted, and unemployed, is a crime too. Look about you, my Lord, from the palace to the cottage; you will find that the bulk of mankind is made to breathe the air of this atmosphere, to roam about this globe, and to consume, like the courtiers of *Alcinous*, the fruits of the earth. *Nos numerus fumus & fruges consumere nati.* When they have trod this insipid round a certain number of years, and begot others to do the same after them, they have lived: and if they have performed, in some tolerable degree, the ordinary moral duties of life, they have done all they were born to do. Look about you again, my Lord, nay look into your own breast, and you will find that there are superior spirits, men who shew even from their infancy, tho' it be not always perceived by others, perhaps not always felt by themselves, that they were born for something more, and better. These are the men to whom the part I mentioned is assigned. Their talents denote their *general designation*: and the opportunities of conforming themselves to it, that arise in the course of things, or that are presented to them by any circumstances of rank and situation in the society to which they belong, denote the *particular vocation*, which is not lawful for them to resist nor even to neglect. The duration of the lives of such men as these is to be determined, I think, by the length and importance of the parts they act, not by the number of years that pass between their coming into the world, and their going out of it. Whether the piece be of three, or five acts, the part may be long: and he, who sustains it thro the whole, may be said to die in the fulness of years; whilst he, who declines it sooner, may be said not to live out half his days.

I have sometimes represented to myself the *vulgar*, who are accidentally distinguished by the titles of king and subject, or lord and vassal, of nobleman and peasant; and the *few* who are distinguished by nature so essentially from the herd of mankind, that (figure apart) they seem to be of another species, in this manner. The former come into the world, and continue in it, like *Dutch travellers* in a foreign country. Everything they meet has the grace of novelty: and they are fond alike of every thing that is new. They wander about from one object, to another, of vain curiosity, or inelegant pleasure. If they are industrious, they shew their industry in copying signs, and collecting mottos and epitaphs. They loiter, or they trifle away their whole time: and their presence or their absence would be equally unperceived, if caprice or accident did not raise them often to stations, wherein their stupidity, their vices, or their follies, make them a public misfortune. The latter come into the world, or at least continue in it after the effects of surprize and inexperience are over, like men who are sent on more important errands. They observe with distinction, they admire with knowledge. They may indulge themselves in pleasure; but as their industry is not employed about trifles, so their amusements are not made the business of their lives. Such men cannot pass unperceived thro a country. If they retire from the world, their splendor accompanies them, and enlightens even the obscurity of their retreat. If they take a part in public life, the effect is never indifferent. They either appear like ministers of divine vengeance, and their course thro the world is marked by desolation and oppression, by poverty and servitude: or they are the guardian angels of the country they inhabit, busy to avert even the most distant evil, and to maintain or to procure peace, plenty, and, the greatest of human blessings, liberty.

From the observation, that superiority of parts is often employed to do superior mischief, no consequence can be drawn against the truth I endeavour to establish. Reason collects the will of God from the constitution of things, in this as in other cases; but in no case does the Divine power impel us necessarily to conform ourselves to this will: and, therefore, from the misapplication of superior parts to hurt, no argument can be drawn against this position, that they were given for the good of mankind. Reason deceives us not: we deceive ourselves, and suffer our wills to be determined by other motives. MONTAIGNE or CHARRON would say, *l'homme se pipe*, 'man is at once his own sharper, and his own bubble.' Human nature is her own bawd, says TULLY, *blanda conciliatrix & quasi lena sui*. He who considers the universal wants, imperfections, and vices of his kind, must agree that men were intended not only for society, but to unite in commonwealths, and to submit to laws: *legum idcirco omnes servi sumus, ut liberi esse possimus*. And yet this very man will be seduced by his own passions, or the passions and examples of others, to think, or to act as if he thought, the very contrary. So he who is conscious of superior endowments, such as render him more capable than the generality of men to secure and improve the advantages of social life, by preserving the commonwealth in strength and splendor, even he may be seduced to think, or to act as if he thought, that these endowments were given him for the gratification of his ambition, and his other passions; and that there is no difference between vice and virtue, between a knave and an honest man, but one which a prince, who died not many years ago, asserted, 'that men of great sense were, therefore, knaves, and men of little sense were, therefore, honest'. But in neither of these cases will the truth and reason of things be altered, by such examples of human frailty. It will be still true, and reason will still demonstrate, that all men are directed, by the general constitution of human nature, to submit to government; and that some men are in a particular manner designed to take care of that government on which the common happiness depends. The use that reason will make of such examples will be only this, that since men are so apt in every form of life and every degree of understanding, to act against their interest and their duty too, without benevolence to mankind, or regard to the divine will; it is the more incumbent on those who have this benevolence and this regard at heart, to employ all the means that the nature of government allows, and that rank, circumstances of situation, or superority of talents, give them, to oppose evil, and promote good government; and contribute thus to preserve the moral system of the world, at that point of imperfection at least, which seems to have been prescribed to it by the great Creator of every system of beings.

Passage 1.10
(*from* Oliver Goldsmith, Letter CI, *The Citizen of the World*, 1762)

From Lien Chi Altangi, to Fum Hoam, first president of the Ceremonial Academy at Pekin, in China
In every society some men are born to teach, and others to receive instruction; some to work, and others to enjoy in idleness the fruits of their industry; some to govern, and others to obey. Every people, how free soever, must be contented to give up part of their liberty and judgment to those who govern, in exchange for their hopes of security; and the motives which first influenced their choice in the election of their governors should ever be weighed against the succeeding apparent inconsistencies of their conduct. All cannot be rulers, and men are generally best governed by a few. In making way thro' the intricacies of business, the smallest obstacles are apt to retard the execution of what is to be planned by a multiplicity of counsels; the judgment of one alone being always fittest for winding through the labyrinths of intrigue, and the obstructions of disappointment. A serpent, which, as the fable observes, is furnished with one head and many tails, is much more capable of subsistence and expedition, than another, which is furnished with but one tail and many heads.

Obvious as these truths are, the people of this country seem insensible of their force. Not satisfied with the advantages of internal peace and opulence, they still murmur at their governors, and interfere in the execution of their designs; as if they wanted to be something more than happy. But as the Europeans instruct by argument, and the Asiatics mostly by narration, were I to address them, I should convey my sentiments in the following story.

Takupi had long been Prime Minister of Tipartala, a fertile country that stretches along the western confines of China. During his administration, whatever advantages could be derived from arts, learning, and commerce, were seen to bless the people; nor were the necessary precautions of providing for the security of the state forgotten. It often happens, however, that when men are possessed of all they want, they then begin to find torment from imaginary afflictions, and lessen their present enjoyments, by foreboding that those enjoyments are to have an end. The people now therefore endeavoured to find out grievances; and after some search, actually began to think themselves aggrieved. A petition against the enormities of Takupi was carried to the throne in due form; and the Queen who governed the country, willing to satisfy her subjects, appointed a day, in which his accusers should be heard, and the Minister should stand upon his defence.

The day being arrived, and the Minister brought before the tribunal, a carrier, who supplied the city with fish, appeared among the number of his accusers. He exclaimed, that it was the custom, time immemorial, for carriers to bring their fish upon an horse in a hamper; which being placed on one side, and balanced by a stone on the other, was thus conveyed with ease and safety: but that the prisoner, moved either by a spirit of innovation, or perhaps bribed by the hamper-makers, had obliged all carriers to use the stone no longer, but balance one hamper with another; an order entirely repugnant to the customs of all antiquity, and those of the kingdom of Tipartala in particular.

The carrier finished; and the whole court shook their heads at the innovating Minister: when a second witness appeared. He was inspector of the city buildings, and accused the disgraced favourite of having given orders for the demolition of an ancient ruin, which obstructed the passage thro' one of the principal streets. He observed, that such buildings were noble monuments of barbarous antiquity; contributed finely to shew how little their ancestors understood of architecture: and for that reason such monuments should be held sacred, and suffered gradually to decay.

The last witness now appeared. This was a widow, who had laudably attempted to burn herself upon her husband's funeral pile. But the innovating minister had prevented the execution of her design, and was insensible to her tears, protestations, and entreaties.

The Queen could have pardoned the two former offences; but this last was considered as so gross an injury to the sex, and so directly contrary to all the customs of antiquity, that it called for immediate justice. 'What, cried the Queen, not suffer a woman to burn herself when she thinks proper? The sex are to be very prettily tutored, no doubt, if they must be restrained from entertaining their female friends now and then with a friend's wife, or roasted acquaintance. I sentence the criminal to be banished from my presence for ever for his injurious treatment of the sex.'

Takupi had been hitherto silent, and spoke only to shew the sincerity of his resignation. 'Great Queen, cried he, I acknowledge my crime; and since I am to be banished, I beg it may be to some ruined town, or desolate village in the country I have governed. I shall find some pleasure in improving the soil, and bringing back a spirit of industry among the inhabitants.' His request appearing reasonable, it was immediately complied with; and a courtier had orders to fix upon a place of banishment, answering the Minister's description. After some months search, however, the enquiry proved fruitless; neither a desolate village, nor a ruined town, was found in the whole kingdom. *Alas*, said Takupi to the Queen, *How can that country be ill governed which has neither a desolate village, nor a ruined town in it?* The Queen perceived the justice of his expostulation, and the Minister was received into more than former favour.

Passage 1.11

(*from* Oliver Goldsmith, 'Of the Pride and Luxury of the Middling Class of People', *The Bee*, 1759)

Of all the follies and absurdities which this great metropolis labours under, there is not one, I believe, at present, appears in a more glaring and ridiculous light than the pride and luxury of the middling class of people; their eager desire of being seen in a sphere far above their capacities and circumstances, is daily, nay hourly instanced by the prodigious numbers of mechanics, who flock to the races, and gaming-tables, brothels, and all public diversions this fashionable town affords.

You should see a grocer, or a tallow-chandler sneak from behind the compter, clap on a laced coat and a bag, fly to the EO table, throw away fifty pieces with some sharping man of quality, while his industrious wife is selling a penny-worth of sugar, or a pound of candles, to support her fashionable spouse in his extravagances.

I was led into this reflection by an odd adventure, which happened to me the other day at Epsom races, where I went, not through any desire, I do assure you, of laying betts, or winning thousands; but at the earnest request of a friend who had long indulged the curiosity of seeing the sport, very natural for an Englishman. When we had arrived at the course, and had taken several turns to observe the different objects that made up this whimsical groupe, a figure suddenly darted by us, mounted and dressed in all the elegance of those polite gentry who come to shew you they have a little money, and rather than pay their just debts at home, generously come abroad to bestow it on gamblers and pickpockets. As I had not an opportunity of viewing his face till his return, I gently walked after him, and met him as he came back, when, to my no small surprise, I beheld, in this gay Narcissus, the visage of Jack Varnish, an humble vender of prints. Disgusted at the sight, I pulled my friend by the sleeve, pressed him to return him, telling him all the way, that I was so enraged at the fellow's impudence, I was resolved never to lay out another penny with him.

And now, pray sir, let me beg of you to give this a place in your paper, that Mr Varnish may understand he mistakes the thing quite, if he imagines horse-racing commendable in a tradesman; and that he who is revelling every night in the arms of a common strumpet (though blessed with an indulgent wife) when he ought to be minding his business, will never thrive in this world. He will find himself soon mistaken, his finances decrease, his friends shun him, customers fall off, and himself thrown into a Gaol. I would earnestly recommend this adage to every mechanic in London, 'Keep your shop, and your shop will keep you.' A strict observance of these words will, I am sure, in time, gain them estates. Industry is the road to wealth, and honesty to happiness; and he who strenuously endeavours to pursue them both, may never fear the critic's lash, or the sharp cries of penury and want.

Notes

1. Virgil, *Eclogues*, 7. 69:
These rhymes I did to memory commend,
When vanquish'd Thyrsis did in vain contend (Dryden)

2. Juvenal, *Satires*, 3.1-2: Although confounded by the departure of my old Friend, I cannot but commend him.

3. Juvenal, *Satires*, 8. 24-6: Do you prove yourself stainless in life, one who holds fast to the right both in word and deed? I acknowledge you as a lord.

4. Tacitus, *Histories*, i, 1: It is a rare blessing of the times when you can think what you like and can say what you think.

2 COMMERCE AND INDUSTRY

These passages provide a number of interesting points of comparison with the more specialised economic writings represented in the next section. The essays from *The Review*, *The Spectator* and *The Freeholder* in particular, share many of the preoccupations of that later writing. In *The Review* Defoe introduces the general reader to some of the principles of commerce, and explains its importance in society. In passage 2.1 he presents it as the natural agency by which God's provision becomes apparent and beneficial to men: '*Nature Natureing*, which I call GOD' produces different 'Species of things' in different parts of the world. They require the operations of trade to bring them into harmony, and the merchant has the task of organising these operations. Through trade he 'by his Correspondence reconciles that infinite Variety, which, as I noted, has by the Infinite Wisdom of Providence, been scattred over the Face of the World'.

These arguments are paralleled in the essays from *The Spectator* and *The Freeholder*. In *The Adventurer* No. 67 (passage 2.6), Johnson takes an account of the multifarious commercial activities of London as the basis for a moral reflection on the advantages of civilised over primitive societies, and on the plenitude of God's design of the world. The essay incorporates a description of the economic hierarchy of society, in which 'the refuse of part of mankind furnishes a subordinate class with the materials necessary to their support'. The relation between this description and the larger moral discussion is well worth examining.

The extract from *The Idea of a Patriot King* stands in contrast to these passages in its insistence that trade is declining for lack of the regulation and encouragement that could be afforded by the ideal statesman, the Patriot King.

Passages 2.7a, 2.7b and 2.8 provide accounts of industrial production in West Yorkshire and the West of England. The extracts from Defoe's *Tour* are unreservedly celebratory of the benefits of industry; the passage from Tucker's *Instructions for Travellers* gives a more qualified analysis of the labour problems involved. The passages compare interestingly with Smith's account of the division of labour in passage 3.9, and with Young's comments on the conduct of industrial workers in passage 4.11.

Passage 2.1
(Daniel Defoe, 'Of TRADE in General', *The Review*, Vol. III, No. 2, 3 January 1706)

Trade is a general Exchange of the Necessaries and Utensils of Life, from and between Person and Person, Place and Place.

The Principal Subjects of Trade are Included, in Provisions, House-Furniture, and Cloathing; and they are handed from Place to Place, by an Infinite and incessant Circulation; they are attended with a vast Variety of Handicrafts, to Furnish Tools to make Vessels to Convey, and Instruments to produce and preserve.

'Twould be Foreign to the Design of these Papers, to give an *Index* of the several Arts, into which Trade is thus subdivided. I shall go on farther upon the Generals, and then come to Particulars of another sort.

Generally speaking, all the Innumerables of Trade, come under these two Heads; Natural Produce, and Manufacture. The different Climates and Soil in the World, have, by the Wisdom and Direction of *Nature Natureing*, which I Call GOD, produc'd such differing Species of things, all of them in their kind equally Necessary, or at least Useful and Desirable; as insensibly preserves the Dependance, of the most Remote Parts of the World upon one another; and at least makes them useful to each other, and Contributing to one another's Convenience, Necessity, or Delight.

And here I might digress to good purpose, in letting out, how the most Plentiful Country, receives from the most Barren; how every Nation has something to fetch from, and something to send to one another; every Nation something to spare, which another Country wants, and finds something wanting, another Country can spare; and this occasions Exchanging with those Countries, to the Advantage of both; and that we call TRADE. This necessarily implies Convenience for Portage, and that we call Navigation; and thus General Negoce began to be improv'd by Humane Industry, to Strange and Unaccountable Enlargements.

This Variety also, is not only Natural, but Artificial; and as the Climates and Soil, have produc'd in every Country different Growths or Species of things; so the differing Genius of the People of every Country, prompts them to different Improvements, and to different Customs. They Eat, Wear, and Dwell after differing Manners; and as all People, Tenacious of their own way, seek what qualifies them best to pursue it; they seek to Foreign Climates to furnish themselves, with what they cannot have so much to their purpose, or so suited to their occasions or Inclinations at Home; and this is again Revolv'd into necessary

Correspondence, they must send to those Countries some Equivalent, to satisfie the People for what they take from them; and thus we are again brought home to TRADE.

To Examine this Variety a little, may not be Unpleasant, nor in its end Unprofitable to the Reader; because it will tend to open our particular Scenes of Trade, of which in Course, I shall come to Treat more Particularly and Largely, than perhaps is expected.

The Variety, both of the Produce and Manufactures of the several Countries, are the Foundations of Trade, and I Entitle Providence to it; not only as it is found in Nature, but as it is found in Customs and Consequences of things; for GOD in whose Infinite foreknowledge, all the Accidents of Time are always present, who in one Infinite Substantial Essential NOW, in which is not past or future, must be suppos'd to foreknow that Natural Causes consider'd, *and to Natural Causes, he had in his Infinite Wisdom by Laws of Nature, submitted all the Variety of Consequences*; the Generations of the World, could not subsist in the Manner prescrib'd, without the Mutual Assistance, and Concurrence of one another. The bare Produce of the Earth, in many of our Neighbouring Countries, could by no means have Maintain'd the Numbers of People, which the Consequences of Trade have brought together to Answer for this Navigable Rivers, as well as a Navigable Sea, has made the Communication of Remote Parts Practicable; and Floaty Bodies are adapted for Vessels, that the Light Bodies may bear the Heavy, and Goods that will not bear it, may be fenc'd from the Inconvenience of Weather, and preserv'd fit for Use and Convenience.

The Rivers and Roads, are as the Veins and Arteries, that Convey Wealth, like the Blood, to all the Parts of the World; and this Wealth is the Life of Kingdoms and Towns; the Support of their People, and Test of their Power.

I wonder sometimes, at the Ignorance of those People and Nations, whose Gentry pretend to Despise Families rais'd by Trade; Why should that, which is the Wealth of the World, the Prosperity and Health of Kingdoms and Towns, be accounted Dishonourable?

If we Respect Trade, as it is understood by Merchandizing; it is certainly the most Noble, most instructive, and Improving of any way of Life. The Artificers or Handicrafts-Men, are indeed Slaves; the Gentlemen are the Plowmen of the Nation, but the Merchant is the Support, and Improver of Power, Learning, and Fortunes.

A True-Bred Merchant, is a Universal Scholar his Learning Excells the meer Scholar in Greek and Latin, as much as that does the Illiterate Person, that cannot Write or Read: He Understands Languages without

Books, Geography without Maps; his Journals and Trading Voyages delineate the World; his Foreign Exchanges, Protests and Procurations, speak all Tongues; he sits in his Counting-House, and Converses with all Nations, and keeps up the most exquisite and extensive part of human Society in a Universal Correspondence.

He is qualified for all sorts of Employment in the State, by a General Knowledge of things and Men; he remits and draws such vast Sums, that he Transacts more Value than a large Exchequer.

By the Number of these Cities, rise out of nothing, and decay again into Villages: If Trade abandons a Port; if the Merchants quit the place, it languishes of course, and dies like Man in a Consumption, insensibly; if these flock to a Town, Home-trade crowds upon them; Seamen increase; People flock in, and the Village soon becomes a City.

In Nations and Empires 'tis the same; what infinite Crowds of People flock into *Holland*; Cities without Number, and Towns thick like the Houses in other Countries, that the whole Country seems to be one populous City; People in such Multitude; that all the Land in the Country can't find Butter and Cheese for them; much less maintain them.

All these attend upon Trade by Trade, they possess the World, and have greater Stocks of Goods in each Country's Growth, than the Countries from whence they have them can show.

Their Rivers are throng'd with Shipping like a Weed; their Naval Stores are inexhaustible; they can build a Navy, and fit it to Sea, sooner than any Nation in the World; and yet have neither the Timber or Plank, the Iron-Work or Cordage, the Pitch or the Tar, the Hemp or the Rosin, in any part of the Country.

All this is done by Trade; the Merchant makes a wet Bog become a populous State; enriches Beggars, enobles Mechannicks, raises not Families only, but Towns, Cities, Provinces and Kingdoms.

How then can that be dishonourable that it in its kind is the support of the World, and by and from which Nations and Kingdoms are made to differ from one another; are made to excel one another, and be too strong, because too rich for one another.

The Merchant by his Correspondence reconciles that Infinite Variety, which, as I noted, has by the Infinite Wisdom of Providence, been scattred over the Face of the World.

If *England* has Wool, and *Spain* has Oil, *Spain* sends her Oil over to *England* to enable *England* to work that Wool into Cloth, Bays, Sayes, Perpets and Stuffs; and so they may be sent over to *Spain* for their Clothing.

Has *Spain* Wine, *England* has her Beer and fine Ale, which in those

Countries where there they have Wine, is justly esteem'd before it: And again, we send for their Wines to drink here, our Prelates encling to seek those Liquors which we must fetch from abroad.

We Cloth all the Islands and Continent of *America*; and they in return, furnish us with Sugars and Tobaccoes, things by Custom becoming as useful to us, as our Cloths is to them: Trade carries the very Soil away, and transposes the World in Parts, removing Mountains, and carrying them over the Sea into other Countries; what a Quantity of the *Terra Firma* has been carried from *New-Castle* in *Coles*; whose Ashes lie mix'd with the Soil in most parts of the World; what Cavities and Chasms in the Bowels of the Earth have we made for our Tin, Lead and Iron; in the respective Countries of *Cornwel*, *Darby* and *Sussex*.

These we carry abroad, and with them we purchase and bring back the Woods of *Norway*; the Silks of *Italy* and *Turky*; the Wines and Brandies of *France*, the Wines, Oil, and Fruit of *Spain*; the Druggs of *Persia*; the Spices of *India*; the Sugars of *America*; the Toys and Gaiety of *China* and *Japan*.

An infinite Variety might here be run through; every Country Communicates to its other corresponding Country what they want; and these can spare them *vice versa*; receive from that Country again, what of their Growth these want; and not a Country so barren, so useless, but something is to be found there that can be had no where else.

All the World could not have thought of such an encreasing Trade, as has been establish'd in our Colonies of *America*; for Tobacco and Sugar and abundance of useful things; the Cocheneal, Cocoa, Bark and Drugs of *America*; the Elephants Teeth of *Africa*; the Fish of *New-foundland* and *New-England*; the Whales from uninhabitable *Greenland*, and the like; no Nation so hot or so cold, but it contributes something to another, by which Wealth is advanced, People benefited and imploy'd; and this in its true Original call'd, TRADE.

In the Pursuit of this Matter of General Trade, the Nature of the thing led Mankind to a Necessity of a General Medium of Trade; and the Original of this is found in this absolute Necessity: For example, one County Demands more Goods from another, than it can pay for in Goods of its own Growth or Procuring, or than that Country will take in Exchange: now Trade labouring under this Dilemma, Necessity drove Men to form a Medium of Trade; something whose Value being always intrinsick, would be accepted every where, and that always must attend to form the Balance and pay the overplus; and this is, MONEY.

When this Money could not be either readily as to Time, or sufficiently as to Quantity, be procur'd; the Honour and Character of the

Persons, raised from Experience of Probity and punctual Payment, made the Men easy; and in Confidence of the Integrity of the Person Trading, he will be content with to Morrow, which cannot with convenience be had to Day; and accordingly he stays the Day appointed, and then receives it; *and this we call CREDIT*; of both which in our ensuing Discourse.

Passage 2.2
(*from* Daniel Defoe, *The Review*, Vol. VIII, No. 16, 1 May 1711)

My Time is so little that I can spare upon the Subject of Trade, and the Scene so large, that I own, I can but touch at Things as I go; yet I cannot but bestow a few Lines upon the Subject of our Credit; a Thing I touch'd more largely when I thought it in some Danger, and say the less to it, now I think it secure.

I confess, I have thought one of the Pleasant Things in the World, is to see Men struggling against themselves grow happy, by being defeated of their own Desires, Rich, by having their Interest Ruin'd, and safe, by having their own Measures Cross'd and Disappointed – To see them, like a Man in the Water that cannot swim, struggling to drown himself, and endeavouring to pull him under Water that comes to save him – This, indeed, I take to be the Case of our high-Hat Gentlemen, that would fain have thrown the Heels of our Bank up, and with it have Ruin'd both it and themselves.

Those Gentlemen talk'd loud of Credit, but understood it so ill, that really a Man would rather have pitied them, than have laugh'd at them, because they had a great deal of Money at Stake to lose – Did ever Men that had any Money in the Stock thrive so earnestly to Ruin that Stock, as these? Did ever Men that had a Cargo in the Ship, bore a Hole in the Bottom? – What wretched stuff was it, to hear these Men talk of Credit without Trade, and Banks without Money? And this has been all their Cry – It is true, Land is a Fund – Unhappy is the *Examiner*, to bestow so much Wit on so dull an Argument! *What makes Land a Fund?* Let any Man go back and Enquire what was Land in the Days of *Henry* I? The Ground stood just where it does now; the sweet Dews of Heaven, the refreshing Showers, the warm Beams of the Sun, all invigorated the Earth as much, as constantly, and as seasonably as they do now – But where was the Fund? – What was the Rent? Where the Improvement? – Alas for the Ignorance of our Men of Learning! – *Land is a Fund!* But what had your Land been without Trade? Go dig your Lead-Mines in *Wales*, and turn them all into Silver, as *Sir HM has done into Dross*, and see how Rich you will be; shear your Sheep, and see what you will do with the Wooll; Till Trade brought you Gold and Silver, and fetch'd away your Manufactures, found Vent for the Produce, and Labour for your People, What was all your Wealth? – Your Natives must have wander'd Abroad, and been *Hirelings* and *Mauls* for *Europe, as the Swiss are to this Day*: Your Gentry and Nobility might have been Kings and Princes at Home, and the poor People Drones and Slaves – But where had been your Fund? Where your Wealth? – *It is Trade* has made your Commons Rich, your Merchants Numerous, your Poor able to maintain themselves: *It is Trade* has made you Great, Strong, Terrible Abroad, and busie at Home: *It is Trade* has kept your People from wandring like *Vagabonds* on the Face of the Earth; People Consume the Produce, Trade has fill'd you with People, the Produce raises the Rent, and the Rent makes the Land a Fund; mark the Climax – Your Land might go a begging but for Trade; and for the Landed Men to rail at Trade, is like the Members Mutinying against the Belly – 'Tis from Trade as the Magazine, that Land receives its Value and Life – *Land is a Fund of Wealth*, that's true; but Trade is the Fund of Land, from your Trade, springs your Land's Wealth – Let such Men but View the Land in other Countries; What was the Land in *Barbadoes* good for, when the Island was, unpossess'd by us? – It was as Rich as now, the Fund was there – But that Trade gave that Fund a Value – It was a Fund and no Fund – A Fund of nothing; and take Trade from that Island now, with all its Wealth, and what will it be good for still? Will it Feed and Employ 60,000 *Negroes*, *&c.* in a Place of but 25 Leagues round?

Stop but Trade in *England*, and see what your Lands will soon come to! – Let no more Cloaths or Stuffs be made, or in general, no more Wooll spun, except for private Use; no more Ships built, no more Correspondence with Foreign Nations, no Exportations or Circulation – And let any Man but imagine what a State this Nation will soon be in! – The Poor would eat up the Rich, the Land would not feed the Multitude; your Rich Trading and Encroaching Neighbours, would hire and Entertain all your Youth, who would fly to them for Bread, and being Arm'd by them, would come back and Conquer you; your Provisions, of course, would fail, *that failing*, Rents of Lands must fall – Customs, Excises, and Taxes, would fail of course, all your Subsidies must lie upon Land, your Gentry would sink, a Thousand Pounds a Year in Land wou'd not be worth a Hundred, and Where then is your Landed Fund?

I blush for the Ignorance of those Men, that would contemn Trade to raise Land – No, no, Gentlemen, if you will have Land be a Fund, you must Encourage Trade; Land and Trade are like the Monster of *Glasgow*, of which I have often spoken, on another Occasion; it had one Body from the Navel downwards, but two Bodies from the Navel upwards – They had different Hands to Work, different Heads to Contrive, and, *no doubt*, different Souls to Direct; they receiv'd Nourishment two different Ways, and had two Stomachs to digest, but they had but one pair of Legs to walk with, one Belly to receive and vent, one Receptacle; and from hence it follow'd that they had but one and the same Life.

The Foolish Creature would sometimes, just *like our Landed Men and Trading Men*, Quarrel with itself; one Side would be for going this Way, and the other that, an Evidence it had two Wills – And *What was the Consequence?* why the Legs were fain to stand still till the Heads were agreed, for there being but one pair of Feet, and the Locomotive Faculty receiving its orders from the Will – and there being two Wills, till they concurr'd, the Legs were perfectly Useless.

Would to God our People would consider how apt this Creature was form'd to describe our Case; Really, good People, if Trade and Land, which are the Wealth of this Nation, are divided and differ, the whole Body will soon stand still – And this, like the Circulation in the Body, will throw the whole into Appoplexies, dead palsies, and every Mortal Disease.

Wretched Folly! Land despise Trade! and Trade set up against Land? – Can any Thing be more absurd? Is not Trade the Nurse of Land? And is not Land the Nourishment of Trade? Does not Land supply the Materials of Trade? And does not Trade enable the Land to supply these Materials? Land produces Wool, Corn, Cattle, Timber, Hemp, Metals, and Minerals; Trade produces a Market for all these, gives a Price to them, brings Home Silver to Circulate that Trade, and feeds the People who take off these Provisions at a Price, and by this, Land lives – What would Land be without it?

The Monster I tell you of, was really born at, or near *Glasgow*, and liv'd many Years in that unhappy Conjunction – Came at last to this miserable End – And is an Emblem to our purpose in its End, as it was in its Life; one of the Bodies died before the other – *What was to be done then?* What Course to be taken to preserve the Living Part? – Indeed nothing – No – Nature had it not in her Power, Art could give no help, the Living Body was ty'd fast to the Dead – it mourn'd, it griev'd, it wept, it struggled, it pin'd, but *it could not be*; the Mortification convey'd itself on gradually to the Living Part, it Languish'd, and became a Carcass by meer Natural Consequence.

Let your Landed Men that would crush our Trade, take the Hint –

Whenever Trade dies, Land will, of course, feel the beginnings of Death – Land will pine, fade, Languish, and at last, die into its Original Poverty, and its meer Native Condition.

Trade then, is the Life of the Land's Wealth, and Land will be no Fund without it; and those People that think to make Land a Fund, must cherish Trade to support the Value or Rent or Land, or they destroy that Fund themselves.

Passage 2.3
(Joseph Addison, *The Spectator*, No. 69, 19 May 1711)

Hic segetes, illic veniunt felicius uvae:
Arborei foetus alibi, atque injussa virescunt
Gramina. Nonne vides, croceos ut Tmolus odores,
India mittit ebur, molles sua thura Sabaei?
At Chalybes nudi ferrum, virosaque Pontus
Castorea, Eliadum palmas Epirus equarum?
Continuo has leges aeternaque foedera certis
Imposuit Natura locis . . .

Vir.[1]

There is no Place in the Town which I so much love to frequent as the *Royal-Exchange*. It gives me a secret Satisfaction, and, in some measure, gratifies my Vanity, as I am an *Englishman*, to see so rich an Assembly of Country-men and Foreigners consulting together upon the private Business of Mankind, and making this Metropolis a kind of *Emporium* for the whole Earth. I must confess I look upon High-Change to be a great Council, in which all considerable Nations have their Representatives. Factors in the Trading World are what Ambassadors are in the Politick World; they negotiate Affairs, conclude Treaties, and maintain a good Correspondence between those wealthy Societies of Men that are divided from one another by Seas and Oceans, or live on the different Extremities of a Continent. I have often been pleased to hear Disputes adjusted between an Inhabitant of *Japan* and an Alderman of *London*, or to see a Subject of the *Great Mogul* entering into a League with one of the *Czar* of *Muscovy*. I am infinitely delighted in mixing with these several Ministers of Commerce, as they are distinguished by their different Walks and different Languages: Sometimes I am justled among a Body of *Armenians*: Sometimes I am lost in a Crowd of *Jews*, and sometimes make one in a Groupe of *Dutch-men*. I am a *Dane*, *Swede*, or *French-Man* at different times, or rather fancy my self like the old Philosopher, who upon being asked what Country-man he was, replied, That he was a Citizen of the World.

Though I very frequently visit this busie Multitude of People, I am known to no Body there but my Friend, Sir ANDREW, who often smiles upon me as he sees me bustling in the Croud, but at the same time connives at my Presence without taking any further notice of me. There is indeed a Merchant of *Egypt*, who just knows me by sight, having formerly remitted me some Mony to *Grand Cairo*; but as I am not versed in the Modern *Coptick*, our Conferences go no further than a Bow and a Grimace.

This grand Scene of Business gives me an infinite Variety of solid and substantial Entertainments. As I am a great Lover of Mankind, my Heart naturally overflows with Pleasure at the sight of a prosperous and happy Multitude, insomuch that at many publick Solemnities I cannot forbear expressing my Joy with Tears that have stolen down my Cheeks. For this reason I am wonderfully delighted to see such a Body of Men thriving in their own private Fortunes, and at the same time promoting the Publick Stock; or in other Words, raising Estates for their own Families, by bringing into their Country whatever is wanting, and carrying out of it whatever is superfluous.

Nature seems to have taken a particular Care to disseminate her Blessings among the different Regions of the World, with an Eye to this mutual Intercourse and Traffick among Mankind, that the Natives of the several Parts of the Globe might have a kind of Dependance upon one another, and be united together by their common Interest. Almost every *Degree* produces something peculiar to it. The Food often grows in one Country, and the Sauce in another. The Fruits of *Portugal* are corrected by the Products of *Barbadoes*: The Infusion of a *China* Plant sweetned with the Pith of an *Indian* Cane: The *Philippick* Islands give a Flavour to our *European* Bowls. The single Dress of a Woman of Quality is often the Product of an hundred Climates. The Muff and the Fan come together from the different Ends of the Earth. The Scarf is sent from the Torrid Zone, and the Tippet from beneath the Pole. The Brocade Petticoat rises out of the Mines of *Peru*, and the Diamond Necklace out of the Bowels of *Indostan*.

If we consider our own Country in its natural Prospect, without any of the Benefits and Advantages of Commerce, what a barren uncomfortable Spot of Earth falls to our Share! Natural Historians tell us, that no Fruit grows originally among us, besides Hips and Haws, Acorns and Pig-Nutts, with other Delicacies of the like Nature; That our Climate of itself, and without the Assistances of Art, can make no further Advances towards a Plumb than to a Sloe, and carries an Apple to no greater a Perfection than a Crab: That our Melons, our Peaches, our Figs, our Apricots, and Cherries, are Strangers among us, imported in different Ages, and naturalized in our *English* Gardens; and that they would all degenerate and fall away into the Trash of our own Country, if they were wholly neglected by the Planter, and left to the Mercy of our Sun and Soil. Nor has Traffick more enriched our Vegetable World, than it has improved the whole Face of Nature among us. Our Ships are laden with the Harvest of every Climate: Our Tables are stored with Spices, and Oils, and Wines: Our Rooms are filled with Pyramids of *China*, and adorned with the Workmanship of *Japan*: Our Morning's-Draught comes to us from the remotest Corners of the Earth: We repair our Bodies by the Drugs of *America*, and repose our selves under *Indian* Canopies. My Friend Sir ANDREW calls the Vineyards of *France* our Gardens; the Spice-Islands our Hot-Beds; the *Persians* our Silk-Weavers, and the *Chinese* our Potters. Nature indeed furnishes us with the bare Necessaries of Life, but Traffick gives us a great Variety of what is Useful, and at the same time supplies us with everything that is Convenient and Ornamental. Nor is it the least part of this our Happiness, that whilst we enjoy the remotest Products of the North and South, we are free from those Extremities of Weather which give them Birth; That our Eyes are refreshed with the green Fields of *Britain*, at the same time that our Palates are feasted with Fruits that rise between the Tropicks.

For these Reasons there are not more useful Members in a Commonwealth than Merchants. They knot Mankind together in a mutual Intercourse of good Offices, distribute the Gifts of Nature, find Work for the Poor, add Wealth to the Rich, and Magnificence to the Great. Our *English* Merchant converts the Tin of his own Country into Gold, and exchanges his Wooll for Rubies. The *Mahometans* are cloathed in our *British* Manufacture, and the Inhabitants of the Frozen Zone warmed with the Fleeces of our Sheep.

When I have been upon the *'Change*, I have often fancied one of our old Kings standing in Person, where he is represented in Effigy, and looking down upon the wealthy Concourse of People with which that Place is every Day filled. In this Case, how would he be surprized to hear all the Languages of *Europe* spoken in this little Spot of his former Dominions, and to see so many private Men, who in his Time would have been the Vassals of some powerful Baron, Negotiating like Princes for greater Sums of Mony than were formerly to be met with in the Royal Treasury! Trade, without enlarging the *British* Territories, has given us a kind of additional Empire: It has multiplied the Number of the Rich, made our Landed Estates infinitely more Valuable than they were formerly, and added to them an Accession of other Estates as Valuable as the Lands themselves.

Passage 2.4
(Joseph Addison, *The Freeholder*, No. 42, 14 May 1716)

O Fortunatos Mercatores!
Hor.[2]

Several Authors have written on the Advantage of Trade in general; which is indeed so copious a Subject, that as it is impossible to exhaust it in a short Discourse, so it is very difficult to observe any thing New upon it. I shall, therefore, only consider Trade in this Paper, as it is absolutely necessary and essential to the Safety, Strength, and Prosperity of our own Nation.

In the first Place, as we are an Island accommodated on all Sides with convenient Ports, and encompassed with navigable Seas, we should be inexcusable, if we did not make these Blessings of Providence and Advantages of Nature turn to their proper Account. The most celebrated Merchants in the World, and those who make the greatest Figure in Antiquity, were situated in the little Island of *Tyre*, which, by the prodigious Increase of its Wealth and Strength at Sea, did very much influence the most considerable Kingdoms and Empires on the neighbouring Continent, and gave birth to the *Carthaginians*, who afterwards exceeded all other Nations in Naval Power. The old *Tyre* was indeed seated on the Continent, from whence the Inhabitants, after having been besieged by the Great King of *Assyria* for the Space of thirteen Years, withdrew themselves and their Effects into the Island of *Tyre*; where, by the Benefit of such a Situation, a Trading People were enabled to hold out for many Ages against the Attempts of their Enemies, and became the Merchants of the World.

Further; as an Island, we are accessible on every Side, and exposed to perpetual Invasions; against which it is impossible to fortify ourselves sufficiently without such a Power at Sea, as is not to be kept up, but by a People who flourish in Commerce. To which we must add, that our inland Towns being destitute of Fortifications, it is our indispensable Concern to preserve this our Naval Strength, which is as a general Bulwark to the *British* Nation.

Besides; as an Island, it has not been thought agreeable to the true *British* Policy to make Acquisitions upon the Continent. In lieu, therefore, of such an Increase of Dominion, it is our Business to extend to the utmost our Trade and Navigation. By this Means we reap the Advantages of Conquest, without Violence or Injustice; we not only strengthen ourselves, but gain the Wealth of our Neighbours in an honest Way; and, without any Act of Hostility, lay the several Nations, of the World under a kind of Contribution.

Secondly, Trade is fitted to the Nature of our Country, as it abounds with a great Profusion of Commodities of its own Growth very convenient for other Countries, and is naturally destitute of many Things suited to the Exigences, Ornaments and Pleasures of Life, which may be fetched from Foreign Parts. But that which is more particularly to be remarked, our *British* Products are of such Kinds and Quantities, as can turn the Balance of Trade to our Advantage, and enable us to sell more to Foreigners than we have occasion to buy from them.

To this we must add, that by extending a well-regulated Trade, we are as great Gainers by the Commodities of many other Countries, as by those of our own Nation; and by supplying foreign Markets with the Growth and Manufactures of the most distant Regions, we receive the same Profit from them, as if they were the Produce of our own Island.

Thirdly, We are not a little obliged to Trade, as it has been a great Means of civilizing our Nation, and banishing out of it all the Remains of its antient Barbarity. There are many bitter Sayings against Islanders in general, representing them as fierce, treacherous and inhospitable. Those who live on the Continent have such Opportunities of a frequent Intercourse with Men of different Religions and Languages, and who live under different Laws and Governments, that they become more kind, benevolent, and open-hearted to their Fellow-Creatures, than those who are the Inhabitants of an Island, that hath not such Conversations with the rest of the Species. *Caesar*'s Observation upon our Fore-fathers is very much to our present Purpose; who remarks, That those of them who lived upon the Coast, or in the Sea-Port Towns, were much more Civilized, than those who had their Dwellings in the Inland Country, by reason of frequent Communications with their Neighbours on the Continent.

In the last Place. Trade is absolutely necessary for us, as our Country is very populous. It employs Multitudes of Hands both by Sea and Land, and furnishes the poorest of our Fellow-Subjects with the Opportunities of gaining an honest Livelihood. The Skilful or Industrious find their Account in it: And many, who have no fixed Property in the Soil of our Country, can make themselves Masters of as considerable Estates, as those who have the greatest Portions of the Land descending to them by Inheritance.

If what has been often charged upon us by our Neighbours has any Truth in it, That we are prone to Sedition and delight in Change, there is no cure more proper for this Exit than Trade, which thus supplies Business to the Active, and Wealth to the Indigent. When Men are easy in their Circumstances, they are naturally Enemies to Innovations: And indeed we see in the Course of our *English* Histories, many of our popular Commotions have taken their Rise from the Decay of some Branch of Commerce, which created Discontents among Persons concerned in the Manufactures of the Kingdom. When Men are sower'd with Poverty, and unemploy'd, they easily give into any Prospect of Change which may better their Condition, and cannot make it much worse.

Passage 2.5
(*from* Henry St John, Viscount Bolingbroke, *The Idea of a Patriot King*, c. 1740)

The situation of *Great Britain*, the character of her people, and the nature of her government, fit her for trade and commerce. Her climate and her soil make them necessary to her well-being. By trade and commerce we grew a rich and powerful nation, and by their decay we are growing poor and impotent. As trade and commerce enrich, so they fortify, our country. The sea is our barrier, ships are our fortresses, and the mariners, that trade and commerce alone can furnish, are the garrisons to defend them. *France* lies under great disadvantages in trade and commerce, by the nature of her government. Her advantages, in situation, are as great at least as ours. Those that arise, from the temper and character of her people, are a little different perhaps, and yet upon the whole equivalent. Those of her climate and her soil are superior to ours, and indeed to those of any *European* nation. The *United Provinces* have the same advantages that we have in the nature of their government, more perhaps in the temper and character of their people, less to be sure in their situation, climate, and soil. But, without descending into a longer detail of the advantages and disadvantages attending each of these nations in trade and commerce, it is sufficient for my present purpose to observe, that *Great Britain* stands in a certain middle between the other two, with regard to wealth and *power* arising from these springs. A less, and a less constant, application to the improvement of these may serve the ends of *France*; a greater is necessary in this country; and a greater still in *Holland*. The *French* may improve their natural wealth and power by the improvement of trade and commerce. We can have no wealth, nor power by consequence, as *Europe* is now constituted, without the improvement of them, nor in any degree but proportionably to this improvement. The *Dutch* cannot subsist without them. They bring wealth to other nations, and are necessary to the well-being of them; but they supply the *Dutch* with food and raiment, and are necessary even to their being.

The result of what has been said is, in general, that the wealth and power of all nations depending so much on their trade and commerce, and every nation being, like the three I have mentioned, in such different circumstances of advantage or disadvantage in the pursuit if this common interest; a good government, and therefore the government of a PATRIOT KING, will be directed constantly to make the most of every advantage that nature has given or art can procure, towards the improvement of trade and commerce. And this is one of the principal criterions by which we are to judge, whether governors are in the true interest of the people, or not.

It results, *in particular*, that *Great Britain* might improve her wealth and power in a proportion superior to that of any nation who can be deemed her rival, if the advantages she has were as wisely cultivated, as they will be in the reign of a PATRIOT KING. To be convinced more thoroughly of this truth, a very short process of reasoning will suffice. Let any man, who has knowledge enough for it, first compare the natural state of *Great Britain*, and of the *United Provinces*, and then their artificial state together; that is, let him consider minutely the advantages we have by the situation, extent, and nature of our island, over the inhabitants of a few salt marshes gained on the sea, and hardly defended from it: and after that, let him consider how nearly these provinces have raised themselves to an equality of wealth and power with the kingdom of *Great Britain*. From whence arises this difference of improvement? It arises plainly from hence: the *Dutch* have been, from the foundation of their common-wealth, a nation of *patriots and merchants*. The spirit of that people has not been diverted from these two objects, the defence of their liberty, and the improvement of their trade and commerce; which have been carried on by them with uninterrupted and unslackened application, industry, order, and oeconomy. In Great Britain the case has not been the same, in either respect; but here we confine ourselves to speak of the last alone.

Trade and commerce, such as they were in those days, had been sometimes, and in some instances, before the reign of Queen ELIZABETH, encouraged and improved: but the great encouragements were given, the great extensions and improvements were made, by that glorious princess. To her we owe that spirit of domestic and foreign trade which is not quite extinguished. It was she who gave that rapid motion to our whole mercantile system which is not entirely ceased. They both flagged under her successor; were not revived under his son; were checked, diverted, clogged, and interrupted, during our civil wars: and began to exert new vigour after the restoration, in a long course of peace; but met with new difficulties, too, from the confirmed rivalry of the *Dutch*, and the growing rivalry of the *French*. To one of these the pusillanimous character of JAMES the first gave many scandalous occasions: and the other was favoured by the conduct of CHARLES the second, who never was in the true interest of the people he governed. From the revolution to the death of queen ANNE, however trade and commerce might be aided and encouraged in other respects, they were necessarily subjected to depredations abroad, and over-loaded by taxes at home, during the course of two great wars. From the accession of the late king to this hour, in the midst of a full peace, the debts of the nation continue much the same, the taxes have been encreased, and for eighteen years of this time we have tamely suffered continual depredations from the most contemptible maritime power in *Europe*, that of *Spain*.

A PATRIOT KING will neither neglect, nor sacrifice, his country's interest. No other interest, neither a foreign nor a domestic, neither a public nor a private, will influence his conduct in government. He will not multiply taxes wantonly, nor keep up those unnecessarily which necessity has laid, that he may keep up legions of tax-gatherers. He will not continue national debts, by all sorts of political and other profusion; nor, more wickedly still, by a settled purpose of oppressing and impoverishing the people; that he may with greater ease corrupt some, and govern the whole, according to the dictates of his passions and arbitrary will. To give ease and encouragement to manufactory at home, to assist and protect trade abroad, to improve and keep in heart the national colonies, like so many farms of the mother country, will be principal and constant parts of the attention of such a Prince. The wealth of the nation he will most justly esteem to be his wealth, the power his power, the security and the honour, his security and honour: and, by the very means by which he promotes the two first, he will wisely preserve the two last; for by these means, and by these alone, can the great advantage of the *situation* of this kingdom be taken and improved.

Passage 2.6
(Samuel Johnson, *The Adventurer*, No. 67, 26 June 1753)

Inventas-vitam excoluere per artes.
Virg.[3]

That familiarity produces neglect, has been long observed. The effect of all external objects, however great or splendid, ceases with their novelty: the courtier stands without emotion in the royal presence; the rustic tramples under his foot the beauties of the spring, with little attention to their colour or their fragrance; and the inhabitant of the coast darts his eye upon the immense diffusion of waters, without awe, wonder, or terror.

Those who have past much of their lives in this great city, look upon its opulence and its multitudes, its extent and variety, with cold indifference; but an inhabitant of the remoter parts of the kingdom is immediately distinguished by a kind of dissipated curiosity, a busy endeavour to divide his attention amongst a thousand objects, and a wild confusion of astonishment and alarm.

The attention of a new-comer is generally first struck by the multiplicity of cries that stun him in the streets, and the variety of merchandise and manufactures which the shopkeepers expose on every hand; and he is apt, by unwary bursts of admiration, to excite the merriment and contempt of those, who mistake the use of their eyes for effects of their understanding, and confound accidental knowledge with just reasoning.

But, surely, these are subjects on which any man may without reproach employ his meditations: the innumerable occupations, among which the thousands that swarm in the streets of London are distributed, may furnish employment to minds of every cast, and capacities of every degree. He that contemplates the extent of this wonderful city, finds it difficult to conceive, by what method plenty is maintained in our markets, and how the inhabitants are regularly supplied with the necessaries of life; but when he examines the shops and warehouses, sees the immense stores of every kind of merchandise piled up for sale, and runs over all the manufactures of art and products of nature, which are every where attracting his eye and soliciting his purse, he will be inclined to conclude, that such quantities cannot easily be exhausted, and that part of mankind must soon stand still for want of employment, till the wares already provided shall be worn out and destroyed.

As Socrates was passing through the fair at Athens, and casting his eyes over the shops and customers, 'how many things are here,' says he, 'that I do not want!' The same sentiment is every moment rising in the mind of him that walks the streets of London, however inferior in philosophy to Socrates: he beholds a thousand shops crouded with goods, of which he can scarcely tell the use, and which, therefore, he is apt to consider as of no value; and, indeed, many of the arts by which families are supported, and wealth is heaped together, are of that minute and superfluous kind, which nothing but experience could evince possible to be prosecuted with advantage, and which, as the world might easily want, it could scarcely be expected to encourage.

But so it is, that custom, curiosity, or wantonness, supplies every art with patrons, and finds purchasers for every manufacture; the world is so adjusted, that not only bread, but riches may be obtained without great abilities, or arduous performances: the most unskilful hand and unenlightened mind have sufficient incitements to industry; for he that is resolutely busy, can scarcely be in want. There is, indeed, no employment, however despicable, from which a man may not promise himself more than competence, when he sees thousands and myriads raised to dignity, by not other merit than that of contributing to supply their neighbours with the means of sucking smoke through a tube of clay; and others raising contributions upon those, whose elegance disdains the grossness of smoky luxury, by grinding the same materials into a powder, that may at once gratify and impair the smell.

Not only by these popular and modish trifles, but by a thousand unheeded and evanescent kinds of business, are the multitudes of this city preserved from idleness, and consequently from want. In the endless variety of tastes and circumstances that diversify mankind, nothing is so superfluous, but that some one desires it; or so common, but that some one is compelled to buy it. As nothing is useless but because it is in improper hands, what is thrown away by one is gathered up by another; and the refuse of part of mankind furnishes a subordinate class with the materials necessary to their support.

When I look round upon those who are thus variously exerting their qualifications, I cannot but admire the secret concatenation of society, that links together the great and the mean, the illustrious and the obscure; and consider with benevolent satisfaction, that no man, unless his body or mind be totally disabled, has need to suffer the mortification of seeing himself useless or burdensome to the community: he that will diligently labour, in whatever occupation, will deserve the sustenance which he obtains, and the protection which he enjoys; and may lie down every night with the pleasing consciousness, of having contributed something to the happiness of life.

Contempt and admiration are equally incident to narrow minds: he whose comprehension can take in the whole subordination of mankind, and whose perspicacity can pierce to the real state of things through the thin veils of fortune or of fashion, will discover meanness in the highest stations, and dignity in the meanest; and find that no man can become venerable but by virtue, or contemptible but by wickedness.

In the midst of this universal hurry, no man ought to be so little influenced by example, or so void of honest emulation, as to stand a lazy spectator of incessant labour; or please himself with the mean happiness of a drone, while the active swarms are buzzing about him: no man is without some quality, by the due application of which he might deserve well of the world; and whoever he be that has but little in his power, should be in haste to do that little, lest he be confounded with him that can do nothing.

By this general concurrence of endeavours, arts of every kind have been so long cultivated, that all the wants of man may be immediately supplied; idleness can scarcely form a wish which she may not gratify by the toil of others, or curiosity dream of a toy which the shops are not ready to afford her.

Happiness is enjoyed only in proportion as it is known; and such is the state or folly of man, that it is known only by the experience of its contrary: we who have long lived amidst the conveniences of a town immensely populous, have scarce an idea of a place where desire cannot be gratified by money. In order to have a just sense of this artificial plenty, it is necessary to have passed some time in a distant colony, or those parts of our island which are thinly inhabited: he that has once known how many trades every man in such situations is compelled to exercise, with how much labour the products of nature must be accommodated to human use, how long the loss or defect of any common utensil must be endured, or by what aukward expedients it must be supplied, how far men may wander with money in their hands before any can sell them what they wish to buy, will know how to rate at its proper value the plenty and ease of a great city.

But that the happiness of man may still remain imperfect, as wants in this place are easily supplied, new wants likewise are easily created: every man, in surveying the shops of London, sees numberless instruments and conveniences, of which, while he did not know them, he never felt the need; and yet, when use has made them familiar, wonders how life could be supported without them. Thus it comes to pass, that our desires always increase with our possessions; the knowledge that something remains yet unenjoyed, impairs our enjoyment of the good before us.

They who have been accustomed to the refinements of science, and multiplications of contrivance, soon lose their confidence in the unassisted powers of nature, forget the paucity of our real necessities, and overlook the easy methods by which they may be supplied. It were a speculation worthy of a philosophical mind, to examine how much is taken away from our native abilities, as well as added to them by artificial expedients. We are so accustomed to give and receive assistance, that each of us singly can do little for himself; and there is scarce any one amongst us, however contracted may be his form of life, who does not enjoy the labour of a thousand artists.

But a survey of the various nations that inhabit the earth will inform us, that life may be supported with less assistance, and that the dexterity, which practice enforced by necessity produces, is able to effect much by very scanty means. The nations of Mexico and Peru erected cities and temples without the use of iron; and at this day the rude Indian supplies himself with all the necessaries of life: sent like the rest of mankind naked into the world, as soon as his parents have nursed him up to strength, he is to provide by his own labour for his own support. His first care is to find a sharp flint among the rocks; with this he undertakes to fell the trees of the forest; he shapes his bow, heads his arrows, builds his cottage, and hollows his canoe, and from that time lives in a state of plenty and prosperity; he is sheltered from the storms, he is fortified against beasts of prey, he is enabled to persue the fish of the sea, and the deer of the mountains – and as he does not know, does not envy the happiness of polished nations, where gold can supply the want of fortitude and skill, and he whose laborious ancestors have made him rich, may lie stretched upon a couch, and see all the treasures of all the elements poured down before him.

This picture of a savage life, if it shews how much individuals may perform, shews likewise how much society is to be desired. Though the perseverance and address of the Indian excite our admiration, they nevertheless cannot procure him the conveniences which are enjoyed by the vagrant beggar of a civilized country; he hunts like a wild beast to satisfy his hunger; and when he lies down to rest after a successful chace, cannot pronounce himself secure against the danger of perishing in a few days; he is, perhaps, content with his condition, because he knows not that a better is attainable by a man; as he that is born blind does not long for the perception of light, because he cannot conceive the advantages which light would afford him: but hunger, wounds and weariness are real evils, though he believes them equally incident to all his fellow creatures; and when a tempest compels him to lie starving in his hut, he cannot justly be concluded equally happy with those whom art has exempted from the power of chance, and who make the foregoing year provide for the following.

To receive and to communicate assistance, constitutes the happiness of human life. man may indeed preserve his existence in solitude, but can enjoy it only in society: the greatest understanding of an individual, doomed to procure food and cloathing for himself, will barely supply him with expedients to keep off death from day to day; but as one of a large community performing only his share of the common business, he gains leisure for intellectual pleasures, and enjoys the happiness of reason and reflection.

Passage 2.7a
(*from* Daniel Defoe, *A Tour thro' the whole Island of Great Britain*, 1724-7)

From hence to *Leeds*, and every way to the Right hand and the Left, the Country appears busy, diligent, and even in a hurry of Work, they are not scattered and dispersed as in the Vicaridge of *Hallifax*, where the Houses stand one by one; but in Villages, those Villages large, full of Houses, and those Houses thronged with People, for the whole Country is infinitely populous.

A noble Scene of Industry and Application is spread before you here, and which, joined to the Market at Leeds, where it chiefly centers, is such a surprising thing, that they who have pretended to give an Account of *Yorkshire*, and have left this out, must betray an Ignorance not to be accounted for, or excused; 'tis what is well worth the Curiosity of a Stranger to go on purpose to see; and many Travellers and Gentlemen have come over from *Hamburgh*, nay, even from *Leipsick* in *Saxony*, on purpose to see it.

And this brought me from the Villages where this Manufacture is wrought, to the Market where it is sold, which is at *Leeds*.

Leeds is a large, wealthy and populous Town, it stands on the North Bank of the River *Aire*, or rather on both Sides the River, for there is a large Suburb or Part of the Town on the South Side of the River, and the whole is joined by a stately and prodigiously strong Stone Bridge, so large, and so wide, that formerly the Cloth Market was kept in neither Part of the Town, but on the very Bridge it self; and therefore the Refreshment given the Clothiers by the Inn-keepers, of which I shall speak presently, is called the *Brigg-shot* to this Day.

The Encrease of the Manufactures and of the Trade, soon made the Market too great to be confined to the Brigg or Bridge, and it is now kept in the High-street, beginning from the Bridge, and running up North almost to the Market-House, where the ordinary Market for Provisions begins, which also is the greatest of its kind in all the North of *England*, except *Hallifax*, of which I have spoken already, nay, the People at *Leeds* will not allow me to except *Hallifax*, but say, that theirs is the greatest Market, and not the greatest Plenty only, but the best of all Kinds of Provisions are brought hither.

But this is not the Case; it is the Cloth Market I am now to describe, which is indeed a Prodigy of its Kind and is not to be equalled in the World. The Market for Serges at Exeter is indeed a wonderful Thing, and the Value sold there is very great; but then the Market there is but once a Week, here it is twice a Week, and the Quantity of Goods vastly great too.

The Market it self is worth describing, tho' no Description can come up to the Thing it self; however, take a Sketch of it with its Customs and Usages as follows:

The Street is a large, broad, fair and well-built Street, beginning, as I have said, at the Bridge, and ascending gently to the North.

Early in the Morning, there are Tressels placed in two Rows in the Street, sometimes two Rows on a Side, but always one Row at least; then there are Boards laid cross those Tressels, so that the Boards lie like long Counters on either Side, from one end of the Street to the other.

The Clothiers come early in the Morning with their Cloth; and as few Clothiers bring more than one Piece, the Market being so frequent, they go into the Inns and Publick-Houses with it, and there set it down.

At seven a Clock in the Morning, the Clothiers being supposed to be all come by that time, even in the Winter, but the Hour is varied as the Seasons advance (in the Summer earlier, in the Depth of Winter a little later) I take it, at a Medium, and as it was when I was there, at six or seven, I say, the Market Bell rings; it would surprize a Stranger to see in how few Minutes, without hurry or noise, and not the least disorder, the whole Market is fill'd; all the Boards upon the Tressels are covered with Cloth, close to one another as the Pieces can lie long ways by one another, and behind every Piece of Cloth, the Clothier standing to sell it.

This indeed is not so difficult, when we consider that the whole Quantity is brought into the Market as soon as one Piece, because as the Clothiers stand ready in the Inns and Shops just behind, and that there is a Clothier to every Piece, they have no more to do, but, like a Regiment drawn up in Line, every one takes up his Piece, and has about five Steps to march to lay it upon the first Row of Boards, and perhaps ten to the second Row; so that upon the Market Bell ringing, in half a quarter of an Hour the whole Market is fill'd, and Rows of Boards cover'd, and the Clothiers stand ready.

As soon as the Bell has done Ringing, the Merchants and Factors, and Buyers of all Sorts, come down, and coming along the Spaces between the Rows of Boards, they walk up the Rows, and down as their Occasions direct. Some of them have their foreign Letters of Orders, with Patterns feal'd on them, in Rows, in their Hands; and with those they match Colours, holding them to the Cloths as they think they agree to: when they see any Cloths to their Colours, or that suit their occasions, they reach over to the Clothier and whisper, and in the fewest Words imaginable the Price is stated; one asks, the other bids; and 'tis agree, or nor agree, in a Moment.

The Merchants and Buyers generally walk down and up twice on each Side of the Town, and in little more than an Hour all the Business is done; in less than half an Hour you will perceive the Cloths begin to move off, the Clothier taking it up upon his Shoulder to carry it to the Merchant's House; and by half an hour after eight a Clock the Market Bell rings again; immediately the Buyers disappear, the Cloth is all sold, or if here and there a Piece happens not to be bought, 'tis carried back into the Inn, and, in a quarter of an Hour, there is not a Piece of Cloth to be seen in the Market.

Thus, you see, Ten or Twenty thousand Pounds value in Cloth, and sometimes much more, bought and sold in little more than an Hour, and the Laws of the Market the most strictly observed as ever I saw done in any Market in *England*; for,

1. Before the Market Bell rings, no Man shews a Piece of Cloth, nor can the Clothiers sell any but in open Market.

2. After the Market Bell rings again, no Body stays a Moment in the Market, but carries his Cloth back if it be not sold.

3. And that which is most admirable is, 'tis all managed with the most profound Silence, and you cannot hear a Word spoken in the whole Market, I mean, by the Persons buying and selling; 'tis all done in whisper.

The reason of this Silence, is chiefly because the Clothiers stand so near to one another; and 'tis always reasonable that one should not know what another does, for that would be discovering their Business, and exposing it to one another.

If a Merchant has bidden a Clothier a Price, and he will not take it, he may go after him to his House, and tell him he has considered of it, and is willing to let him have it; but they are not to make any new Agreement for it, so as to remove the Market from the Street to the Merchant's House.

By nine a Clock the Boards are taken down, the Tressels are removed, and the Street cleared, so that you see no Market or Goods any more than if there had been nothing to do; and this is done twice a Week. By this quick Return the Clothiers are constantly supplied with Money, their Workmen are duly paid, and a prodigious Sum circulates thro' the County every Week.

If you should ask upon all this, where all these Goods, as well here as at *Wakefield*, and at *Hallifax*, are vented and disposed of? It would require a long Treatise of Commerce to enter into that Part: But that I may not bring you into the Labyrinth, and not show you the way out, I shall, in three short Heads, describe the Consumption, for there are three Channels by which it goes:

1. For the home Consumption; their Goods being, as I may say, every where made use of, for the cloathing the ordinary People, who cannot go to the Price of the fine Medley Cloths made, as I formerly gave you Account, in the Western Counties of *England*. There are for this purpose a Set of travelling Merchants in *Leeds*, who go all over *England* with Droves of Pack Horses, and to all the Fairs and Market Towns over the whole Island, I think I may say none excepted. Here they supply not the common People by Retail, which would denominate them Pedlars indeed, but they supply the Shops by Wholesale or whole Pieces; and not only so, but give large Credit too, so that they are really travelling Merchants, and as such they sell a very great Quantity of Goods; 'tis ordinary for one of these Men to carry a thousand Pounds value of Cloth with them at a time, and having sold it at the Fairs or Towns where they go, they send their Horses back for as much more, and this very often in a Summer, for they chuse to travel in the Summer, and perhaps towards the Winter time, tho' as little in Winter as they can, because of the badness of the Roads.

2. Another Sort of Buyers are those who buy to send to London; either by Commissions from *London*, or they give Commissions to Factors and Warehouse-keepers in *London* to sell for them; and these drive also a very great Trade: These Factors and Warehouse-keepers not only supply all the Shop-keepers and Wholesale Men in *London*, but sell also very great Quantities to the Merchants, as well for Exportation to the *English* Colonies in *America*, which take off great Quantities of those

course Goods, especially *New England*, *New York*, *Virginia*, *&c.* as also to the *Russia* Merchants, who send an exceeding Quantity to *Petersburgh*, *Riga*, *Dantzic*, *Narva*, and to *Sweden* and *Pomerania*.

3. The third Sort of Buyers, and who are not less considerable than the other, are truly Merchants, that is to say, such as receive Commissions from Abroad to buy Cloth for the Merchants chiefly in *Hamburgh*, and in *Holland*, and from several other Parts; and these are not only many in Number, but some of them are very considerable in their Dealings, and correspond as far as *Nuremberg*, *Frankfort*, *Leipsick*, and even to *Vienna* and *Ausburgh*, in the farthest Provinces of *Germany*.

On Account of this Trade it was, that some Years ago an Act of Parliament was obtained for making the Rivers *Aire* and *Calder* Navigable; by which a Communication by Water was opened from *Leeds* and *Wakefield* to *Hull*, and by which means all the Woollen Manufactures which those Merchants now export by Commission, as above, is carried by Water to *Hull*, and there shipped for *Holland*, *Bremen*, *Hamburgh*, and the *Baltick*. And thus you have a brief Account, by what Methods this vast Manufacture is carried off, and which way they find a Vent for it.

There is another Trade in this part of the Country, which is now become very considerable since the opening the Navigation of these Rivers, and that is, that from hence they carry Coals down from *Wakefield* (especially) and also from *Leeds*, at both which they have a very great Quantity, and such, as they told me could never be exhausted. These they carry quite down into the *Humber*, and then up the *Ouse* to *York*, and up the *Trent*, and other Rivers, where there are abundance of large Towns, who they supply with Coals; with this Advantage too, that whereas the *Newcastle* Coals pay four Shillings *per* Chaldron Duty to the Publick; these being only called *River Borne* Coal, are exempted, and pay nothing; though, strictly speaking, they are carried on the Sea too, for the *Humber* is properly the *Sea*. But they have been hitherto exempted from the Tax, and so they carry on the Trade to their very great Profit and Advantage.

I need not add, that by the same Navigation they receive all their heavy Goods, as well such as are Imported at *Hull*, as such as come from *London*, and such as other Counties supply, as *Butter*, *Cheese*, *Lead*, *Iron*, *Salt*; all Sorts of *Grocery*, as *Sugars*, *Tobacco*, *Fruit*, *Spice*, *Hops*, *&c.* *Oyl*, *Wine*, *Brandy*, *Spirits*, and every Sort of heavy or bulky Goods.

The Town of *Leeds* is very large, and, as above, there are abundance of wealthy Merchants in it. Here are two Churches, and two large

Meeting-Houses of Dissenters, and six or seven Chapels of Ease, besides Dissenters Chapels, in the adjacent, depending Villages; so that *Leeds* may not be much inferior to *Hallifax* in Numbers of People: It is really a surprising Thing to see what Numbers of People are thronged together in all the Villages about these Towns; and how busy they all are, being fully employed in this great Manufacture.

Passage 2.7b
(*from* Defoe, *Tour*, 1724-7)

In the low Country, on the other Side *Mendip Hills*, lies *Chedder*, a Village pleasantly situated under the very Ridge of the Mountains; before the Village is a large Green, or Common, a Piece of Ground, in which the whole Herd of the Cows, belonging to the Town, do feed; the Ground is exceeding rich, and as the whole Village are Cowkeepers, they take care to keep up the Goodness of the Soil, by agreeing to lay large Quantities of Dung for manuring, and inriching the Land.

The Milk of all the Town Cows, is brought together every Day into a common Room, where the Persons appointed, or trusted for the Management, measure every Man's Quantity, and set it down in a Book; when the Quantities are adjusted, the Milk is all put together, and every Meal's Milk makes One Cheese, and no more, so that the Cheese is bigger, or less, as the Cows yield more, or less, Milk. By this Method, the Goodness of the Cheese is preserved, and, without all Dispute, it is the best Cheese that *England* affords, if not, that the whole World affords.

As the Cheeses are, by this means, very large, for they often weigh a Hundred Weight, sometimes much more, so the poorer Inhabitants, who have but few Cows, are obliged to stay the longer for the Return of their Milk; for no Man has any such Return, 'till his Share comes to a whole Cheese, and then he has it; and if the Quantity of his Milk deliver'd in, comes to above a Cheese, the Overplus rests in Account to his Credit, 'till another Cheese comes to his Share; and thus every Man has equal Justice, and though he should have but one Cow, he shall, in Time, have One whole Cheese. This Cheese is often sold for Six Pence to Eight Pence *per* Pound, when the *Cheshire* Cheese is sold but for Two Pence and Two Pence Halfpenny.

Here is a deep, frightful Chasm in the Mountain, in the Hollow of which, the Road goes, *by which they travel* towards *Bristol*; and out of the same Hollow springs a little River, which flows with such a full Stream, that *it is said*, it drives Twelve Mills within a Quarter of a Mile of the Spring; but this is not to be understood, without supposing it to fetch some winding Reaches in the Way; there would not, otherwise, be Room for Twelve Mills to stand, and have any Head of Water *above the Mill*, within so small a Space of Ground. The Water of this Spring, grows quickly into a River, and runs down into the Marshes, and joins another little River called *Axe*, and *Axbridge*, and thence into the *Bristol Channel*, or *Severn Sea*.

I must now turn *East*, and *South-East*, for I resolved not to go up the Hills of *Mendip* at all, this Journey, leaving that Part to another Tour, when I shall give an Account of these Mountains, as also of the Cities of *Bath* and *Bristol*, to which they are very near, all in One Letter.

I come now to that Part of the Country, which joins itself to *Wiltshire*, which I reserved, in particular, to this Place, in order to give some Account of the *Broad-Cloth* Manufacture, which I several Times mentioned in my first Journey, and which is carried on here, and that to such a Degree, as deserves a Place in all the Descriptions, or Histories, which shall be given of this Country.

As the *East*, and *South* Parts of *Wiltshire* are, as I have already observed, all Hilly, spreading themselves far and wide, in Plains, and Grassy Downs, for breeding, and feeding, vast Flocks of Sheep, and a prodigious Number of them: And as the *West* and *North* Parts of *Somersetshire* are, on the contrary, Low, and Marshy, or Moorish, for feeding, and breeding, of black Cattle, and Horses, or for Lead-mines, *&c*. So all the *South West* Part of *Wiltshire*, and the *East* Part of *Somersetshire*, are low and flat, being a rich, inclosed Country, full of Rivers and Towns, and infinitely populous, insomuch, that some of the Market Towns are equal to Cities in Bigness, and superior to them in Numbers of People.

This low, flat Country, contains Part of the Three Counties of *Somerset*, *Wilts*, and *Gloucester*, and that the Extent of it may be the easier understood by those who know any thing of the Situation of the Country, it reaches from *Cirencester* in the *North*, to *Sherburn* on the Edge of *Dorsetshire South*, and from the *Devizes East*, to *Bristol West*, which may take in about Fifty Miles in Length where longest, and Twenty in Breadth where narrowest.

In this Extent of Country, we have the following Market Towns, which are principally employed in the Clothing Trade, that is to say, in that Part of it, which I am now speaking of; namely, Fine Medley, or mix'd Cloths, such as are usually worn in *England* by the better Sort of People; and, also, exported in great Quantities to *Holland*, *Hamburgh*, *Sweden*, *Denmark*, *Spain*, *Italy*, *&c.* The principal Clothing Towns in this Part of the Country, are these,

Somersetshire	*Frome, Pensford, Philip's Norton, Bruton, Shepton Mallet, Castle Carey,* and *Wincanton.*
Wiltshire	*Malmesbury, Castlecomb, Chippenham, Caln, Devizes, Bradford, Trubridge, Westbury, Warminster, Meer.*
Dorsetshire	*Gillingham, Shaftsbury, Bemister,* and *Bere, Sturminster, Shireborn.*
Gloucester	*Cirencester, Tetbury, Marshfield, Minchinghampton,* and *Fairford.*

These Towns, as they stand thin, and at considerable Distance from one another; for, except the Two Towns of *Bradford* and *Trubridge*, the other stand at an unusual Distance; I say, these Towns are interspers'd with a very great Number of Villages, I had almost said, innumerable Villages, Hamlets, and scattered Houses, in which, generally speaking, the spinning Work of all this Manufacture is performed by the poor People; the Master Clothiers, who generally live in the greater Towns, sending out the Wooll Weekly to their Houses, by their Servants and Horses, and, at the same Time, bringing back the Yarn that they have spun and finished, which then is fitted for the Loom.

The increasing and flourishing Circumstances of this Trade, are happily visible by the great Concourse of People to, and Increase of Buildings and Inhabitants in these principal clothing Towns where this Trade is carried on, and the Wealth of the Clothiers. The Town of *Froom*, or, as it is written in our Maps, *Frome Sellwood*, is a Specimen of this, which is so prodigiously increased within these last Twenty or Thirty Years, that they have built a New Church, and so many New Streets of Houses, and those Houses are so full of Inhabitants, that *Frome* is now reckoned to have more People in it, than the City of *Bath*, and some say, than even *Salisbury* itself, and if their Trade continues to increase for a few Years more, as it has done for those past, it is very likely to be one of the greatest and wealthiest Inland Towns in *England*.

I call it an Inland Town, because it is particularly distinguish'd as such, being, not only no Sea-Port, but not near any Sea-Port, having no manner of Communication by Water, no Navigable River at it, or near it. Its Trade is wholly Clothing, and the Cloths they make, are generally speaking, all conveyed to *London*: *Blackwell-Hall* is their Market, and thither they send up the Gross of their Clothing Product; and, if we may believe Common Fame, there are above Ten thousand People in *Frome* now, more than lived in it Twenty Years ago, and yet it was a considerable Town then too.

Here are, also, several large Meeting-Houses, as well as Churches, as there are, generally, in all the manufacturing, trading Towns in *England*, especially in the *Western* Counties.

The *Devizes* is, next to this, a large and important Town, and full of Wealthy Clothiers; but this Town has, lately, run pretty much into the Drugget-making-Trade; a Business, which has made some Invasion upon the Broad-Cloth Trade, and great Quantities of Druggets are worn in *England*, as also, exported beyond the Seas, even in the Place of our Broad-Cloths, and where they usually were worn and exported; but this is much the same as to the Trade still; for as it is all a Woollen Manufacture, and that the Druggets may properly be called Cloth, though Narrow, and of a different Make, so the Makers are all called Clothiers.

The River *Avon*, a noble and large fresh River, branching itself into many Parts, and receiving almost all the Rivers on that Side the Hills, waters this whole fruitful Vale; and the Water of this River seems particularly qualified for the Use of the Clothiers; that is to say, for dying the best Colours, and for fulling and dressing the Cloth, so that the Clothiers generally plant themselves upon this River, but especially the Dyers, as at *Trubridge*, and *Bradford*, which are the Two most eminent Cloathing Towns in that Part of the Vale for the making fine *Spanish* Cloths, and of the nicest Mixtures.

From these Towns *South*, to *Westbury*, and to *Warminster*, the same Trade continues, and the finest Medley *Spanish* Cloths, not in *England* only, but in the whole World, are made in this Part. They told me at *Bradford*, That it was no extraordinary Thing to have Clothiers in that Country worth, from Ten thousand, to Forty thousand Pounds a Man, and many of the great Families, who now pass for Gentry in those Counties, have been originally raised from, and built up by this truly noble Manufacture.

If I may speak here from the Authority of the Antient Inhabitants of the Place, and who have been curious Observers upon this Subject, the Country which I have now described, as principally imploy'd in, and maintained by this Prodigy of a Trade, contains Two million, Three hundred and Thirty Acres of Land, and has in it Seven hundred Eighty-Eight Parishes, and Three hundred and Seventy-four thousand People. It is true, that this is all guess-work; but I must confess myself very willing to believe, that the Reckoning is far short of the Account; for the County is exceeding large and populous.

Passage 2.8
(*from* Josiah Tucker, *Instructions for Travellers*, 1758)

Q. What Machines are used to abridge the Process of a Manufacture, so that one person can do the Work of many? And what is the Consequence of this Abridgment both regarding the Price, and the Numbers of Persons employed?

A. Few Countries are equal, perhaps none excel the *English* in the Numbers and Contrivance of their Machines to abridge Labour. Indeed the *Dutch* are superior to them in the Use and Application of Wind-Mills for sawing Timber, expressing Oil, making Paper, and the like. But in regard to Mines and Metals of all Sorts, the *English* are uncommonly dexterous in their Contrivance of the mechanic Powers; some being calculated for landing the Ores out of Pits, such as Cranes and Horse-Engines: Others again for draining off superfluous Water, such as Water Wheels and Steam Engines: Others again for easing the Expence of Carriage, such as Machines to run on inclined Planes, or Roads down Hill with wooden Frames, in order to carry many Tons of Materials at a Time. And to these must be added the various Sorts of Levers used in different Processes Also the Brass Battery Works, the Slitting Mills, Plate, and Flatting Mills, and those for making Wire of different Fineness. Yet all these, curious as they may seem, are little more than Preparations or Introductions for further Operations. Therefore when we still consider, that at *Bermingham, Wolverhampton, Sheffield*, and other Manufacturing Places, almost every Master Manufacturer hath a new Invention of his own, and is daily improving on those of others; we may aver with some Confidence, that those Parts of *England* in which these Things are to be seen, exhibit a Specimen of practical Mechanics scarce to be paralleled in any Part of the World. As to Machines in the Woollen, and Stuff Way, nothing very considerable hath been of late attempted; owing in a great Measure to the mistaken Notions of the infatuated Populace, who, not being able to see farther than the first Link of the Chain, consider all such Inventions, as taking the Bread out of their Mouths; and therefore never fail to break out into Riots, and Insurrections, whenever such Things are proposed. In regard to the Silk Manufacture, the Throwsting Mills, especially the grand one at *Derby*, are eminent Proofs of the Abridgment of that Species of Labour: And some Attempts have been lately made towards helping forward the Cotton and Linen Manufactures by means of certain Engines.

In regard to the other Part of the Query, *viz.* What is the Consequence of this Abridgment of Labour, both regarding the Price of the Goods, and the Number of Persons employed? The Answer is very short and full, *viz.* That the Price of Goods is thereby prodigiously lowered from what otherwise it must have been; and that a much greater Number of Hands are employed. The first of these is a Position universally assented to; but the other, though nothing more than a Corollary of the former, is looked upon by the Majority of Mankind, and even by some Persons of great Name and Character, as a monstrous Paradox. We must therefore endeavour to clear away these Prejudices Step by Step. And the first Step, that Cheapness, *cæteris paribus*, is an Inducement to buy, – and that many Buyers cause a great Demand, – and that a great Demand brings on a great Consumption – which great Consumption must necessarily employ a vast Variety of Hands, whether the original Material is considered, or the Number and Repair of Machines, or the Materials out of which those Machines are made, or the Persons necessarily employed in tending upon and conducting them: Not to mention those Branches of the Manufacture, Package, Porterage, Stationary Articles, and Bookkeeping, *&c. &c.* which must inevitably be performed by human Labour. But to come to some determinate and striking Instance, let us take the Plow, the Harrow, the Cart, the Instruments for Threshing and Winnowing, and the Mills for Grinding and Boulting, as so many Machines for abridging Labour in the Process of making Bread: I ask, do these Machines prevent, or create Employment for the People? And would there have been as many Persons occupied in raising of Corn, and making of Bread, if no such Engines had been discovered? – The obvious Reply to this Query is, That probably the wheaten Loaf had been confined to one, or two Families in a State, who, on Account of this superior Rank, and vast Revenues, could have afforded to give an extravagant Price for their delicious Morsel: But it is impossible, that under such Circumstances, it ever could have become the common Food of the Kingdom. The same Remark would hold good, were it to be applied to the Art of Printing, and to the Numbers of People, from first to last, therein employed: For Printing is nothing more than a Machine to abridge the Labour, and reduce the Price of Writing. – But Examples are endless; and surely enough has been said, to convince any reasonable Man, though even the great Author of *L'Esprit des Loix* should once be of a different Mind, that that System of Machines, which so greatly reduces the Price of Labour, as to enable the Generality of a People to become Purchasers of the Goods, will in the End, though not immediately, employ more Hands in the Manufacture, than could possibly have found Employment, had no such Machines been invented. And every manufacturing Place, when duly considered, is an Evidence in this Point.

Q. Is that Labour, which is still to be performed by the human Kind, so judiciously divided, that Men, Women, and Children have their respective Shares in Proportion to their Strength, Sex, and Abilities? And is every Branch so contrived, that there is no Waste of Time, or unnecessary Expence of Strength or Labour? Moreover, what good Consequences attend these Circumstances in such Parts of the Kingdom, where they are observed, and what bad ones in other Parts, where they are not?

A. In many Provinces of the Kingdom, particularly, *Staffordshire*, *Warwickshire*, and certain Districts of *Yorkshire*, with the Town of *Manchester*, *Norwich*, and some others, the Labour, for the most Part, is very properly proportioned, and great Judgment appears in the Methods and Contrivances for bringing the several Parts of the Manufacture so within the Reach of each other, that no Time should be wasted in passing the Goods to be manufactured from Hand to Hand, and that no unnecessary Strength should be employed. For an Instance of both Kinds, take one among a Thousand at *Birmingham*, *viz.* When a Man stamps a metal Button by means of an Engine, a Child stands by him to place the Button in readiness to receive the Stamp, and to remove it when received, and then to place another. By these means the Operator can stamp at least double the Number, which he could otherwise have done, had he been obliged to have stopped each Time to have shifted the Buttons: And as his Gettings may be from 14d to 18d and the Child's from a Penny to 2*d per* Day for doing the same Quantity of Work, which must have required double the Sum, had the Man alone been employed; this single Circumstance saves about 80, or near 100 *per Cent* at the same Time that it trains up Children to an Habit of Industry, almost as soon as they can speak. And hence it is, that the *Bijoux d'Angleterre*, or the *Birmingham* Toys, are rendered so exceedingly cheap as to astonish all *Europe*; and that the Roman Catholic Countries are supplied with such vast Quantities of Crucifixes, Agnus Dei's, *&c.* from *England*. A Dozen of these Crucifixes, as I am informed, being to be sold, in the wholesale Way, for 7½d. – But the good Effects of this proportioning of Labour to different Strengths and Sexes, is still more extensive than it at first appears. For in *Birmingham* the Numbers of poor Women on the Pay-Bill, compared to those of poor Men, are hardly as three to two; whereas in *Bristol*, where no such good Polities obtain, the Numbers are upwards of four to one; and in many Parts of *London*, it is still much worse: So great is the Difference, and such the Expensiveness and heavy Burdens of a wrong Conduct even in this Respect: not to mention, that Prostitution and Debauchery seem to be an unavoidable Consequence in the female Sex of Poverty and Idleness, when they are young; and when they grow old, what Refuge can they have, if they do not soon rot with their Diseases, but the Parish Pay?

Q. In those Towns and Places, where great Manufactures are carried on, are there many independent Masters, and few Journeymen to each Master? or few independent Masters, and many Journeymen? And what is the Difference, in regard to Morals, Cheapness and Goodness of Work, Extent of Trade, Rioting, Mobbing and the like?

A. This Matter is better illustrated by comparing the same Manufacture, and the Consequences attending it, under the different Circumstances here referred to. In many Parts of *Yorkshire*, the Woollen Manufacture is carried on by small Farmers and Freeholders: These People buy some Wool, and grow some; their Wives, Daughters, and Servants spin it in the long Winter Nights, and at such Times when not employed in their Farms and Dairies; the Master of the Family either sells this Produce in the Yarn Market, or hath it wove up himself. It is then milled, cleansed, and brought to Market, generally to the Town of *Leeds*; but when sold there, he can be paid for no greater Number of Yards than the Cloth will measure, after having been well soaked in Water: By which means all Frauds in Stretching, Tentering, *&c.* are effectually prevented. The Persons who buy this Cloth, generally act upon Commission at a very low Rate; and afterwards cause the Cloth to be dyed (if it was not dyed in the Wool) and to be properly dressed and finished. Thus, the whole passes through various Hands independently of each other. And though in Fact the Spinner, Weaver, Millman, Dyer, Dresser, *&c.* are all of them the Journeymen of the Agent or Commissioner, who stands in the Stead of him who is the Clothier in other Places; yet by acting thus upon a distinct Footing, they conceive themselves as far independent of him, and of each other, as any Buyer or Seller whatever. And being thus independent, they are all Rivals, all animated with the same Desire of bringing their Goods to Market upon the cheapest Terms, and of excelling one another. Their Journeymen likewise, if they have any, being so little removed from the Degree and Condition of their Masters, and likely to set up for themselves by the Industry and Frugality of a few Years, have no Conception that they are embarked in an Interest opposite to that of their Masters, or that they are called upon to enter into Clubs and Combinations against them. Thus it is, that the working People are generally Moral, Sober, and Industrious; that the Goods are well made, and exceedingly Cheap; and that a Riot or a Mob is a Thing hardly known among them. Whereas in *Gloucestershire*, *Wiltshire*, and *Somersetshire*, the Manufacture is carried on by a quite different Process, and the Effects are accordingly; *viz.* One Person, with a great Stock and large Credit, buys the Wool, pays for the Spinning, Weaving, Milling, Dying, Shearing, Dressing, *&c. &c.* That is, he is Master of the whole Manufacture from first to last, and perhaps employs a thousand Persons under him. This is the Clothier, whom all the Rest are to look upon as their Paymaster. But will they not also sometimes look upon him as their Tyrant? And as great Numbers of them work together in the same Shop, will they not have it the more in their Power to vitiate and corrupt each other, to cabal and associate against their Masters, and to break out into Mobs and Riots upon every little Occasion? The Event hath fully shewed, and is now shewing, that these Conjectures are too frequently supported by Facts. Besides, as the Master is placed so high above the Condition of the Journeyman, both their Conditions approach much nearer to that of a Planter and Slave in our *American* Colonies, than might be expected in such a Country as *England*; and the Vices and Tempers belonging to each Condition are of the same Kind, only in an inferior Degree. The Master, for Example, however well-disposed in himself, is naturally tempted by his Situation to be proud and over-bearing, to consider his People as the Scum of the Earth, whom he has a Right to squeeze whenever he can; because they ought to be kept low, and not rise up in Competition with their Superiors. The Journeymen on the contrary, are equally tempted by their Situation, to envy the high Station, and superior Fortunes of their Masters; and to envy them the more, in Proportion as they find themselves deprived of the Hopes of advancing themselves to the same Degree by any Stretch of Industry, or superior Skill. Hence their Self-Love takes a wrong Turn, destructive to themselves, and others. They think it no Crime to get as much Wages, and to do as little for it as they possibly can, to lie and cheat, and do any other bad Thing; provided it is only against their Master, whom they look upon as their common Enemy, with whom no Faith is to be kept. The Motives to Industry, Frugality, and Sobriety are all subverted by this one Consideration, *viz.* That they shall always be chained to the same Oar, and never be but Journeymen. Therefore their only Happiness is to get Drunk, and to make Life pass away with as little Thought as possible. This being the Case, is it to be wondered at, that the Trade in *Yorkshire* should flourish, or the Trade in *Somersetshire*, *Wiltshire*, and *Gloucestershire* be found declining every Day? The real Surprize would be to discover, that such Causes did not produce such Effects: And if ever the Manufactures in the North should adopt the bad Policy of the West, and *vice versa*, Things will come round again.

Q. Are the Manufactures of *England*, those especially in the Toy, Jewelry, Cabinet, Furniture, and Silk Way, chiefly adapted for high or middling Life? and what Species of People make up the Bulk of the Customers?

A. England being a free Country, where Riches got by Trade are no Disgrace, and where Property is also safe against the Prerogative either of Prince or Nobles, and where every Person may make what Display he pleases of his Wealth, without incurring a higher *Taille*, Poll, or Capitation the next Year for so doing; – the Manufactures of the Kingdom accommodate themselves, if I may so speak, to the Constitution of it: That is, they are more adapted for the Demands of Peasants and Mechanics, in order to appear in warm Circumstances; – for Farmers, Freeholders, Tradesmen, and Manufacturers in middling Life; – and for wholesale Dealers, Merchants, and all Persons of Landed Estates, to appear in genteel Life; than for the Magnificence of Palaces, or the Cabinets of Princes. Thus it is, according to the very Spirit of our Constitution, that the *English* of these several Denominations have better Conveniences in their Houses, and affect to have more in Quantity of clean, neat Furniture, and a greater Variety (such as Carpets, Screens, Window Curtains, Chamber Bells, polished Brass Locks, Fenders, *&c. &c.* (Things hardly known Abroad among Persons of such a Rank) than are to be found in any other Country in *Europe*, *Holland* excepted.) Moreover, as the Demand is great and continual, the Numbers of Workmen and their greater Experience excite the higher Emulation, and cause them to excel the Mechanics of other Countries in these Sorts of Manufactures. In a Word, it is a true Observation, that almost the whole Body of the People of *Great Britain* may be considered either as the Customers *to*, or the Manufacturers *for* each other: A very happy Circumstance this, on which the Wealth and Prosperity of a Nation greatly depends. – Were an Inventory to be taken of the Houshold Goods and Furniture of a Peasant, or Mechanic in *France*, and of a Peasant, or Mechanic in *England*, the latter would be found, upon an Average, to exceed the former in Value at least as three to one.

Notes

1. Virgil, *Georgics*, 1.54-61:
This ground with *Bacchus*, that with *Ceres* suits:
That other loads the Trees with happy Fruits.
A fourth with Grass, unbidden, decks the Ground:
Thus *Tmolus* is with yellow Saffron crown'd:

India, black Ebon and white Ivory bears:
And soft *Idume* weeps her od'rous Tears.
Thus *Pontus* sends her Beaver Stones from far;
And naked *Spanyards* temper Steel for War.
Epirus for th'*Elean* Chariot breeds.
(In hopes of Palms,) a Race of running Steeds.
This is the Orig'nal Contract; these the Laws
Impos'd by Nature, and by Nature's Cause,
On sundry Places.

Dryden

2. Horace, *Satires*, I.i.4: O happy traders!
3. Virgil, *Acneid*, VI.663: They polish life by useful arts.

3 THE ECONOMY AND THE SOCIAL ORDER

The first two readings in this section (passages 3.1 and 3.2) show some of the characteristics of 'traditional' humanist writing about trade, luxury and public morality: the rest belong to the new forms of economic writing that develop in the period. The pieces from Mandeville (passages 3.3 a, b and c) are the concluding lines of *The Grumbling Hive*, in which the 'moral' of the whole poem is laid out, and two of the prose 'Remarks', expanding and explaining points from earlier in the poem. The later passages show considerable areas of disagreement with Mandeville's argument, and with each other. However, they also reveal a number of the shared preoccupations which characterise political economy.

The essays by Hume are from the enormously influential *Essays Moral Political and Literary*. They mark a transition from general 'polite' discussion of economic affairs to the more specialised debates in political economy, and broach various questions which are central to the development of the new discipline. These are most fully explored in Adam Smith's *Wealth of Nations* (passages 3.9 a and b). The first has been discussed in the introduction; the second provides an account of the historical evolution of society in the wake of developments in the market. Both can be compared with the discussions of the social establishment and of the economy in Chapters 1 and 3.

The extracts from Josiah Tucker's *Elements of Commerce* and Sir James Steuart's *Principles of Political Oeconomy* discuss some of the problems in the relation between the state and the market economy. The passage from Ferguson comes from the *Essay on the History of Civil Society*, an early 'sociological' account of social development. It provides an interesting commentary on the issues dealt with in political economy, in which the residue of humanism and the influence of the new discipline itself are both clear.

Passage 3.1

(*from* George Berkeley, *An Essay towards preventing the Ruin of Great Britain*, 1721)

Frugality of Manners is the Nourishment and Strength of Bodies politic.

It is that by which they grow and subsist, until they are corrupted by Luxury; the natural Cause of their Decay and Ruin. Of this we have Examples in the *Persians*, *Lacaedemonians*, and *Romans*: not to mention many later Governments which have sprung up, continued a while, and then perished by the same natural Causes. But these are, it seems, of no use to us; and, in spight of them, we are in a fair Way of becoming ourselves, another useless Example to future Ages.

Men are apt to measure national Prosperity by Riches, it would be righter to measure it by the Use that is made of them. Where they promote an honest Commerce among Men, and are Motives to Industry and Virtue, they are without doubt of great Advantage; but where they are made (as too often happens) an Instrument to Luxury, they enervate and dispirit the bravest People. So just is that Remark of *Machiavel*, that there is no Truth in the common Saying; Money is the Nerves of War; and though we may subsist tolerably for a Time among corrupt Neighbours, yet if ever we have to do with a hardy, temperate, religious Sort of Men, we shall find to our Cost, that all our Riches are but a poor Exchange for that Simplicity of Manners which we despise in our Ancestors. This sole Advantage hath been the main Support of all the Republics that have made a Figure in the World; and perhaps it might be no ill Policy in a Kingdom to form itself upon the Manners of a Republic.

Simplicity of Manners may be more easily preserved in a Republic than a Monarchy; but if once lost, may be sooner recovered in a Monarchy, the Example of a Court being of great Efficacy, either to reform or to corrupt a People; that alone were sufficient to discountenance the wearing of Gold or Silver, either in Cloaths or Equipage, and if the same were prohibited by Law, the saving so much Bullion would be the smallest Benefit of such an Institution; there being nothing more apt to debase the Virtue and good Sense of our Gentry of both Sexes, than the trifling Vanity of Apparel, which we have learned from *France*, and which hath had such visible ill Consequences on the Genius of that People. Wiser Nations have made it their Care to shut out this Folly by severe Laws and Penalties, and its spreading among us can forbode no good, if there be any Truth in the Observation of one of the Ancients, that the direct Way to ruin a Man is to dress him up in fine Cloaths.

It cannot be denied that Luxury of Dress giveth a light Behaviour to our Women, which may pass for a small Offence, because it is a common one, but is in truth the Source of great Corruptions. For this very Offence the Prophet *Isaiah* denounced a severe Judgment against the Ladies of his Time. I shall give the Passage at length; 'moreover, the

LORD saith, because the Daughters of *Zion* are haughty, and walk with stretched forth Necks and wanton Eyes, walking and mincing as they go, and making a Tinkling with their Feet; therefore the LORD will smite with a Scab the Crown of the Head of the Daughters of *Zion*, and the LORD will discover their secret Parts. In that Day the LORD will take away the Bravery of their tinkling Ornaments about their Feet, and their Cauls and their round Tires like the Moon, the Chains, and the Bracelets, and the Mufflers, the Bonnets, and the Ornaments of the Legs, and the Head-bands, and the Tablets, and the Ear-rings, the Rings and Nose-jewels, the changeable Suits of Apparel, and the Mantles, and the Wimples, and the crisping Pins, the Glasses, and the fine Linen, and the Hoods and the Vails. And it shall come to pass that instead of a sweet Smell there shall be a Stink; and instead of a Girdle a Rent; and instead of well set Hair, baldness; and instead of a Stomacher, a Girding of Sackcloth; and Burning instead of Beauty': The Scab, the Stench, and the Burning are terrible pestilential Symptoms, and our Ladies would do well to consider, they may chance to resemble those of *Zion*, in their Punishment as well as their Offence.

But Dress is not their only Thing to be reformed, sumptuary Laws are useful in many other Points. In former Times the natural Plainness and good Sense of the *English* made them less necessary. But ever since the luxurious Reign of King *Charles* the second, we have been doing Violence to our Natures, and are by this Time so much altered for the worse, that it is to be feared, the very same Dispositions that make them necessary, will for ever hinder them from being enacted or put in Execution.

A private Family in difficult Circumstances, all Men agree, ought to melt down their Plate, walk on Foot, retrench the Number of their Servants, wear neither Jewels nor rich Cloaths, and deny themselves expensive Diversions; and why not the Public? had any Thing like this been done, our Taxes had been less, or which is the same Thing, we should have felt them less. But it is very remarkable, that Luxury was never at so great a Height, nor spread so generally through the Nation, as during the Expence of the late Wars, and the heavy Debt that still lyeth upon us.

This Vice draweth after it a Train of Evils which cruelly infest the Public; Faction, Ambition, Envy, Avarice, and that of the worst kind, being much more hurtful in its Consequences, though not so infamous as Penury. It was the great Art of Cardinal *Richelieu*, by encouraging Luxury and Expence to impoverish the *French* Nobility, and render them altogether dependent on the Crown, which hath been since very successfully effected. These and many more Considerations shew the Necessity there is for sumptuary Laws, nor can any Thing be said against them in this Island, which might not with equal Force be objected in other Countries, which have nevertheless judged the public Benefit of such Institutions, to be of far greater Importance than the short Sufferings of a few, who subsist by the Luxury of others.

It is evident, that old Taxes may be better born, as well as new ones raised by sumptuary Laws judiciously framed, not to damage our Trade, but retrench our Luxury. It is evident, that for want of these, Luxury (which like the other Fashions, never faileth to descend) hath infected all Ranks of People, and that this enableth the *Dutch* and *French* to undersell us, to the great Prejudice of our Traffic. We cannot but know that in our present Circumstances, it should be our Care, as it is our Interest, to make Poverty tolerable; in short, we have the Experience of many Ages to convince us, that a corrupt luxurious People must of themselves fall into Slavery, although no Attempt be made upon them. These and the like obvious Reflections should, one would think, have forced any People in their Senses upon frugal Measures.

But we are doomed to be undone. Neither the plain Reason of the Thing, nor the Experience of past Ages, nor the Examples we have before our Eyes, can restrain us from imitating, not to say surpassing, the most corrupt and ruined People, in those very Points of Luxury that ruined them. Our Gaming, our Operas, our Masquerades, are, in spight of our Debts and Poverty, become the Wonder of our Neighbours. If there be any Man so void of all Thought and common Sense, as not to see where this must end, let him but compare what *Venice* was at the League of *Cambray*, with what it is at present, and he will be convinced, how truly those fashionable Pastimes are calculated to depress and ruin a Nation.

Passage 3.2a

(*from* John Brown, 'Of the Ruling Manners of the Times', *An Estimate of the Manners and Principles of the Times*, 1757)

(This passage follows Brown's 'Estimate' of 'liberty', 'humanity' and 'justice'.)

Having made this prefatory Estimate of those remaining Manners which may demand Esteem and Applause, let us now proceed to the ruling Manners of the Times; from which this Age and Nation derives its present and particular Complexion.

It may be necessary to remark, that this designed Estimate extends not to the comparative Excellence of Manners and Principles, considered in every View, and in all their Variety of near and remote Effects. It relates not to the immediate Happiness or Misery, which Individuals, Families, or Nations, may derive from the Force of prevailing Principles and Manners. These Effects branch out into an Infinity of intricate Combinations, which cannot be comprehended in the present, but will make a material Part of some future Enquiry. This Estimate, therefore, confines itself to such Consequences only, as affect the *Duration* of the *public State*: So that the leading Question will be, 'How far the present ruling Manners and Principles of this Nation may tend to its Continuance or Destruction.'

In Consequence of this Restriction, the Manners and Principles of the common People will scarce find a Place in the Account. For though the Sum total of a Nation's immediate Happiness must arise, and be estimated, from the Manners and Principles of the Whole; yet the Manners and Principles of those who *lead*, not of those who *are led*; of those who *govern*, not of those who *are governed*; of those, in short, who *make* Laws or *execute* them, will ever determine the Strength or Weakness, and therefore the Continuance or Dissolution of a State.

For the blind Force or Weight of an ungoverned Multitude can have no steady nor rational Effect, unless some *leading Mind* rouze it into Action, and *point* it to its proper *End*: without this, it is either a *brute* and random *Bolt*, or a *lifeless Ball* sleeping in the *Cannon*: It depends on some superior *Intelligence*, to give it both *Impulse* and *Direction*.

Indeed, were the *People* remarkably corrupt, they might properly make a Part of this Enquiry: But in most of those important Circumstances to which this Estimate refers, they are in general much more irreproachable than their Superiors in Station; especially, if we except the lower Ranks of those who live in great Towns. It will therefore be unnecessary to mark the Character of their Principles of Manners, unless where they appear evidently poisoned by the Example or other Influence of the higher Ranks in Life.

Now the slightest Observation, if attended with Impartiality, may convince us, that the Character of the Manners of this Age and Nation, is by no means that of *abandoned Wickedness* and *Profligacy*. This Degree of Degeneracy, indeed, is often imputed to the Times: But, to what Times hath it *not* been imputed? Present Objects are naturally magnified to the human Eye, while remote ones, though larger in Dimensions, vanish into nothing. Hence the Speculative and Virtuous, in every Age, confining their Views to their own Period, have been apt to aggravate its Manners into the highest Degree of Guilt; to *satyrize*, rather than *describe*; to throw their respective Times into one dark Shade of *Horror*, rather than mark their peculiar *Colour* and *Complexion*.

Here, a large Field of Comparison and Debate would open, were it necessary or even expedient to enter upon it. We might cast our Eye upon the Manners of ROME, CARTHAGE, and many other States, in their last declining Period; where we should behold such tragic Scenes of Cruelty, Impiety, and Oppression, as would confound the most sanguine Advocate for the Manners of Antiquity. But, in Truth, there can be no Occasion for this Display of *Profligacy*. For if the previous Estimate, already given, be just, if the Spirit of *Liberty*, *Humanity*, and *Equity*, be in a certain Degree yet left among us, some of the most essential Foundations of abandoned Wickedness and Profligacy can have no Place: For these are *Servility*, *Cruelty*, and *Oppression*. How far we may be from this last Period of Degeneracy, it is certain, we are not arrived at it. Whenever this fatal Time approaches, it will come distinguished by its proper and peculiar Characters; and whoever shall estimate such Times, will find himself under the same Circumstance with the great Historian, who, in the profligate Period of declining Rome, tells us he had nothing to relate, but 'false Accusations, bloody Proscriptions, treacherous Friendships, and the Destruction of the Innocent'.

This, we may truly affirm, is far from the Character of the Manners of our Times: which, on a fair Examination, will probably appear to be that of a '*vain*, *luxurious*, and *selfish* EFFEMINACY'.

Passage 3.2b

(*from* Brown, 'The Conclusion', *Estimate*, 1757)

The Character, Effects, and Sources of our Manners and Principles, being thus laid open, the Writer had it in his Thoughts to have proceeded to the Consideration of '*their most practicable Remedies*'. But as the Closet-*Projects* of retired and speculative Men, often *are*, and always are *regarded*, as *chimerical*; he was therefore unwilling, at present, to hazard the Discredit of such an Attempt.

However, lest his Attempt should be deemed more visionary than perhaps it is, he judged it not improper to hint at some of the leading Principles on which it is built. And with this View, the following Reflections are submitted to the Consideration of the Public.

The World has been long amused with a trite and hacknied Comparison between the Life of Man, and that of States; in which it is pretended that they both proceed in the same irrevocable Manner; from Infancy to Maturity, from Maturity to Death: A Comparison, perhaps as groundless as it is common. The human Body contains, in its very Texture, the Seeds of certain Dissolution. That is, tho' you set aside all the possible Accidents arising from Intemperance, from the Influence of the Elements, the Climate, and every other external and contingent Cause, the human Frame itself, after a certain Period, would grow into Rigidity, the Fluids would decrease, the Solids accumulate, the Arteries *ossify*, the Blood stagnate, and the Wheels of Life stand still.

But in Societies, of whatever Kind, there seems no such necessary or essential Tendency to Dissolution. The human Body is *naturally* mortal; the political, only so by *Accident*: Internal Disorders or Diseases may arise; External Violence may attack or overpower: but these Causes, tho' always to be expected, are wholly incidental: the first is precisely of the same Nature as Intemperance, the second as the Influence of the external Elements, on the human Body. But there appears nothing in the internal Construction of any State, that tends inevitably to Dissolution, analogous to those Causes in the human Frame, which lead to certain Death.

This Observation seems confirmed by History: Where you see States, which, after being sunk in Corruption and Debility, have been brought back to the Vigour of their first Principles: But you must have recourse to Fables, for medicated Old Age, restored to Infancy or Youth.

If this be true, it seems not altogether chimerical, tho' confessedly difficult, to bring about the Reformation of a State. To lay down general Rules, in such a Case, would be like giving a Panacea; the very *Empiricism* of Politics. The Remedies must be suited to the Disease.

We have seen, that the ruling Evils of our Age and Nation have arisen from the unheeded Consequences of our Trade and Wealth. That these have produced effeminate Manners, and occasioned Loss of Principle: That these have brought on a national Debility. But would the lessening this exorbitant Trade and Wealth bring back Manners and Principles, and restore the Nation's Strength? – I very much Question the Event.

But whatever the Consequences might be at *Home*, those *Abroad* would certainly be fatal. The *French* are every Day gaining upon us in Commerce; and if ours should lessen, theirs would increase to our Destruction.

Thus are we fallen into a kind of Dilemma: If our Commerce be maintained or increased, its Effects bid fair to destroy us: If Commerce be discouraged and lessened, the growing Power of our Enemy threatens the same Consequence.

There seems, then, no other Expedient than this, 'That Commerce and Wealth be not discouraged in their *Growth* but checked and *controuled in their Effects*.'

And even in attempting this, Care must be had, lest in controuling the Effects of Commerce, we should destroy Commerce itself.

We see how strongly the natural Effects of Trade and Wealth are controuled in *France*, by proper Checks and counteracting Principles: Yet mere Imitation is always a narrow, and often an effectual Scheme. Besides, as our Constitution is of a superior Nature, so our Manners and Principles must be adapted to it, ere it can obtain it's proper Strength.

The Virtues yet left among us, and enumerated above, may be a possible Foundation for such a Change.

There are two different Kinds of Remedies, which might in due Time be applied. The first are radical, general, and lasting: The latter, palliative, particular, and temporary.

The first seem totally impracticable at *present*: For as they suppose a Change of Manners and Principles, this may justly be regarded as an impossible Event, during the present Age, and rather to be wished than hoped for, in the next.

The palliative, particular, and temporary Remedies, may seem more practicable at this Juncture. I mean, those which are of the coercive Kind; which work by opposed Passions, or by destroying the Opportunities or Occasions of Evil. Where the ruling Mischiefs lie among the People, these Remedies, with proper Care, may easily be administered. Thus we have lately seen the salutary Effects of a new Kind of Police, established by a useful Magistrate in the City of *London*; by which, the reigning Evil of *Street-Robberies* hath been almost wholly suppressed; altho' we may reasonably suppose, the Disposition towards them remains as strong as ever.

But where the ruling Mischief desolates the Great, there, even the palliative Remedies cannot easily be applied: The Reason is manifest: A coercive Power is wanting: They who should cure the Evil are the very Delinquents: And moral or political Physic is what no distempered Mind will ever administer to itself.

Necessity therefore, and *Necessity alone*, must in such a Case be the Parent of Reformation. So long as degenerate and unprincipled Manners can support themselves, they will be deaf to Reason, blind to Consequences, and obstinate in the *long* established Pursuit of *Gain and Pleasure*. In such Minds, the Idea of a Public has no Place; and therefore can never be a Curb to private Gratification: Nor can such Minds be ever awakened from their fatal Dream, till either the Voice of an abused People rouse them into Fear; or the State itself totter, thro' the general Incapacity, Cowardice, and Disunion of those who should support it.

Whenever this compelling Power, *Necessity*, shall appear, then, and not till then, may we hope that our Deliverance is at hand. Effeminacy, Rapacity, and Faction, will then be ready to resign the Reins they would now usurp: One common Danger will create one common Interest: Virtue may rise on the Ruins of Corruption; and a despairing Nation yet be saved, by the Wisdom, the Integrity, and unshaken Courage, of some great Minister.

Passage 3.3a

(*from* Bernard Mandeville, 'The Grumbling Hive', *The Fable of the Bees*, 1714-25)

THE
MORAL

Then leave Complaints: Fools only strive
To make a Great an Honest Hive
T'enjoy the World's Conveniencies,
Be fam'd in War, yet live in Ease,
Without great Vices, is a vain
EUTOPIA seated in the Brain.
Fraud, Luxury and Pride must live,
While we the Benefits receive:
Hunger's a dreadful Plague, no doubt,
Yet who digests or thrives without?
Do we not owe the Growth of Wine
To the dry shabby crooked Vine?
Which, while its Shoots neglected stood,
Chok'd other Plants, and ran to Wood;
But blest us with its noble Fruit,
As soon as it was ty'd and cut:
So Vice is beneficial found,
When it's by Justice lopt and bound;
Nay, where the People would be great,
As necessary to the State,
As Hunger is to make 'em eat.
Bare Virtue can't make Nations live
In Splendor; they, that would revive

A Golden Age, must be as free,
For Acorns, as for Honesty.

Passage 3.3b
(*from* Mandeville, 'Remark L', *Bees*, 1714-25)

If every thing is to be Luxury (as in strictness it ought) that is not immediately necessary to make Man subsist as he is a living Creature, there is nothing else to be found in the World, no not even among the naked Savages; of which it is not probable that there are any but what by this time have made some Improvements upon their former manner of Living; and either in the Preparation of their Eatables, the ordering of their Huts, or otherwise, added something to what once sufficed them. This Definition every body will say is too rigorous; I am of the same Opinion; but if we are to abate one Inch of this Severity, I am afraid we shan't know where to stop. When People tell us they only desire to keep themselves sweet and clean, there is no understanding what they would be at; if they made use of these Words in their genuine proper literal Sense, they might soon be satisfy'd without much cost or trouble, if they did not want Water: But these two little Adjectives are so comprehensive, especially in the Dialect of some Ladies, that no body can guess how far they may be stretcht. The Comforts of Life are likewise so various and extensive, that no body can tell what People mean by them, except he knows what sort of Life they lead. The same obscurity I observe in the words Decency and Conveniency, and I never understand them unless I am acquainted with the Quality of the Persons that make use of them. People may go to Church together, and be all of one Mind as much as they please, I am apt to believe that when they pray for their daily Bread, the Bishop includes several things in that Petition which the Sexton does not think on.

By what I have said hitherto I would only shew, that if once we depart from calling every thing Luxury that is not absolutely necessary to keep a Man alive, that then there is no Luxury at all; for if the wants of Men are innumerable, then what ought to supply them has no bounds; what is call'd superfluous to some degree of People, will be thought requisite to those of higher Quality; and neither the World nor the Skill of Man can produce any thing so curious or extravagant, but some most Gracious Sovereign or other, if it either eases or diverts him, will reckon it among the Necessaries of Life; not meaning every Body's Life, but that of his Sacred Person.

It is a receiv'd Notion, that Luxury is as destructive to the Wealth of the whole Body Politic, as it is to that of every individual Person who is guilty of it, and that a National Frugality enriches a Country in the same manner as that which is less general increases the Estates of private Families. I confess, that tho' I have found Men of much better Understanding than myself of this Opinion, I cannot help dissenting from them in this Point. They argue thus: We send, say they, for Example to *Turkey* of Woollen Manufactury, and other things of our own Growth, a Million's worth every Year; for this we bring back Silk, Mohair, Drugs, &c. to the value of Twelve Hundred Thousand Pounds, that are all spent in our own Country. By this, say they, we get nothing; but if most of us would be content with our own Growth, and so consume but half the quantity of those Foreign Commodities, then those in *Turkey*, who would still want the same quantity of our Manufactures, would be forc'd to pay ready Money for the rest, and so by the Balance of that Trade only, the Nation should get Six Hundred Thousand Pounds *per Annum*.

To examine the force of this Argument, we'll suppose (what they would have) that but half the Silk, &c. shall be consumed in *England* of what there is now; we'll suppose likewise, that those in *Turkey*, tho' we refuse to buy above half as much of their Commodities as we used to do, either can or will not be without the same quantity of our Manufactures they had before, and that they'll pay the Balance in Money; that is to say, that they shall give us as much Gold or Silver, as the value of what they buy from us exceeds the value of what we buy from them. Tho' what we suppose might perhaps be done for one Year, it is impossible it should last: Buying is Bartering, and no Nation can buy Goods of others that has none of her own to purchase them with. *Spain and Portugal*, that are yearly supply'd with new Gold and Silver from their Mines, may for ever buy for ready Money as long as their yearly increase of Gold and Silver continues, but then Money is their Growth and the Commodity of the Country. We know that we could not continue long to purchase the Goods of other Nations, if they would not take our Manufactures in Payment for them; and why should we judge otherwise of other Nations? If those in *Turkey* then had no more Money fall from the Skies than we, let us see what would be the consequence of what we supposed. The Six Hundred Thousand Pounds in Silk, Mohair, &c. that are left upon their Hands the first Year, must make those Commodities fall considerably: Of this the *Dutch* and *French* will reap the Benefit as much as our selves; and if we continue to refuse taking their Commodities in Payment for our Manufactures, they can Trade no longer with us, but must content themselves with buying what they want of such Nations as are willing to take what we refuse, tho' their Goods are much worse than ours, and thus our Commerce with *Turkey* must in few Years be infallibly lost.

But they'll say, perhaps, that to prevent the ill consequence I have shew'd, we shall take the *Turkish* Merchandize as formerly, and only be so frugal as to consume but half the quantity of them our selves, and send the rest Abroad to be sold to others. Let us see what this will do, and whether it will enrich the Nation by the balance of that Trade with Six Hundred Thousand Pounds. In the first Place, I'll grant them that our People at Home making use of so much more of our own Manufactures, those who were employ'd in Silk, Mohair, &c. will get a living by the various Preparations of Woollen Goods. But in the second, I cannot allow that the Goods can be sold as formerly; for suppose the Half that is wore at Home to be sold at the same Rate as before, certainly the other Half that is sent Abroad will want very much of it: For we must send those Goods to Markets already supply'd; and besides that there must be Freight, Insurance, Provision, and all other Charges deducted, and the Merchants in general must lose much more by this Half that is re-shipp'd, than they got by the Half that is consumed here. For tho' the Woollen Manufactures are our own Product, yet they stand the Merchant that ships them off to Foreign Countries, in as much as they do the Shopkeeper here that retails them: so that if the Returns for what he sends Abroad repay him not what his Goods cost him here, with all other Charges, till he has the Money and a good Interest for it in Cash, the Merchant must run out, and the Upshot would be, that the Merchants in general finding they lost by the *Turkish* Commodities they sent Abroad, would ship no more of our Manufactures than what would pay for as much Silk, Mohair, &c. as would be consumed here. Other Nations would soon find Ways to supply them with as much as we should send short, and some where or other dispose of the Goods we should refuse: So that all we should get by this Frugality would be, that those in *Turkey* would take but half the Quantity of our Manufactures of what they do now, while we encourage and wear their Merchandizes, without which they are not able to purchase ours.

Passage 3.3c
(*from* Mandeville, 'Remark Y', *Bees*, 1714-25)

Since the first Edition of this Book, several have attack'd me with Demonstrations of the certain Ruin, which excessive Luxury must bring upon all Nations, who yet were soon answered, when I shewed them the Limits within which I had confined it; and therefore that no Reader for the future may misconstrue me on this Head, I shall point at the Cautions I have given, and the Proviso's I have made in the former as well as this present Impression, and which if not overlooked, must prevent all rational Censure, and obviate several Objections that otherwise might be made against me. I have laid down as Maxims never to be departed from, that the Poor should be kept strictly to Work, and that it was Prudence to relieve their Wants, but Folly to cure them; that Agriculture and Fishery should be promoted in all their Branches in order to render Provisions, and consequently Labour cheap. I have named Ignorance as a necessary Ingredient in the Mixture of Society: From all which it is manifest that I could never have imagined, that Luxury was to be made general through every part of a Kingdom. I have likewise required that Property should be well secured, Justice impartially administered, and in every thing the Interest of the Nation taken care of: But what I have insisted on the most, and repeated more than once, is the great Regard that is to be had to the Balance of Trade, and the Care the Legislature ought to take that the Yearly Imports never exceed the Exports; and where this is observed, and the other things I spoke of are not neglected, I still continue to assert that no Foreign Luxury can undo a Country: The height of it is never seen but in Nations that are vastly populous, and there only in the upper part of it, and the greater that is the larger still in proportion must be the lowest, the Basis that supports all, the multitude of Working Poor.

Those who would too nearly imitate others of Superior Fortune must thank themselves if they are ruin'd. This is nothing against Luxury; for whoever can subsist and lives above his Income is a Fool. Some Persons of Quality may keep three or four Coaches and Six, and at the same time lay up Money for their Children: while a young Shopkeeper is undone for keeping one sorry Horse. It is impossible there should be a rich Nation without Prodigals, yet I never knew a City so full of Spendthrifts, but there were Covetous People enough to answer their Number. As an Old Merchant breaks for having been extravagant or careless a great while, so a young Beginner falling into the same Business gets an Estate by being saving or more industrious before he is Forty Years Old: Besides that the Frailties of Men often work by Contraries: Some Narrow Souls can never thrive because they are too stingy, while longer Heads amass great Wealth by spending their Money freely, and seeming to despise it. But the Vicissitudes of Fortune are necessary, and the most lamentable are no more detrimental to Society than the Death of the

Individual Members of it. Christnings are a proper Balance to Burials. Those who immediately lose by the Misfortunes of others are very sorry, complain and make a Noise; but the others who get by them, as there always are such, hold their Tongues, because it is odious to be thought the better for the Losses and Calamities of our Neighbour. The various Ups and Downs compose a Wheel that always turning round gives motion to the whole Machine. Philosophers, that dare extend their Thoughts beyond the narrow compass of what is immediately before them, look on the alternate Changes in the Civil Society no otherwise than they do on the risings and fallings of the Lungs; the latter of which are as much a Part of Respiration in the more perfect Animals as the first; so that the fickle Breath of never-stable Fortune is to the Body Politick, the same as floating Air to a living Creature.

Avarice then and Prodigality are equally necessary to the Society. That in some Countries, Men are more generally lavish than in others, proceeds from the difference in Circumstances that dispose to either Vice, and arise from the Condition of the Social Body as well as the Temperament of the Natural. I beg Pardon of the attentive Reader, if here in behalf of short Memories I repeat some things, the Substance of which they have already seen in Remark (Q). More Money than Land, heavy Taxes and scarcity of Provisions, Industry, Laboriousness, an active and stirring Spirit, Ill-nature and Saturnine Temper; Old Age, Wisdom, Trade, Riches, acquired by our own Labour, and Liberty and Property well secured, are all Things that dispose to Avarice. On the contrary, Indolence, Content, Good-nature, a Jovial Temper, Youth, Folly, Arbitrary Power, Money easily got, Plenty of Provisions and the Uncertainty of Possessions, are Circumstances that render men prone to Prodigality: Where there is the most of the first the prevailing Vice will be Avarice, and Prodigality where the other turns the Scale; but a National Frugality there never was nor never will be without a National Necessity.

Sumptuary Laws may be of use to an indigent Country, after great Calamities of War, Pestilence, or Famine, when Work has stood still, and the Labour of the Poor been interrupted; but to introduce them into an opulent Kingdom is the wrong way to consult the Interest of it. I shall end my Remarks on the Grumbling Hive with assuring the Champions of National Frugality that it would be impossible for the *Persians* and other Eastern People to purchase the vast Quantities of fine *English* Cloth they consume, should we load our Women with less Cargo's of *Asiatick* Silks.

Passage 3.4
(*from* David Hume, *Of Commerce*, 1742)

THE greater part of mankind may be divided into two classes; that of *shallow* thinkers, who fall short of the truth, and that of *abstruse* thinkers, who go beyond it. The latter class are by far the most rare; and I may add, by far the most useful and valuable. They suggest hints, at least, and start difficulties, which they want, perhaps, skill to pursue; but which may produce fine discoveries, when handled by men who have a more just way of thinking. At worst, what they say is uncommon; and if it should cost some pains to comprehend it, one has, however, the pleasure of hearing something that is new. An author is little to be valued, who tells us nothing but what we can learn from every coffee-house conversation.

All people of *shallow* thought are apt to decry even those of *solid* understanding, as *abstruse* thinkers, and metaphysicians, and refiners; and never will allow anything to be just which is beyond their own weak conceptions. There are some cases, I own, where an extraordinary refinement affords a strong presumption of falsehood, and where no reasoning is to be trusted but what is natural and easy. When a man deliberates concerning his conduct in any *particular* affair, and forms schemes in politics, trade, oeconomy, or any business in life, he never ought to draw his arguments too fine, or connect too long a chain of consequences together. Something is sure to happen, that will disconcert his reasoning, and produce an event different from what he expected. But when we reason upon *general* subjects, one may justly affirm, that our speculations can scarcely ever be too fine, provided they be just; and that the difference between a common man and a man of genius is chiefly seen in the shallowness or depth of the principles upon which they proceed. General reasonings seem intricate, merely because they are general; nor is it easy for the bulk of mankind to distinguish, in a great number of particulars, that common circumstance in which they all agree, or to extract it, pure and unmixed, from the other superfluous circumstances. Every judgment or conclusion, with them, is particular. They cannot enlarge their view to those universal propositions, which comprehend under them an infinite number of individuals, and include a whole science in a single theorem. Their eye is confounded with such an extensive prospect; and the conclusions, derived from it, even though clearly expressed, seem intricate and obscure. But however intricate they may seem, it is certain, that general principles, if just and sound, must always prevail in the general course of things, though they may fail in particular cases; and it is the chief business of philosophers to regard the general course of things. I may add, that it is also the chief business of politicians; especially in the domestic government of the state, where the public good, which is, or ought to be their object, depends on the concurrence of a multitude of causes; not, as in foreign politics, on accidents and chances and the caprices of a few persons. This therefore makes the difference between *particular* deliberations and *general* reasonings, and renders subtility and refinement much more suitable to the latter than to the former.

I thought this introduction necessary before the following discourses on *commerce, money, interest, balance of trade, &c.* where, perhaps, there will occur some principles which are uncommon, and which may seem too refined and subtile for such vulgar subjects. If false, let them be rejected: But no one ought to entertain a prejudice against them, merely because they are out of the common road.

The greatness of a state, and the happiness of its subjects, how independent soever they may be supposed in some respects, are commonly allowed to be inseparable with regard to commerce; and as private men receive greater security, in the possession of their trade and riches, from the power of the public, so the public becomes powerful in proportion to the opulence and extensive commerce of private men. This maxim is true in general; though I cannot forbear thinking, that it may possibly admit of exceptions, and that we often establish it with too little reserve and limitation. There may be some circumstances, where the commerce and riches and luxury of individuals, instead of adding strength to the public, will serve only to thin its armies, and diminish its authority among the neighbouring nations. Man is a very variable being, and susceptible of many different opinions, principles, and rules of conduct. What may be true, while he adheres to one way of thinking, will be found false, when he has embraced an opposite set of manners and opinions.

The bulk of every state may be divided into *husbandmen* and *manufacturers*. The former are employed in the culture of the land; the latter work up the materials furnished by the former, into all the commodities which are necessary or ornamental to human life. As soon as men quit their savage state, where they live chiefly by hunting and fishing, they must fall into these two classes; though the arts of agriculture employ *at first* the most numerous part of the society. Time and experience improve so much these arts, that the land may easily maintain a much greater number of men, than those who are immediately employed in its culture, or who furnish the more necessary manufactures to such as are so employed.

If these superfluous hands apply themselves to the finer arts, which are commonly denominated the arts of *luxury*, they add to the happiness of the state; since they afford to many the opportunity of receiving enjoyments, with which they would otherwise have been unaquainted. But may not another scheme be proposed for the employment of these superfluous hands? May not the sovereign lay claim to them, and employ them in fleets and armies, to encrease the dominions of the state abroad, and spread its fame over distant nations? It is certain that the fewer desires and wants are found in the proprietors and labourers of land, the fewer hands do they employ; and consequently the superfluities of the land, instead of maintaining tradesmen and manufacturers, may support fleets and armies to a much greater extent, than where a great many arts are required to minister to the luxury of particular persons. Here therefore seems to be a kind of opposition between the greatness of the state and the happiness of the subject. A state is never greater than when all its superfluous hands are employed in the service of the public. The ease and convenience of private persons require, that these hands should be employed in their service. The one can never be satisfied, but at the expence of the other. As the ambition of the sovereign must entrench on the luxury of individuals; so the luxury of individuals must diminish the force, and check the ambition of the sovereign.

Nor is this reasoning merely chimerical; but is founded on history and experience. The republic of SPARTA was certainly more powerful than any state now in the world, consisting of an equal number of people; and this was owing entirely to the want of commerce and luxury. The HELOTES were the labourers: The SPARTANS were the soldiers or gentlemen. It is evident, that the labour of the HELOTES could not have maintained so great a number of SPARTANS, had these latter lived in ease and delicacy, and given employment to a great variety of trades and manufactures. The like policy may be remarked in ROME. And indeed, throughout all ancient history, it is observable, that the smallest republics raised and maintained greater armies, than states consisting of triple the number of inhabitants, are able to support at present. It is computed, that, in all EUROPEAN nations, the proportion between soldiers and people does not exceed one to a hundred. But we read, that the city of ROME alone, with its small territory, raised and maintained, in early times, ten legions against the LATINS. ATHENS, the whole of whose dominions was not larger than YORKSHIRE, sent to the expedition against SICILY near forty thousand men. DIONYSIUS the elder, it is said, maintained a standing army of a hundred thousand foot and ten thousand horse, besides a large fleet of four hundred sail;

though his territories extended no farther than the city of SYRACUSE, about a third of the island of SICILY, and some sea-port towns and garrisons on the coast of ITALY and ILLYRICUM. It is true, the ancient armies, in time of war, subsisted much upon plunder: But did not the enemy plunder in their turn? which was a more ruinous way of levying a tax, than any other that could be devised. In short, no probable reason can be assigned for the great power of the more ancient states above the modern, but their want of commerce and luxury. Few artizans were maintained by the labour of the farmers, and therefore more soldiers might live upon it. LIVY says, that ROME, in his time, would find it difficult to raise as large an army as that which, in her early days, she sent out against the GAULS and LATINS. Instead of those soldiers who fought for liberty and empire in CAMILLUS'S time, there were, in AUGUSTUS'S days, musicians, painters, cooks, players, and tailors; and if the land was equally cultivated at both periods, it could certainly maintain equal numbers in the one profession as in the other. They added nothing to the mere necessaries of life, in the latter period more than in the former.

It is natural on this occasion to ask, whether sovereigns may not return to the maxims of ancient policy, and consult their own interest in this respect, more than the happiness of their subjects? I answer, that it appears to me, almost impossible; and that because ancient policy was violent, and contrary to the more natural and usual course of things. It is well known with what peculiar laws SPARTA was governed, and what a prodigy that republic is justly esteemed by every one, who has considered human nature as it has displayed itself in other nations, and other ages. Were the testimony of history less positive and circumstantial, such a government would appear a mere philosophical whim or fiction, and impossible ever to be reduced to practice. And though the ROMAN and other ancient republics were supported on principles somewhat more natural, yet was there an extraordinary concurrence of circumstances to make them submit to such grievous burthens. They were free states; they were small ones; and the age being martial, all their neighbours were continually in arms. Freedom naturally begets public spirit, especially in small states; and this public spirit, this *amor patriæ*, must encrease, when the public is almost in continual alarm, and men are obliged, every moment, to expose themselves to the greatest dangers for its defence. A continual succession of wars makes every citizen a soldier: He takes the field in his turn: And during his service he is chiefly maintained by himself. This service is indeed equivalent to a heavy tax; yet is it less felt by a people addicted to arms, who fight for honour and revenge more than pay, and are unacquainted with gain and industry as well as pleasure. Not to mention the great equality of fortunes among the inhabitants of the ancient republics, where every field, belonging to a different proprietor, was able to maintain a family, and rendered the numbers of citizens very considerable, even without trade and manufactures.

But though the want of trade and manufactures, among a free and very martial people, may *sometimes* have no other effect than to render the public more powerful, it is certain, that, in the common course of human affairs, it will have a quite contrary tendency. Sovereigns must take mankind as they find them, and cannot pretend to introduce any violent change in their principles and ways of thinking. A long course of time, with a variety of accidents and circumstances, are requisite to produce those great revolutions, which so much diversify the face of human affairs. And the less natural any set of principles are, which support a particular society, the more difficulty will a legislator meet with in raising and cultivating them. It is his best policy to comply with the common bent of mankind, and give it all the improvement of which it is susceptible. Now, according to the most natural course of things, industry and arts and trade encrease the power of the sovereign as well as the happiness of the subjects; and that policy is violent, which aggrandises the public by the poverty of individuals. This will easily appear for a few considerations, which will present to us the consequences of sloth and barbarity.

Where manufactures and mechanic arts are not cultivated, the bulk of the people must apply themselves to agriculture; and if their skill and industry encrease, there must arise a great superfluity from their labour beyond what suffices to maintain them. They have no temptation, therefore, to encrease their skill and industry; since they cannot exchange that superfluity for any commodities, which may serve either to their pleasure or vanity. A habit of indolence naturally prevails. The greater part of the land lies uncultivated. What is cultivated, yields not its utmost for want of skill and assiduity in the farmers. If at any time the public exigencies require, that great numbers should be employed in the public service, the labour of the people furnishes now no superfluities, by which these numbers can be maintained. The labourers cannot encrease their skill and industry on a sudden. Lands uncultivated cannot be brought into tillage for some years. The armies, mean while, must either make sudden and violent conquests, or disband for want of subsistence. A regular attack or defence, therefore, is not to be expected from such a people, and their soldiers must be as ignorant and unskilful as their farmers and manufacturers.

Every thing in the world is purchased by labour; and our passions are the only causes of labour. When a nation abounds in manufactures and mechanic arts, the proprietors of land, as well as the farmers, study agriculture as a science, and redouble their industry and attention. The superfluity, which arises from their labour, is not lost; but is exchanged with manufactures for those commodities, which men's luxury now makes them covet. By this means, land furnishes a great deal more of the necessaries of life, than what suffices for those who cultivate it. In times of peace and tranquility, this superfluity goes to the maintenance of manufacturers, and the improvers of liberal arts. But it is easy for the public to convert many of these manufacturers into soldiers, and maintain them by that superfluity, which arises from the labour of the farmers. Accordingly we find, that this is the case in all civilized governments. When the sovereign raises an army, what is the consequence? He imposes a tax. This tax obliges all the people to retrench what is least necessary to their subsistence. Those, who labour in such commodities, must either enlist in the troops, or turn themselves to agriculture, and thereby oblige some labourers to enlist for want of business. And to consider the matter abstractedly, manufactures encrease the power of the state only as they store up so much labour, and that of a kind to which the public may lay claim, without depriving any one of the necessaries of life. The more labour, therefore, is employed beyond mere necessaries, the more powerful is any state; since the persons engaged in that labour may easily be converted to the public service. In a state without manufactures, there may be the same number of hands; but there is not the same quantity of labour, nor of the same kind. All the labour is there bestowed upon necessaries, which can admit of little or no abatement.

Thus the greatness of the sovereign and the happiness of the state are, in a great measure, united with regard to trade and manufactures. It is a violent method, and in most cases impracticable, to oblige the labourer to toil, in order to raise from the land more than what subsists himself and family. Furnish him with manufactures and commodities, and he will do it of himself. Afterwards you will find it easy to seize some part of his superfluous labour, and employ it in the public service, without giving him his wonted return. Being accustomed to industry, he will think this less grievous, than if, at once, you obliged him to an augmentation of labour without any reward. The case is the same with regard to the other members of the state. The greater is the stock of labour of all kinds, the greater quantity may be taken from the heap, without making any sensible alteration in it.

A public granary of corn, a storehouse of cloth, a magazine of arms; all these must be allowed real riches and strength in any state. Trade and industry are really nothing but a stock of labour, which in times of peace and tranquillity, is employed for the ease and satisfaction of individuals; but in the exigencies of state, may, in part, be turned to public advantage. Could we convert a city into a kind of fortified camp, and infuse into each breast so martial a genius, and such a passion for public good, as to make every one willing to undergo the greatest hardships for the sake of the public; these affections might now, as in ancient times, prove alone a sufficient spur to industry, and support the community. It would then be advantageous, as in camps, to banish all arts and luxury; and, by restrictions on equipage and tables, make the provisions and forage last longer than if the army were loaded with a number of superfluous retainers. But as these principles are too disinterested and too difficult to support, it is requisite to govern men by other passions, and animate them with a spirit of avarice and industry, art and luxury. The camp is, in this case, loaded with a superfluous retinue; but the provisions flow in proportionably larger. The harmony of the whole is still supported; and the natural bent of the mind being more complied with, individuals, as well as the public find their account in the observance of those maxims.

Passage 3.5
(*from* David Hume, *Of Refinement in the Arts*, 1742)

The liberties of ENGLAND, so far from decaying since the improvements in the arts, have never flourished so much as during that period. And though corruption may seem to encrease of late years; this is chiefly to be ascribed to our established liberty, when our princes have found the impossibility of governing without parliament, or of terrifying parliaments by the phantom of prerogative. Not to mention, that this corruption or venality prevails much more among the electors than the elected; and therefore cannot justly be ascribed to any refinement in luxury.

If we consider the matter in a proper light, we shall find, that a progress in the arts is rather favourable to liberty, and has a natural tendency to preserve, if not produce a free government. In rude unpolished nations, where the arts are neglected, all labour is bestowed on the cultivation of the ground; and the whole society is divided into two classes, proprietors of land, and their vassals or tenants. The latter are necessarily dependent, and fitted for slavery and subjection; especially where they possess no riches, and are not valued for their knowledge in agriculture; as must always be the case where the arts are neglected. The former naturally erect themselves into petty tyrants; and must either submit to an absolute master, for the sake of peace and order; or if they will preserve their independency, like the ancient barons, they must fall into feuds and contests among themselves, and throw the whole society into such confusion, as is perhaps worse than the most despotic government. But where luxury nourishes commerce and industry, the peasants, by a proper cultivation of the land, become rich and independent; while the tradesmen and merchants acquire a share of the property, and draw authority and consideration to that middling rank of men, who are the best and firmest basis of public liberty. These submit not to slavery, like the peasants, from poverty and meanness of spirit; and having no hopes of tyrannizing over others, like the barons, they are not tempted, for the sake of that gratification, to submit to the tyranny of their sovereign. They covet equal laws, which may secure their property, and preserve them from monarchical, as well as aristocratical tyranny.

The lower house is the support of our popular government; and all the world acknowledges, that it owed its chief influence and consideration to the encrease of commerce, which threw such a balance of property into the hands of the commons. How inconsistent then is it to blame so violently a refinement in the arts, and to represent it as the bane of liberty and public spirit!

To declaim against present times, and magnify the virtue of remote ancestors, is a propensity almost inherent in human nature: And as the sentiments and opinions of civilized ages alone are transmitted to posterity, hence it is that we meet with so many severe judgments pronounced against luxury, and even science; and hence it is that at present we give so ready an assent to them. But the fallacy is easily perceived, by comparing different nations that are contemporaries; where we both judge more impartially, and can better set in opposition those manners, with which we are sufficiently acquainted. Treachery and cruelty, the most pernicious and most odious of all vices, seem peculiar to uncivilized ages; and by the refined GREEKS and ROMANS were ascribed to all the barbarous nations, which surrounded them. They might justly, therefore, have presumed, that their own ancestors, so highly celebrated, possessed no greater virtue, and were as much inferior to their posterity in honour and humanity, as in taste and science. An ancient FRANK or SAXON may be highly extolled: But I believe every man would think his life or fortune much less secure in the hands of a MOOR or TARTAR, than in those of a FRENCH or ENGLISH gentleman, the rank of men the most civilized in the most civilized nations.

We come now to the *second* position which we propose to illustrate, to wit, that, as innocent luxury, or a refinement in the arts and conveniences of life, is advantageous to the public; so wherever luxury ceases to be innocent, it also ceases to be beneficial; and when carried a degree farther, begins to be a quality pernicious, though, perhaps, not the most pernicious, to political society.

Let us consider what we call vicious luxury. No gratification, however sensual, can of itself be esteemed vicious. A gratification is only vicious, when it engrosses all a man's expence, and leaves no ability for such acts of duty and generosity as are required by his situation and fortune. Suppose, that he correct the vice, and employ part of his expence in the education of his children, in the support of his friends, and in relieving the poor: would any prejudice result to society? On the contrary, the same consumption would arise; and that labour, which, at present, is employed only in producing a slender gratification to one man, would relieve the necessitous, and bestow satisfaction on hundreds. The same care and toil that raise a dish of peas at CHRISTMAS, would give bread to a whole family during six months. To say, that, without a vicious luxury, the labour would not have been employed at all, is only to say, that there is some other defect in human nature, such as indolence, selfishness, inattention to others, for which luxury, in some measure, provides a remedy; as one poison may be an antidote to another. But virtue, like wholesome food, is better than poisons, however corrected.

Suppose the same number of men, that are present in GREAT BRITAIN, with the same soil and climate; I ask, is it not possible for them to be happier, by the most perfect way of life that can be imagined, and by the greatest reformation that Omnipotence itself could work in their temper and disposition? To assert, that they cannot, appears evidently ridiculous. As the land is able to maintain more than all its present inhabitants, they could never, in such a UTOPIAN state, feel any other ills than those which arise from bodily sickness; and these are not the half of human miseries. All other ills spring from some vice, either in ourselves or others; and even many of our diseases proceed from the same origin. Remove the vices, and the ills follow. You must only take care to remove all the vices. If you remove part, you may render the matter worse. By banishing *vicious* luxury, without curing sloth and an indifference to others, you only diminish industry in the state, and add nothing to men's charity or their generosity. Let us, therefore, rest contented with asserting, that two opposite vices in a state may be more advantageous than either of them alone; but let us never pronounce vice in itself advantageous. Is it not very inconsistent for an author to assert in one page, that moral distinctions are inventions of politicians for public interest; and in the next page maintain, that vice is advantageous to the public? And indeed it seems upon any system of morality, little less than a contradiction in terms, to talk of a vice, which is in general beneficial to society.

I thought this reasoning necessary, in order to give some light to a philosophical question, which has been much disputed in ENGLAND. I call it a *philosophical* question, not a *political* one. For whatever may be the consequence of such a miraculous transformation of mankind, as would endow them with every species of virtue, and free them from every species of vice; this concerns not the magistrate, who aims only at possibilities. He cannot cure every vice by substituting a virtue in its place. Very often he can only cure one vice by another; and in that case, he ought to prefer what is least pernicious to society. Luxury, when excessive, is the source of many ills; but is in general preferable to sloth and idleness, which would commonly succeed in its place, and are more hurtful both to private persons and to the public. When sloth reigns, a mean uncultivated way of life prevails amongst individuals, without society, without enjoyment. And if the sovereign, in such a situation, demands the service of his subjects, the labour of the state suffices only to furnish the necessaries of life to the labourers, and can afford nothing to those who are employed in the public service.

Passage 3.6a

(*from* Josiah Tucker, Introduction, *The Elements of Commerce and Theory of Taxes*, 1755)

As the natural Disposition of Mankind to *Commerce* hath been set forth at large in the *Preliminary Discourse*, and as *Self-Love* is known to be the great Mover in human Nature, it may not be improper to begin with the following Observation; *viz.* That every Legislature should consider these two Principles as the Foundation of their future Proceedings, or as Materials in the Stores of Nature for them to work upon. They cannot *create* new Powers or Faculties in human Nature; but they can cultivate and improve those that are already subsisting: They can, by a proper Application of their Influence and Authority, prune away Luxuriances, and check the Progress of *unbearing* Branches, at the same Time that they promote and encourage the Growth of every Thing good and useful in Society. Now when the legislative Powers act upon this Plan, they will consider, That a lasting and extensive *National Commerce* is no otherwise to be obtained, than by a prudent Direction of the Passion of Self-Love to its *proper Objects*, – by *confining* it to those Objects, – and there giving it all possible *Assistance* and *Incouragement*. The passion of Self-Love therefore must be taken hold of by some Method or other; and so *trained* or *guided* in its Operations, that its Activity may never be mischievous, but always productive of the public Welfare. When Things are brought to that pass, the Consequences will be, that every Individual (whether he intends it or not) will be promoting the Good of his Country, and of Mankind in general, while he is pursuing his own private Interest.

But Self-Love is no otherwise to be taken hold of in the Case before us than either by having recourse to PENAL LAWS, or by establishing a JUDICIOUS POLITY. The Business of Penal Laws is to *terrify* or *punish*, but the Use of a judicious Policy is to *incline* and *incourage*: The one is to *deter* the Multitude from offending, the other to lead them by their own *free Choice* to virtuous Industry. This being the Case, it is easy to see which Method deserves the Preference, – especially in a *free* Country. Indeed the Multiplication even of *Penal Laws* would be of no Service, unless you armed the Magistrate with a proportionable Power to put them in Execution. And this, in other Words, would be giving him something too like a *Carte Blanche* to act as he pleases. Such a degree of absolute Power is too great a Trust to be reposed in *Man*: And perhaps is safe and beneficial only in the Hands of that Great Being, whose *Wisdom and Goodness are over all his Works*.

WHEREFORE the only Thing desirable in our Situation, is a *judicious Polity*: – Which may be farther described as a *preventive Regimen* of State, whereby the Temptations to Vice are removed, and such Incouragements given to Virtue, as would induce a Man to execute the proposed Regulations of his own free Choice, without the Appearance of Restraint or Compulsion. Thus a Traveller may be said to *choose that Road*, which the *Public* hath *laid out* for him, when he finds that the *By-Roads* are deep, intricate, and disagreeable, and the other straight, easy, safe, and good. – He prefers the public Road, not because he is *compelled* by any penal Statute, but because he finds his own Advantage in his Compliance, and cannot find it any other way.

This may serve to explain in some measure the great Difference between *Polity* and *Law*: But if any thing is yet wanting to complete the Description, it may be farther suggested, That the one is like a beautiful Machine, which regulates and adjusts its own Motion; and the other a clumsy imperfect Work, which is always out of Order, unless the Maker stands by to correct and amend it. Now from these Hints and Illustrations it plainly appears; that the Influence of the one must be much more extensive and universal than that of the other. And indeed thus it comes to pass, that the *distinguishing* Characteristics of a People chiefly depend on their *National Polity*; whereas the general *System of Laws* makes no such Difference. Antient and modern *Rome*, for Example, do not differ much from each other in the main Tenor of their Laws, relating to the common Principles of Justice and Equity: But as to the whole Body of their Polity, it is in a manner diametrically opposite. And what is the Consequence? – Plainly this; That the very Temper and Genius of the People are changed, and that there is not a greater Contrast in Nature, than between the antient *Romans* and modern *Italians*.

The Subject has hitherto been considered only in a *general* View; *viz.* That Self-Love should be so directed as to promote its own, and the public Interest at the same Time; and that *Polity* is a properer Method than *Penal Laws* for giving it this Direction. – But the immediate Inquiry comes yet to be resolved; *viz.* In what Particulars doth the Public Good consist? And how shall the Passion of Self-Love be directed so as to produce the happy Effects intended? – In answer to the former Part of the Inquiry, it may be proper to observe, That the Good of any State doth plainly arise from the *Increase*, *Imployment*, and Morals of its Subjects; because a *numerous*, *industrious*, and *virtuous* People, cannot fail of Plenty and Content at Home, of Respect and Influence Abroad. And in regard to the Method, or System of Polity, How these great and good Ends are to be obtained, this is to be the Subject of the ensuing Discourse.

Passage 3.6b
(*from* Tucker, Part II, *Elements*, 1755)

National and extensive Commerce is only another Name for the right and useful Imployment of the Individuals: And this Imployment is derived either from the *natural*, or the *artificial* Wants of Mankind. The *natural* Wants, as hath been observed before, are such as belong to Man in common with other Animals: But the *artificial* are peculiar to him as a rational Agent, and a Member of Civil Society: – Though indeed in another Sense these very artificial Wants may be stiled natural, because they arise from the *peculiar Nature* of Man as distinguished from other Creatures. But this being a less intelligible Way of speaking, it would be better to keep to the former Division of Wants, into *natural*, and *artificial*. If therefore a Man is *poor*, he is scarce able to purchase or supply himself with any thing beyond the *bare* Necessaries of Life; so that his Condition will approach the nearer to the *Brutal* State, which admits of no Commerce at all: But if he is *rich*, he need not deny himself the Injoyment of many things both useful and convenient. By which means it comes to pass, That several other Persons, besides himself, may be imployed in making or procuring them. Now if this is the Case, it plainly follows, That the Support and Extension of Commerce must result from the Multiplication of the *artificial* Needs of Mankind.

But as this System of *Commercial Industry* is equally the Plan of Providence with the System of *Morals*, we may rest assured, That both are consistent with each other: And therefore, for the present, let us take it for granted, that they are so; – deferring the Proof till we come to Part III. which is to treat particularly on this Subject: And then it will be fully shewn, That these artificial Needs must be under the Direction of *good Morals*, before they can produce that *beneficial, perpetual* and *extensive* Commerce, which Providence intended by them.

Leaving therefore this Subject till a future Occasion, let us now observe, That all Commercial Imployment may be divided into two kinds, *Husbandry*, and *Manufacture*; the immediate Object of the one being to provide *Food*, and that of the other to procure *Raiment*, and *Dwelling*: And from the CONCURRENCE *of these three* every other Trade, Calling, or Profession derives its Origin and Support. If therefore this is the Case, how wrong must have been that System of Politics, which endeavoured to set Husbandry, and Manufactures at perpetual Variance? How base and disingenuous to stir up Jealousies between them, and to represent the one an Enemy to the other? For in Fact the *Landed*, and the *Trading* Interests are only the different Markets for each other's Produce, the one being the respective *Maker*, and the other the *Consumer*. And consequently, the real Exaltation, or Depression of either, must really exalt, or depress them both.

Indeed, if by the *Landed* Interest is to be understood the Interest of the Gothic Barons (as it formerly subsisted here in *England*) or the Interest of the Lairds of Clans in *Scotland*, – between that Interest and the Commercial there ever was, and ever will be a strong Opposition. For the Power and Importance of these *petty Tyrants* over their Slaves or Vassals, can be no otherwise preserved, than by chaining down the Mass of the People in Slavery and Want. It is therefore their Interest to depress Commerce; because every Increase of Property in the lower and middling Class of People tends to render them more free and independent; – and perhaps at last more considerable than their former Superiors. In short, the poorer the Inhabitants of a Country, the greater by *Comparison* is the Baron, the Laird of the Clan, or the Landed Squire. Granting therefore that the Estates of such *Old English Gentry*, who value themselves on the Antiquity of their Houses, would be bettered by the Introduction of Trade and Manufactures, and that they themselves would enjoy more of the Conveniences, Elegancies, and Ornaments of Life, than they otherwise could do; – yet as their *Inferiors* by Birth might sometimes equal, and perhaps surpass them in these Injoyments, the *Country Gentlemen* are strongly tempted to regret this Diminution of their former Importance, and the Eclipsing of their antient Grandeur by the Wealth of these *Upstarts*.

Passage 3.7
(*from* Adam Ferguson, *An Essay on the History of Civil Society*, Part III, Section IV, 1767)

Men are tempted to labour, and to practise lucrative arts, by motives of interest. Secure to the workman the fruit of his labour, give him the prospects of independence or freedom, the public has found a faithful minister in the acquisition of wealth, and a faithful steward in hoarding what he has gained. The statesman in this, as in the case of population itself, can do little more than avoid doing mischief. It is well, if, in the beginnings of commerce, he knows how to repress the frauds to which it is subject. Commerce, if continued, is the branch in which men committed to the effects of their own experience, are least apt to go wrong.

The trader, in rude ages, is short-sighted, fraudulent, and mercenary; but in the progress and advanced state of his art, his views are enlarged, his maxims are established: he becomes punctual, liberal, faithful, and enterprising; and in the period of general corruption, he alone has every virtue, except the force to defend his acquisitions. He needs no aid from the state, but its protection; and is often in himself its most intelligent and respectable member. Even in China, we are informed, where pilfering, fraud, and corruption, are the reigning practice with all the other orders of men, the great merchant is ready to give, and to procure confidence: while his countrymen act on the plans and under the restrictions of a police adjusted to knaves, he acts on the reasons of trade, and the maxims of mankind.

If population be connected with national wealth, liberty and personal security is the great foundation of both: and if this foundation be laid in the state, nature has secured the increase and the industry of its members; the one by desires the most ardent in the human frame; the other by a consideration the most uniform and constant of any that possesses the mind. The great object of policy, therefore, with respect to both, is, to secure to the family its means of subsistence and settlement, to protect the industrious in the pursuit of his occupation; to reconcile the restrictions of police, and the social affections of mankind, with their separate and interested pursuits.

In matters of particular profession, industry, and trade, the experienced practitioner is the master, and every general reasoner is a novice. The object in commerce is to make the individual rich; the more he gains for himself, the more he augments the wealth of his country. If a protection be required, it must be granted; if crimes and frauds be committed, they must be repressed; and government can pretend to no more. When the refined politician would lend an active hand, he only multiplies interruptions and grounds of complaint; when the merchant forgets his own interest to lay plans for his country, the period of vision and chimera is near, and the solid basis of commerce withdrawn. He might be told, perhaps, that while he pursues his advantage, and gives no cause of complaint, the interest of commerce is safe.

The general police of France, proceeding on a supposition that the exportation of corn must drain the country where it has grown, had, till of late, laid that branch of commerce under a severe prohibition. The English landholder and the farmer had sale of their commodity; and the event has shewn, that private interest is a better patron of commerce and plenty, than the refinements of state. One nation lays the refined plan of a settlement on the continent of North America, and trusts little to the conduct of traders and short-sighted men; another leaves men to find their own position in a state of freedom, and to think for themselves. The active industry and the limited views of the one, made a thriving settlement; the great projects of the other were still in idea.

But I willingly quit a subject in which I am not much conversant, and still less engaged by the views which I write. Speculations on commerce and wealth have been delivered by the ablest writers, who have left nothing so important to be offered on the subject, as the general caution, not to consider these articles as making the sum of national felicity, or the principal object of any state.

One nation, in search of gold and precious metals, neglect the domestic sources of wealth, and become dependent on their neighbours for the necessaries of life: another so intent on improving their internal resources, and on increasing their commerce, that they become dependent on foreigners for the defence of what they acquire. It is even painful in conversation to find the interests of trade give the tone to our reasonings, and to find a subject perpetually offered as the great business of national councils, to which any interposition of government is seldom, with propriety, applied, or never beyond the protection it affords.

We complain of a want of public spirit; but whatever may be the effect of this error in practice, in speculation it is none of our faults: we reason perpetually for the public; but the want of national views were frequently better than the possession of those we express: we would have nations, like a company of merchants, think of nothing but the increase of their stock; assemble to deliberate on profit and loss; and, like them too, intrust their protection to a force which they do not possess in themselves.

Because men, like other animals, are maintained in multitudes, where the necessaries of life are amassed, and the store of wealth is enlarged, we drop our regards for the happiness, the moral and political character of a people; and anxious for the herd we would propagate, carry our views no farther than the stall and the pasture. We forget that the few have often made a prey of the many; that to the poor there is nothing so enticing as the coffers of the rich; and that when the price of freedom comes to be paid, the heavy sword of the victor may fall into the opposite scale.

Whatever be the actual conduct of nations in this matter, it is certain, that many of our arguments would hurry us, for the sake of wealth and of population, into a scene where mankind being exposed to corruption, are unable to defend their possessions; and where they are, in the end, subject to oppression and ruin. We cut off the roots, while we would extend the branches, and thicken the foliage.

It is possibly from an opinion that the virtues of men are secure, that some who turn from their attention to public affairs, think of nothing but the numbers and wealth of a people: it is from a dread of corruption, that others think of nothing but how to preserve the national virtues. Human society has great obligations to both. They are opposed to one another only by mistake; and even when united, have not strength sufficient to combat the wretched party, that refers every object to personal interest, and that cares not for the safety or increase of any stock but its own.

Passage 3.8
(*from* Sir James Steuart, Introduction to Part II, *Principles of Political Oeconomy*, 1767)

The principle of self-interest will serve as a general key to this inquiry; and it may, in one sense, be considered as the ruling principle of my subject, and may therefore be traced throughout the whole. This is the main spring, and only motive which a statesman should make use of, to engage a free people to concur in the plans which he lays down for their government.

I beg I may not here be understood to mean, that self-interest should conduct the statesman: by no means. Self-interest, when considered with regard to him, is public spirit; and it can only be called self-interest, when it is applied to those who are to be governed by it.

From this principle, men are engaged to act in a thousand different ways, and every action draws after it certain necessary consequences. The question therefore constantly under consideration comes to be, what will mankind find it their interest to do, under such and such circumstances?

In order to exhaust the subject of political oeconomy, I have proposed to treat the principles of it in relation to circumstances; and as these are infinite, I have taken them by the more general combinations, which modern policy has formed. These, for the sake of order, I have represented as all hanging in a chain of consequences, and depending on one another . . .

I found this the best method for distributing my plan, from which it is natural to infer, that it will also prove the best for enabling my readers to retain it.

I shall do what I can to diversify, by various circumstances, the repetitions which this disposition must lead me into. There is no seeing a whole kingdom, without passing now and then through a town which one has seen before. I shall therefore imitate the traveller, who, upon such occasions, makes his stay very short, unless some new curiosity should happen to engage his attention.

I have said, that self-interest is the ruling principle of my subject, and I have so explained myself, as to prevent any one from supposing, that I consider it as the universal spring of human actions. Here is the light in which I want to represent this matter.

The best way to govern a society, and to engage every one to conduct himself according to a plan, is for the statesman to form a system of administration, the most consistent possible with the interest of every individual, and never to flatter himself that his people will be brought to act in general, and in matters which purely regard the public, from any other principle than private interest. This is the utmost length to which I pretend to carry my position. As to what regards the merit and demerit of actions in general, I think it fully as absurd to say, that no action is truly virtuous, as to affirm, that none is really vicious.

It might perhaps be expected, that, in treating of politics, I should have brought in public spirit also, as a principle of action; whereas all I require with respect to this principle is merely a restraint from it; and even this is, perhaps, too much to be taken for granted. Were public spirit, instead of private utility, to become the spring of action in the individuals of a well-governed state, I apprehend, it would spoil all. Let me explain myself.

Public spirit, in my way of treating this subject, is as superfluous in the governed, as it ought to be all-powerful in the statesman; at least, if it is not altogether superfluous, it is fully as much so, as miracles are in a religion once fully established. Both are admirable at setting out, but would shake every thing loose, were they to continue to be common and familiar. Were miracles wrought every day, the laws of nature would no longer be laws; and were every one to act for the public, and neglect himself, the statesman would be bewildered, and the supposition is ridiculous.

I expect, therefore, that every man is to act for his own interest in what regards the public; and, politically speaking, every one ought to do so. It is the combination of every private interest which forms the public good, and of this the public, that is, the statesman only, can judge. You must love your country. Why? Because it is *yours*. But you must not prefer your own interest to that of your country. This, I agree, is perfectly just and right: but this means no more, than that you are to abstain from acting to its prejudice, even though your own private interest should demand it; that is, you should abstain from unlawful gain. Count Julian, for example, who, from private resentment, it is said, brought the Moors into Spain, and ruined his country, transgressed this maxim. A spy in an army, or in a cabinet, who betrays the secrets of his country, and he who sells his trust, are in the same case: defrauding the state is, among many others, a notorious example of this. To suppose men, in general, honest in such matters, would be absurd. The legislature therefore ought to make good laws, and those who transgress them ought to be speedily, severely, and most certainly punished. This belongs to the coercive part of government, and, falling beyond the limits of my subject, is ever taken for granted.

Were the principle of public spirit carried further; were a people to become quite disinterested; there would be no possibility of governing them. Every one might consider the interest of his country in a different light, and many might join in the ruin of it, by endeavouring to promote its advantages. Were a rich merchant to begin and sell his goods without profit, what would become of trade? Were another to defray the extraordinary expence of some workmen in a hard year, in order to enable them to carry on their industry, without raising their price, what would become of others, who had not the like advantages? Were a man of a large landed estate to sell his grain at a low price in a year of scarcity, what would become of the poor farmers? Were people to feed all who would ask charity, what would become of industry? These operations of public spirit ought to be left to the public, and all that is required of individuals is, not to endeavour to defeat them.

This is the regular distribution of things, and it is this only which comes under my consideration.

In ill-administered governments, I admire as much as any one every act of public spirit, every sentiment of disinterestedness, and nobody can have a higher esteem for every person remarkable for them.

The less attentive any government is to do *their* duty, the more essential it is that every individual be animated by *that* spirit, which then languishes in the very part where it ought to flourish with the greatest strength and vigour; and on the other hand, the more public spirit is shewn in the administration of public affairs, the less occasion has the state for assistance from individuals.

Now as I suppose my statesmen to do his duty in the most minute particulars, so I allow every one of his subjects to follow the dictates of his private interest. All I require is an exact obedience to the laws. This also is the interest of every one; for he who transgresses ought most undoubtedly to be punished: and this is all the public spirit which any perfect government has occasion for.

Passage 3.9a

(*from* Adam Smith, Book I, Chapters 1 and 2, *An Inquiry into the Nature and Causes of the Wealth of Nations*, 1776)

It is the great multiplication of the productions of all the different arts, in consequence of the division of labour, which occasions, in a well-governed society, that universal opulence which extends itself to the lowest ranks of the people. Every workman has a great quantity of his own work to dispose of beyond what he himself has occasion for; and every other workman being exactly in the same situation, he is enabled to exchange a great quantity of his own goods for a great quantity, or, what comes to the same thing, for the price of a great quantity of theirs. He supplies them abundantly with what they have occasion for, and they accommodate him as amply with what he has occasion for, and a general plenty diffuses itself through all the different ranks of the society.

Observe the accommodation of the most common artificer or day-labourer in a civilized and thriving country, and you will perceive that the number of people of whose industry a part, though but a small part, has been employed in procuring him this accommodation, exceeds all computation. The woollen coat, for example, which covers the day-labourer, as coarse and rough as it may appear, is the produce of the joint labour of a great multitude of workmen. The shepherd, the sorter of the wool, the wool-comber or carder, the dyer, the scribbler, the spinner, the weaver, the fuller, the dresser, with many others, must all joint their different arts in order to complete even this homely production. How many merchants and carriers, besides, must have been employed in transporting the materials from some of those workmen to others who often live in a very distant part of the country! How much commerce and navigation in particular, how many ship-builders, sailors, sail-makers, rope-makers, must have been employed in order to bring together the different drugs made use of by the dyer, which often come from the remotest corners of the world! What a variety of labour too is necessary in order to produce the tools of the meanest of those workmen! To say nothing of such complicated machines as the ship of the sailor, the mill of the fuller, or even the loom of the weaver, let us consider only what a variety of labour is requisite in order to form that very simple machine, the shears with which the shepherd clips the wool. The miner, the builder of the furnace for smelting the ore, the feller of the timber, the burner of the charcoal to be made use of in the smelting-house, the brick-maker, the brick-layer, the workmen who attend the furnace, the mill-wright, the forger, the smith, must all of them join their different arts in order to produce them. Were we to examine, in the same manner, all the different parts of his dress and household furniture, the coarse linen shirt which he wears next to his skin, the shoes which cover his feet, the bed which he lies on, and all the different parts which compose it, the kitchen-grate at which he prepares his victuals, the coals which he makes use of for that purpose, dug from the bowels of the earth, and brought to him perhaps by a long sea and a long land carriage, all the other utensils of his kitchen, all the furniture of his table, the knives and forks, the earthern or pewter plates upon which he serves up and divides his victuals, the different hands employed in preparing his bread and his beer, the glass window which lets in the heat and the light, and keeps out the wind and the rain, with all the knowledge and art requisite for preparing that beautiful and happy invention, without which these northern parts of the world could scarce have afforded a very comfortable habitation, together with the tools of all the different workmen employed in producing those different conveniences; if we examine, I say, all these things, and consider what a variety of labour is employed about each of them, we shall be sensible that without the assistance and co-operation of many thousands, the very meanest person in a civilized country could not be provided, even according to, what we very falsely imagine, the easy and simple manner in which he is commonly accommodated. Compared, indeed, with the more extravagant luxury of the great, his accommodation must no doubt appear extremely simple and easy; and yet it may be true, perhaps, that the accommodation of an European prince does not always so much exceed that of an industrious and frugal peasant, as the accommodation of the latter exceeds that of many an African king, the absolute master of the lives and liberties of ten thousand naked savages.

Of the Principle which gives occasion to the Division of Labour

This division of labour, from which so many advantages are derived, is not originally the effect of any human wisdom, which foresees and intends that general opulence to which it gives occasion. It is the necessary, though very slow and gradual consequence of a certain propensity in human nature which has in view no such extensive utility; the propensity to truck, barter, and exchange one thing for another.

Whether this propensity be one of those original principles in human nature, of which no further account can be given; or whether, as seems more probable, it be the necessary consequence of the faculties of reason and speech, it belongs not to our present subject to enquire. It is common to all men, and to be found in no other race of animals, which seem to know neither this nor any other species of contracts. Two greyhounds, in running down the same hare, have sometimes the appearance of acting in some sort of concert. Each turns her towards his companion, or endeavours to intercept her when his companion turns her towards himself. This, however, is not the effect of any contract, but of the accidental concurrence of their passions in the same object at that particular time. Nobody ever saw a dog make a fair and deliberate exchange of one bone for another with another dog. Nobody ever saw one animal by its gestures and natural cries signify to another, this is mine, that yours; I am willing to give this for that. When an animal wants to obtain something either of a man or of another animal, it has no other means of persuasion but to gain the favour of those whose service it requires. A puppy fawns upon its dam, and a spaniel endeavours by a thousand attractions to engage the attention of its master who is at dinner, when it wants to be fed by him. Man sometimes uses the same arts with his brethren, and when he has no other means of engaging them to act according to his inclinations, endeavours by every servile and fawning attention to obtain their good will. He has not time, however, to do this upon every occasion. In civilized society he stands at all times in need of the co-operation and assistance of great multitudes, while his whole life is scarce sufficient to gain the friendship of a few persons. In almost every other race of animals each individual, when it is grown up to maturity, is intirely independent, and in its natural state has occasion for the assistance of no other living creature. But man has almost constant occasion for the help of his brethren, and it is in vain for him to expect it from their benevolence only. He will be more likely to prevail if he can interest their self-love in his favour, and shew them that it is for their own advantage to do for him what he requires of them. Whoever offers to another a bargain of any kind, proposes to do this. Give me that which I want, and you shall have this which you want, is the meaning of every such offer; and it is in this manner that we obtain from one another the far greater part of those good offices which we stand in need of. It is not from the benevolence of the butcher, the brewer, or the baker, that we expect our dinner, but from their regard to their own interest. We address ourselves, not to their humanity but to their self-love, and never talk to them of our own necessities but of their advantages. Nobody but a beggar chuses to depend chiefly upon the benevolence of his fellow-citizens. Even a beggar does not depend upon it entirely. The charity of well-disposed people, indeed, supplies him with the whole fund of his subsistence. But though this principle ultimately provides him with all the necessaries of life which he has occasion for, it neither does nor can provide him with them as he has occasion for them. The greater part of his occasional wants are supplied in the same manner as those of other people, by treaty, by barter, and by purchase. With the money which one man gives him he purchases food. The old cloaths which another bestows upon him he exchanges for other old cloaths which suit him better, or for lodging, or for food, or for money, with which he can buy either food, cloaths, or lodging, as he has occasion.

As it is by treaty, by barter, and by purchase, that we obtain from one another the greater part of those mutual good offices which we stand in need of, so it is this same trucking disposition which originally gives occasion to the division of labour. In a tribe of hunters or shepherds a particular person makes bows and arrows, for example, with more readiness and dexterity than any other. He frequently exchanges them for cattle or for venison with his companions; and he finds at last that he can in this manner get more cattle and venison, than if he himself went to the field to catch them. From a regard to his own interest, therefore, the making of bows and arrows grows to be his chief business, and he becomes a sort of armourer. Another excels in making the frames and covers of their little huts or moveable houses. He is accustomed to be of use in this way to his neighbours, who reward him in the same manner with cattle and with venison, till at last he finds it his interest to dedicate himself entirely to this employment, and to become a sort of house-carpenter. In the same manner a third becomes a smith or a brazier, a fourth a tanner or dresser of hides and skins, the principal part of the clothing of savages. And thus the certainty of being able to exchange all that surplus part of the produce of his own labour, which is over and above his own consumption, for such parts of the produce of other men's labour as he may have occasion for, encourages every man to apply himself to a particular occupation, and to cultivate and bring to perfection whatever talent or genius he may possess for that particular species of business.

The difference of natural talents in different men is, in reality, much less than we are aware of; and the very different genius which appears to distinguish men of different professions, when grown up to maturity, is not upon many occasions so much the cause, as the effect of the division of labour. The difference between the most dissimilar characters, between a philosopher and a common street porter, for example, seems to arise not so much from nature, as from habit, custom, and education. When they came into the world, and for the first six or eight years of their existence, they were, perhaps, very much alike, and neither their parents nor play-fellows could perceive any remarkable difference. About that age, or soon after, they come to be employed in very different occupations. The difference of talents comes then to be taken notice of, and widens by degrees, till at last the vanity of the philosopher is willing to acknowledge scarce any resemblance. But without the disposition to truck, barter, and exchange, every man must have procured to himself every necessary and conveniency of life which he wanted. All must have had the same duties to perform, and the same work to do, and there could have been no such difference of employment as could alone give occasion to any great difference of talents.

As it is this disposition which forms that difference of talents, so remarkable among men of different professions, so it is this same disposition which renders that difference useful. Many tribes of animals acknowledged to be all of the same species, derive from nature a much more remarkable distinction of genius, than what, antecedent to custom and education, appears to take place among men. By nature a philosopher is not in genius and disposition half so different from a street porter, as a mastiff is from a greyhound, or a greyhound from a spaniel, or this last from a shepherd's dog. Those different tribes of animals, however, though all of the same species, are of scarce any use to one another. The strength of the mastiff is not, in the least, supported either by the swiftness of the greyhound, or by the sagacity of the spaniel, or by the docility of the shepherd's dog. The effects of those different geniuses and talents, for want of the power or disposition to barter and exchange, cannot be brought into a common stock, and do not in the least contribute to the better accommodation and conveniency of the species. Each animal is still obliged to support and defend itself, separately and independently, and derives no sort of advantage from that variety of talents with which nature has distinguished its fellows. Among men, on the contrary, the most dissimilar geniuses are of use to one another; the different produces of their respective talents, by the general disposition to truck, barter, and exchange, being brought, as it were, into a common stock, where every man may purchase whatever part of the produce of other men's talents he has occasion for.

Passage 3.9b
(*from* Smith, Book III, Chapter 4, *Inquiry*, 1776)

The introduction of the feudal law, so far from extending, may be regarded as an attempt to moderate the authority of the great allodial lords. It established a regular subordination, accompanied with a long train of services and duties, from the king down to the smallest proprietor. During the minority of the proprietor, the rent, together with the management of his lands, fell into the hands of his immediate superior, and, consequently, those of all great proprietors into the hands of the king, who was charged with the maintenance and education of the pupil, and who, from his authority as guardian, was supposed to have a right of disposing of him in marriage, provided it was in a manner not unsuitable to his rank. But though this institution necessarily tended to strengthen the authority of the king, and to weaken that of the great proprietors, it could not do either sufficiently for establishing order and good government among the inhabitants of the country; because it could not alter sufficiently that state of property and manners from which the disorders arose. The authority of government still continued to be, as before, too weak in the head and too strong in the inferior members, and the excessive strength of the inferior members was the cause of the weakness of the head. After the institution of feudal subordination, the king was as incapable of restraining the violence of the great lords as before. They still continued to make war according to their own discretion, almost continually upon one another, and very frequently upon the king; and the open country still continued to be a scene of violence, rapine, and disorder.

But what all the violence of the feudal institutions could never have effected, the silent and insensible operation of foreign commerce and manufactures gradually brought about. These gradually furnished the great proprietors with something for which they could exchange the whole surplus produce of their lands, and which they could consume themselves without sharing it either with tenants or retainers. All for ourselves, and nothing for other people, seems, in every age of the world, to have been the vile maxim of the masters of mankind. As soon, therefore, as they could find a method of consuming the whole value of their rents themselves, they had no disposition to share them with any other persons. For a pair of diamond buckles perhaps, or for something as frivolous and useless, they exchanged the maintenance, or what is the same thing, the price of the maintenance of a thousand men for a year, and with it the whole weight and authority which it could give them. The buckles, however, were to be all their own, and no other human creature was to have any share of them; whereas in the more antient method of expence they must have shared with at least a thousand people. With the judges that were to determine the preference, this difference was perfectly decisive; and thus, for the gratification of the most childish, the meanest and the most sordid of all vanities, they gradually bartered their whole power and authority.

In a country where there is no foreign commerce, nor any of the finer manufactures, a man of ten thousand a year cannot well employ his revenue in any other way than in maintaining, perhaps, a thousand families, who are all of them necessarily at his command. In the present state of Europe, a man of ten thousand a year can spend his whole revenue, and he generally does so, without directly maintaining twenty people, or being able to command more than ten footmen not worth the commanding. Indirectly, perhaps, he maintains as great or even a greater number of people than he could have done by the antient method of expence. For though the quantity of precious productions for which he exchanges his whole revenue be very small, the number of workmen employed in collecting and preparing it, must necessarily have been very great. Its great price generally arises from the wages of their labour, and the profits of all their immediate employers. By paying that price he indirectly pays all those wages and profits, and thus indirectly contributes to the maintenance of all the workmen and their employers. He generally contributes, however, but a very small proportion to that of each, to very few perhaps a tenth, to many not a hundredth, and to some not a thousandth, nor even a ten thousandth part of their whole annual maintenance. Though he contributes, therefore, to the maintenance of them all, they are all more or less independent of him, because generally they can all be maintained without him.

When the great proprietors of land spend their rents in maintaining their tenants and retainers, each of them maintains entirely all his own tenants and all his own retainers. But when they spend them in maintaining tradesmen and artificers, they may, all of them taken together, perhaps, maintain as great, or, on account of the waste which attends rustick hospitality, a greater number of people than before. Each of them, however, taken singly, contributes often but a very small share to the maintenance of any individual of this great number. Each tradesman or artificer derives his subsistence from the employment, not of one, but of a hundred or a thousand different customers. Though in some measure obliged to them all, therefore, he is not absolutely dependent upon any one of them.

The personal expence of the great proprietors having in this manner gradually increased, it was impossible that the number of their retainers should not as gradually diminish, till they were at last diminished altogether. The same cause gradually led them to dismiss the unnecessary part of their tenants. Farms were enlarged, and the occupiers of land, not withstanding the complaints of depopulation, reduced to the number necessary for cultivating it, according to the imperfect state of cultivation and improvement in those times. By the removal of the unnecessary mouths, and by exacting from the farmer the full value of the farm, a greater surplus, or what is the same thing, the price of a greater surplus, was obtained for the proprietor, which the merchants and manufacturers soon furnished him with a method of spending upon his own person in the same manner as he had done the rest. The same cause continuing to operate, he was desirous to raise his rents above what his lands, in the actual state of their improvement, could afford. His tenants could agree to this upon one condition only, that they should be secured in that possession, for such a term of years as might give them time to recover with profit whatever they should lay out in the further improvement of the land. The expensive vanity of the landlord made him willing to accept of this condition; and hence the origin of long leases.

Even a tenant at will, who pays the full value of the land, is not altogether dependent upon the landlord. The pecuniary advantages which they receive from one another, are mutual and equal, and such a tenant will expose neither his life nor his fortune in the service of the proprietor. But if he has a lease for a long term of years, he is altogether independent; and his landlord must not expect from him even the most trifling service beyond what is either expressly stipulated in the lease, or imposed upon him by the common and known law of the country.

The tenants having in this manner become independent, and the retainers being dismissed, the great proprietors were no longer capable of interrupting the regular execution of justice, or of disturbing the peace of the country. Having sold their birth-right, not like Esau for a mess of pottage in time of hunger and necessity, but in the wantonness of plenty, for trinkets and baubles, fitter to be the play-things of children than the serious pursuits of men, then become as insignificant as any substantial burgher or tradesman in a city. A regular government was established in the country as well as in the city, nobody having sufficient power to disturb its operations in the one, any more than in the other.

It does not, perhaps, relate to the present subject, but I cannot help remarking it, that very old families, such as have possessed some considerable estate from father to son for many successive generations, are very rare in commercial countries. In countries which have little commerce, on the contrary, such as Wales or the highlands of Scotland, they are very common. The Arabian histories seem to be full of genealogies, and there is a history written by a Tartar Khan, which has been translated into several European languages, and which contains scarce any thing else; a proof that antient families are very common among those nations. In countries where a rich man can spend his revenue in no other way than by maintaining as many people as it can maintain, he is not apt to run out, and his benevolence it seems is seldom so violent as to attempt to maintain more than he can afford. But where he can spend the greatest revenue upon his own person, he frequently has no bounds to his expence, because he frequently has no bounds to his vanity, or to his affection for his own person. In commercial countries, therefore, riches, in spite of the most violent regulations of law to prevent their dissipation, very seldom remain long in the same family. Among simple nations, on the contrary, they frequently do without any regulations of law; for among nations of shepherds, such as the Tartars and Arabs, the consumable nature of their property necessarily renders all such regulations impossible.

A revolution of the greatest importance to the publick happiness, was in this manner brought out by two different orders of people, who had not the least intention to serve the publick. To gratify the most childish vanity was the sole motive of the great proprietors. The merchants and artificers, much less ridiculous, acted merely from a view to their own interest, and in pursuit of their own pedlar principle of turning a penny wherever a penny was to be got. Neither of them had either knowledge or foresight of that great revolution which the folly of the one, and the industry of the other, was gradually bringing about.

4 THE POOR

In Dr Johnson's *Dictionary* 'the poor' are defined as 'those who are in the lowest rank of the community; those who cannot subsist but by the charity of others'. However Johnson adds that the term 'is sometimes used with laxity for any not rich'. His definition is worth bearing in mind when reading the passages in this section. In them the category of 'the poor' usually refers to all those outside the property-owning establishment. Within this category each writer draws his own distinctions between the 'labouring' and the 'idle' poor, or between the 'rich' and the 'needy' poor, before considering the relation between each group and established society. The major preoccupation apparent in the passages – no matter which section of the poor they are discussing – is a fear of social insubordination, which is usually countered by demands for increasingly rigorous measures of social control. This preoccupation is equally clear in accounts of the need for restrictions on the movements of the 'begging poor', and in discussions of the appropriate level of wages for their working counterparts.

The passages from *The Guardian* and from *The Fable of the Bees* (passages 4.2 and 4.3) form part of a considerable debate in the period about the advisability of educating the poor. In its advocacy of charity schools, the *Guardian* article is typical of a vein of sentimental humanitarianism that runs through this debate. It employs a familiar moral vocabulary, claiming that the schools will improve the character of the poor, save the age from 'its present Degeneracy and Depravation of Manners' and 'promise us an honest and virtuous Posterity'. At the same time, it concentrates on the gratifying emotional effects that the scene of charity it describes had on 'every Heart that had any Sentiments of Humanity'.

Mandeville's dismissal of this case rests on his claims that the poor are beyond the realms of moral improvement, and that humane sentiments are irrelevant in discussions of the economic management of society. His arguments are echoed by Defoe and Temple (passages 4.4 and 4.6). Both complain about the insubordination of the labouring poor and justify the payment of subsistence wages to them. These justifications are worth examining for their combination of moral judgements (such as Defoe's claim that high wages destroy the virtues of the poor by exposing them to the temptations of luxury), generalisations about human nature (such as Temple's assertion that 'Nothing but necessity can enforce industry. We must take human nature as it is') and pragmatic assessments of the usefulness of a class of subsistence labourers in the economy.

Passages 4.7–4.9 give some idea of the terms in which the poor are discussed in various parts of Johnson's work. The first of them, from his review of Soame Jenyns's *Free Enquiry*, attacks the fashionable doctrines of philosophical optimism espoused by Jenyns and Pope. As Johnson's lengthy quotation from Jenyns shows, this optimism tends to deal with the problem of poverty in society as it does with evil in the world, either by denying its existence or by explaining with apparent ease how it is subsumed in the grand design of the whole. Johnson's insistence on recognising the 'real' conditions of poverty marks an important shift in emphasis away from the philosophical and social arguments of optimism. His emphasis in the last paragraph of the passage on the 'maxims of a commercial nation, which always suppose and promote a rotation of property, and offer every individual a chance of mending his condition by his diligence' compares interestingly with the far more rigidly hierarchic version of the social order that he describes in *The False Alarm* (passage 4.9).

The passage from Goldsmith (passage 4.10) takes a description of ideal poverty as the basis for a Tory polemic against the destructive effects of trade in society. The final passage in the section, from Arthur Young's *Six Weeks' Tour*, continues the earlier debates about wage levels for the labouring poor, introducing a new statistical accuracy in its surveys of wages in the southern counties. Despite Young's claim that 'I mean to deal in facts alone', it shows many traces of its origins in the moral discussions I have outlined elsewhere. The clearest example of this is the analysis that it offers of the effect that London has on the wage market; this employs terms with decided moral connotations throughout. Inflated wage rates in the capital, for instance, are taken to be the result of 'the debauched life of its inhabitants', and are put down to 'the very maxims and principles upon which life is founded in great cities'.

Passage 4.1
(*from* Daniel Defoe, *The Review*, Vol. VI, No. 41, 7 July 1709)

But now I am talking of our Poor, and indeed we are fill'd with the Clamours of our People about our Poor – With the least Reason, and the least Project of Rectification, that ever was seen in any like Case in the World – I might say – it is our rich Poor, not our needy Poor, that are the clamorous and uneasie People of this Nation – And these want sundry Regulations, which I cannot speak to now – However, being thus entered upon the Subject of our Encrease of People, and improving our Lands, I shall lay down a few Heads, in which, I suppose, the general Management of our People in *Britain* is defective, and which, if they suffer'd a due Regulation, would open your Eyes to the several Advantages of Commerce, and to the true Methods of planting and managing not the People you have only, but all those that shall seek Settlement and Refuge among you.

I shall only lay you down Generals at present, and speak to them apart, as Occasion presents.

First, The several Impositions and Encroachments we make upon the industrious Poor in the ordinary Methods of Trade, *whether* by Corporation-Tyranny, as I call it, which confines Men to labour in such or such Places only – A Thing which requires a long *Series* of Regulation in *Britain*; or by the Oppressions of Usury, Tally men, Pawn-brokers, *&c.* a Sort of People, who, as some say, and I am apt to believe, in this very City only, gain 1,000,00*l* yearly, out of the Labour and Industry of the Poor, by horrid Extortions and Barbarisms, which I am very loth to rake into – Such as extravagant Interests, Advance-Money, *&c.* upon Pawns and Pledges – Including a little, *or rather not a little*, *Exchange* Usury, or *Lombard-street* Extortion; such as Discounts on Bills, advancing Money for Customs, *&c.*

We have been told of charitable Endeavours to settle Funds for the easing the Poor in such Cases as these, and delivering them from the Necessity of submitting to such Extravagancies – If such Endeavours are built upon a right Foot, they deserve, and cannot miss of Encouragement, if we have really any Disposition to render Trade flourishing, and make the poorer Sort of our trading labouring People easie.

Secondly, The incredible Swarm of the begging Poor in *South-Britain*, especially where there is so plentiful Provision made for truly necessitous, and such strict, *tho' ill executed,* Laws to punish the vagabond mendicant Poor – And here I cannot but put in a Word, in Behalf of our *North-British* Poor, for whom no Parochial Provision is made, and to note, that, after all we can say of the Poverty of *Scotland*, were the Laws for Maintenance of the Poor the same in *Scotland*, as they are here, or something like it, there would be fewer Beggars there than in any Part of *England* – But to have People beg in *England*, where Wages for Work is so dear, Provision so plentiful, establish'd Allowance to the really indigent so considerable, is a Shame to our Government, and declares, we have the best Laws, the worst executed of any Nation in the World.

Thirdly, The Deficiency in spreading our Manufactures in the most proper Places of *Britain*, by which Means the great Circulation of Trade, which is the Health of our Commerce, is obstructed, and the People drawn in unequal and ill-proportion'd Crowds, from one Part of the Nation to another – This has a great many ill Consequences, both on the Rates of Provisions, the Price of Wages, and indeed on the Manufacture it self – but much more upon the Improvement of Lands, and the Peopling the Nation.

This Head, when I come to treat of it in particular, will lead me to show you a little in *England*, how much it is your Concern to promote and extend Trade Manufactures, and a full Employment, to the People of *Scotland* – Who are and ought now to be esteem'd a Part of your selves, and who, by an Encrease of Commerce, would grow rich in Produce – The Rates of Labour encrease, for Want of which their People fly from home – Their Lands would be improv'd, the Rents and Value rise, the Price of Provisions advance, and that Nation soon be made as populous, and consequently as rich as your selves. Whether you will like to hear of this or no, I know not, nor shall I forbear to tell it you upon that Apprehension.

Passage 4.2

(Richard Steele, *The Guardian*, No. 105, 11 July 1713)

Quod neque in Armeniis tigres fecere latebris:
Perdere nec faetus ausa Leaena suos.
At tenerae faciunt, sed non impune, Puellae;
Saepe suos utero quae necat, ipsa perit.

Ov.[1]

There was no Part of the Show on the Thanksgiving-Day that so much pleased and affected me as the little Boys and Girls who were ranged with so much Order and Decency in that Part of the *Strand* which reaches from the *Maypole* to *Exeter Change*. Such a numerous and Innocent Multitude, cloathed in the Charity of their Benefactors, was a Spectacle pleasing both to God and Man, and a more beautiful expression of Joy and Thanksgiving than could have been exhibited by all the Pomps of a *Roman* Triumph. Never did a more full and unspotted Chorus of Human Creatures join together in a Hymn of Devotion. The

Care and Tenderness which appeared in the Looks of their several Instructors, who were disposed among this little Helpless People, could not forbear touching every Heart that had any Sentiments of Humanity.

I am very sorry that Her Majesty did not see this Assembly of Objects so proper to excite that Charity and Compassion which she bears to all who stand in need of it, tho' at the same time I question not but her Royal Bounty will extend it self to them. A Charity bestowed on the Education of so many of her young Subjects, has more Merit in it than a thousand Pensions to those of a higher Fortune who are in greater Stations in Life.

I have always looked on this Institution of Charity-Schools, which, of late Years, has so Universally prevailed through the whole Nation, as the Glory of the Age we live in, and the most proper Means that can be made use of to recover it out of its present Degeneracy and Depravation of Manners. It seems to promise us an honest and virtuous Posterity: There will be few in the next Generation who will not at least be able to Write and Read, and have not had an early Tincture of Religion. It is therefore to be hoped that the several Persons of Wealth and Quality, who made their Procession through the Members of these new erected Seminaries, will not regard them only as an empty Spectacle, or the Materials of a fine Show, but contribute to their Maintenance and Increase. For my Part, I can scarce forbear looking on the astonishing Victories our Arms have been crowned with to be in some Measure the Blessings returned upon that National Charity which has been so Conspicuous of late, and that the great Successes of the last War, for which we lately offered up our Thanks, were in some Measure occasioned by the several Objects which then stood before us.

Since I am upon this Subject, I shall mention a Piece of Charity which has not been yet exerted among us, and which deserves our Attention the more, because it is practised by most of the Nations about us. I mean a Provision for Foundlings, or for those Children who through want of such a Provision are exposed to the Barbarity of cruel and unnatural Parents. One does not know how to speak on such a Subject without Horror: But what Multitudes of Infants have been made away by those who brought them into the World, and were afterwards either ashamed or unable to provide for them!

There is scarce an Assizes where some unhappy Wretch is not Executed for the Murder of a Child. And how many more of these Monsters of Inhumanity may we suppose to be wholly undiscovered, or cleared for want of Legal Evidence? Not to mention those, who by Unnatural Practices do in some Measure defeat the Intentions of Providence, and destroy their Conceptions even before they see the Light. In all these the Guilt is equal, tho' the Punishment is not so. But to pass by the Greatness of the Crime, (which is not to be expressed by Words) if we only consider it as it robs the Common-wealth of its full Number of Citizens, it certainly deserves the utmost Application and Wisdom of a People to prevent it.

It is certain, that which generally betrays these profligate Women into it, and overcomes the Tenderness which is natural to them on other Occasions, is the fear of Shame, or their Inability to support those whom they give Life to. I shall therefore show how this Evil is prevented in other Countries, as I have learnt from those who have been conversant in the several great Cities of *Europe*.

There are at *Paris*, *Madrid*, *Lisbon*, *Rome*, and many other large Towns, great Hospitals built like our Colleges. In the Walls of these Hospitals are placed Machines, in the Shape of large Lanthorns, with a little Door in the Side of them turned towards the Street, and a Bell hanging by them. The Child is deposited in this Lanthorn, which is immediately turned about into the Inside of the Hospital. The Person who conveys the Child rings the Bell and leaves it there, upon which the proper Officer comes and receives it without making further Enquiries. The Parent or her Friend, who lays the Child there, generally leaves a Note with it, declaring whether it be yet Christned, the Name it should be called by, the particular Marks upon it, and the like.

It often happens that the Parent leaves a Note for the Maintenance and Education of the Child, or takes it out after it has been some Years in the Hospital. Nay, it has been known that the Father has afterwards owned the young Foundling for his Son, or left his Estate to him. This is certain, that many are by this means preserved, and do signal Services to their Country, who without such a Provision might have perished as Abortives, or have come to an untimely End, and perhaps have brought upon their Guilty Parents the like Destruction.

This I think is a Subject that deserves our most Serious Consideration, for which Reason I hope I shall not be thought Impertinent in laying it before my Readers.

Passage 4.3a

(*from* Bernard Mandeville, 'An Essay on Charity, and Charity-schools', *The Fable of the Bees*, 1714-25)

There ought to be a vast disproportion between the Active and Unactive part of the Society to make it Happy, and where this is not regarded the multitude of Gifts and Endowments may soon be excessive and detrimental to a Nation. Charity, where it is too extensive, seldom fails of promoting Sloth and Idleness, and is good for little in the Commonwealth but to breed Drones and destroy Industry. The more Colleges and Alms-houses you build the more you may. The first Founders and Benefactors may have just and good Intentions, and would perhaps for their own Reputations seem to labour for the most laudable Purposes, but the Executors of those Wills, the Governors that come after them, have quite other Views, and we seldom see Charities long applied as it was first intended they should be. I have no design that is Cruel, nor the least aim that savours of Inhumanity. To have sufficient Hospitals for Sick and Wounded I look upon as an indispensible Duty both in Peace and War: Young Children without Parents, Old Age without Support, and all that are disabled from Working, ought to be taken care of with Tenderness and Alacrity. But as on the one hand I would have none neglected that are helpless, and really necessitous without being wanting to themselves, so on the other I would not encourage Beggary or Laziness in the Poor. All should be set to work that are any ways able, and Scrutinies should be made even among the Infirm: Employments might be found out for most of our Lame, and many that are unfit for hard Labour, as well as the Blind, as long as their Health and Strength would allow of it. What I have now under Consideration leads me naturally to that kind of Distraction the Nation has labour'd under for some time, the Enthusiastick Passion for Charity-Schools.

The generality are so bewitched with the Usefulness and Excellency of them, that whoever dares openly oppose them is in danger of being Stoned by the Rabble. Children that are taught the Principles of Religion and can read the Word of God, have a greater Opportunity to improve in Virtue and good Morality, and must certainly be more civiliz'd than others, that are suffer'd to run at random and have no body to look after them. How peverse must be the Judgment of those, who would not rather see Children decently dress'd, with clean Linen at least once a Week, that in an orderly manner follow their Master to Church, than in every open place meet with a Company of Black-guards without Shirts or any thing whole about them, that insensible of their Misery are continually increasing it with Oaths and Imprecations! Can any one doubt but these are the great Nursery of Thieves and Pick-pockets? What Numbers of Felons and other Criminals have we Tried and Convicted every Sessions! This will be prevented by Charity-Schools, and when the Children of the Poor receive a better Education, the Society will in a few Years reap the Benefit of it, and the Nation be clear'd of so many Miscreants as now this great City and all the Country about it are fill'd with.

This is the general Cry, and he that speaks the least Word against it, an Uncharitable, Hard-hearted and Inhuman, if not a Wicked, Profane, and Atheistical Wretch. As to the Comeliness of the Sight, no body disputes it, but I would not have a Nation pay too dear for so transient a Pleasure, and if we might set aside the finery of the Shew, every thing that is material in this popular Oration might soon be answer'd.

As to Religion, the most knowing and polite Part of a Nation have every where the least of it; Craft has a greater Hand in making Rogues than Stupidity, and Vice in general is no where more predominant than where Arts and Sciences flourish. Ignorance is, to a Proverb, counted to be the Mother of Devotion, and it is certain that we shall find Innocence and Honesty no where more general than among the most illiterate, the poor silly Country People. The next to be consider'd, are the Manners and Civility that by Charity-Schools are to be grafted into the Poor of the Nation. I confess that in my Opinion to be in any degree possess'd of what I named is a frivolous if not a hurtful Quality, at least nothing is less requisite in the Laborious Poor. It is not Compliments we want of them, but their Work and Assiduity. But I give up this Article with all my Heart, good Manners we'll say are necessary to all People, but which way will they be furnished with them in a Charity School? Boys there may be taught to pull off their Caps promiscuously to all they meet, unless it be a Beggar: But that they should acquire in it any Civility beyond that I can't conceive.

The Master is not greatly qualify'd, as may be guessed by his Salary, and if he could teach them Manners he has not time for it: While they are at School they are either learning or saying their Lesson to him, or employed in Writing or Arithmetick, and as soon as School is done, they are as much at Liberty as other Poor Peoples Children. It is Precept and the Example of Parents, and those they Eat, Drink and Converse with, that have an Influence upon the Minds of Children: Reprobate Parents that take ill Courses and are regardless of their Children, won't have a mannerly civiliz'd Offspring tho' they went to a Charity-School till they were Married. The honest pains-taking People, be they never so poor, if they have any Notion of Goodness and Decency themselves, will keep their Children in awe, and never suffer them to rake about the Streets, and lie out a-nights. Those who will work themselves, and have any command over their Children, will make them do something or other that turns to Profit as soon as they are able, be it never so little; and such as are so Ungovernable, that neither Words nor Blows can work upon them, no Charity School will mend; Nay, Experience teaches us, that among the Charity-Boys there are abundance of bad ones that Swear and Curse about, and, bar the Clothes, are as much Black-guard as ever *Tower-hill* or St *James's* produc'd.

Passage 4.3b
(*from* Mandeville, *Bees*, 1714-25)

The whole Earth being Curs'd, and no Bread to be had but what we eat in the sweat of our Brows, vast Toil must be undergone before Man can provide himself with Necessaries for his Sustenance and the bare Support of his corrupt and defective Nature as he is a single Creature; but infinitely more to make Life comfortable in a Civil Society, where Men are become taught Animals, and great Numbers of them have by mutual compact framed themselves into a Body Politick; and the more Man's Knowledge increases in this State, the greater will be the variety of Labour required to make him easy. It is impossible that a Society can long subsist, and suffer many of its Members to live in Idleness, and enjoy all the Ease and Pleasure they can invent, without having at the same time great Multitudes of People that to make good this Defect will condescend to be quite the reverse, and by use and patience inure their Bodies to work for others and themselves besides.

The Plenty and Cheapness of Provisions depends in a great measure on the Price and Value that is set upon this Labour, and consequently the Welfare of all Societies, even before they are tainted with Foreign Luxury, requires that it should be perform'd by such of their Members as in the first Place are sturdy and robust and never used to Ease or Idleness, and in the second, soon contented as to the necessaries of Life; such as are glad to take up with the coursest Manufacture in every thing they wear, and in their Diet have no other aim than to feed their Bodies when their Stomachs prompt them to eat, and with little regard to Taste or Relish, refuse no wholesome Nourishment that can be swallow'd when Men are Hungry, or ask any thing for their Thirst but to quench it.

As the greatest part of the Drudgery is to be done by Day-light, so it is by this only that they actually measure the time of their Labour without any thought of the Hours they are employ'd, or the weariness they feel; and the Hireling in the Country must get up in the Morning, not because he has rested enough, but because the Sun is going to rise. This last Article alone would be an intolerable Hardship to Grown People under Thirty, who during Nonage had been used to lie a-bed as long as they could sleep: but all three together make up such a Condition of Life as a Man more mildly Educated would hardly choose; tho' it should deliver him from a Goal or a Shrew.

If such People there must be, as no great Nation can be happy without vast Numbers of them, would not a Wise Legislature cultivate the Breed of them with all imaginable Care, and provide against their Scarcity as he would prevent the Scarcity of Provision itself? No Man would be poor and fatigue himself for a Livelihood if he could help it: The absolute necessity all stand in for Victuals and Drink, and in cold Climates for Clothes and Lodging, makes them submit to any thing that can be bore with. If no body did Want no body would work; but the greatest Hardships are look'd upon as solid Pleasures, when they keep a Man from Starving.

From what has been said it is manifest, that in a free Nation where Slaves are not allow'd of, the surest Wealth consists in a Multitude of laborious Poor; for besides that they are the never-failing Nursery of Fleets and Armies, without them there could be no Enjoyment, and no Product of any Country could be valuable. To make the Society happy and People easy under the meanest Circumstances, it is requisite that great Numbers of them should be Ignorant as well as Poor. Knowledge both enlarges and multiplies our Desires, and the fewer things a Man wishes for, the more easily his Necessities may be supply'd.

The Welfare and Felicity therefore of every State and Kingdom, require that the Knowledge of the Working Poor should be confin'd within the Verge of their Occupations, and never extended (as to things visible) beyond what relates to their Calling. The more a Shepherd, a Plowman or any other Peasant knows of the World, and the things that are Foreign to his Labour or Employment, the less fit he'll be to go through the Fatigues and Hardships of it with Chearfulness and Content.

Reading, Writing and Arithmetick, are very necessary to those, whose Business require such Qualifications, but where People's livelihood has no dependence on these Arts, they are very pernicious to the Poor, who are forc'd to get their Daily Bread by their Daily Labour. Few Children make any Progress at School, but at the same time they are capable of being employ'd in some Business or other, so that every Hour those of poor People spend at their Book is so much time lost to the Society. Going to School in comparison to Working is Idleness, and the longer Boys continue in this easy sort of Life, the more unfit they'll be when grown up for downright Labour, both as to Strength and Inclination. Men who are to remain and end their Days in a Laborious, Tiresome and Painful Station of Life, the sooner they are put upon it at first, the more patiently they'll submit to it for ever after. Hard Labour and the coarsest Diet are a proper Punishment to several kinds of Malefactors, but to impose either on those that have not been used and brought up to both is the greatest Cruelty, when there is no Crime you can charge them with.

Reading and Writing are not attain'd to without some Labour of the Brain and Assiduity, and before People are tolerably vers'd in either, they esteem themselves infinitely above those who are wholly Ignorant of them, often with so little Justice and Moderation as if they were of another Species. As all Mortals have naturally an Aversion to Trouble and Painstaking, so we are all fond of, and apt to over-value those Qualifications we have purchased at the Expence of our Ease and Quiet for Years together. Those who spent a great part of their Youth in learning to Read, Write and Cypher, expect and not unjustly to be employ'd where those Qualifications may be of use to them; the Generality of them will look down upon downright Labour with the utmost Contempt, I mean Labour perform'd in the Service of others in the lowest Station of Life, and for the meanest Consideration. A Man who has had some Education, may follow Husbandry by Choice, and be diligent at the dirtiest and most laborious Work; but then the Concern must be his own, and Avarice, the Care of a Family, or some other pressing Motive must put him upon it; but he won't make a good Hireling and serve a Farmer for a pitiful Reward; at least he is not so fit for it as a Day-Labourer that has always been employ'd about the Plough and Dung Cart, and remembers not that ever he has lived otherwise.

When Obsequiousness and mean Services are required, we shall always observe that they are never so chearfully nor so heartily perform'd as from Inferiors to Superiors; I mean Inferiors not only in Riches and Quality, but likewise in Knowledge and Understanding. A Servant can have no unfeign'd Respect for his Master, as soon as he has Sense enough to find out that he serves a Fool. When we are to learn or to obey, we shall experience in our selves, that the greater Opinion we have of the Wisdom and Capacity of those that are either to Teach or Command us, the greater Deference we pay to their Laws and Instructions. No Creatures submit contentedly to their Equals, and should a Horse know as much as a Man, I should not desire to be his Rider.

Passage 4.4
(*from* Daniel Defoe, 'Letter IV', *The Great Law of Subordination Consider'd*, 1724)

Dear Sir,
I am now to lay down some things for your farther *Admiration* in the particular Behaviour of the *English* Poor, and give me leave, previous to what I have farther to say upon this Head, to add that, 1. This is all, *in spight of double Pay*, at the same Time that their Services are *least*, and their Behaviour *worst*, their Wages are *best*, their pay *largest*, and they have the greatest Obligation laid upon them to be diligent.

This, one would think, should either prevent their Ill-Behaviour, or be a means to reclaim them, when they had broken in upon their Manners; but on the contrary, it is a general Observation at least in the Compass of my particular Knowledge, and I scarce ever knew it fail, *namely*, that I never knew a Servant, or a Workman in *England*, one farthing the better for the Encrease of his Wages; on the contrary, if you advance a Servant's Wages, it is so natural for him to think he deserves it, or that else you would not do it; that instead of mending him, it always makes him worse.

It is a kind of a Proverbial Speech among our People, when they see a dull, heavy Fellow go slowly on in his Business, to say to him, come *mend your Pace*, and I'll *mend your Pay*; but really the Man's return ought to be, do you but mend my Pay first, *and you shall hang me, if I mend my Pace*.

2. Servants and Workmen in *England*, seem to act in the Case of their Master's Bounty, as an old cunning *Cart-Horse* does with the Driver, and his Whip; when the Driver smacks his Whip, the Cart-Horse shakes his Bells; the Driver makes the Horse believe he will strike, and the Cart-Horse makes the Driver believe he'll go; but the Carter does not lash, nor does the Horse mend his Pull; so that the Horse cheats the Driver for his Favour, in which, (by the way), he lets us see that Gratitude is not a natural Principle among Horses.

The Behaviour of the labouring Poor in *England*, is something a-kin to this; and we find that Gratitude is not a natural Principle among the common People; at least, if it is, they are pleas'd to Sin against it in a most unnatural Manner; in a word, their Morals being touch'd as before, that Part of their Virtue, which I call Gratitude, and which is the brightest Part of an honest Man, is in a manner quite sunk among them: But I shall have Occasion to compliment them upon their Gratitude hereafter.

I return now to the most fatal Cause of all this Mischief; I mean the Advance of Wages, for this indeed, is the support of all the Insolence of Servants, as their ruin'd Manners is the Spring of it: Here indeed, they verfie what was by a late Author made part of their Character.

The Lab'ring Poor, in spight of double Pay,
Are saucy, mutinous, and Beggarly.

But to return to the Wages, and here I am to observe, 1. That tho' advancing the Wages of Servants has not been a publick thing done by the Government or Legislature, in the, Nature of a Law.

2. Nor has it been done by a common consent, as some publick things have been done; obtaining thereby the ordinary Sanction of a Law.
3. Nor has it after such a kind of Common Consent been approv'd or confirm'd by any Authority, as a thing which ought to be; no nor lastly,
4. Has it been so much as encourag'd by the Magistrates or Government; on the contrary, it is the common receiv'd Opinion, that it ought not to be so; and that it spoils Servants in the main, and yet guided by we know not what Fate, every-body comes into it; the Servants encroach, and demand high Wages, and the People generally comply with it, and so the Evil is grown insensibly upon us, till it is become a receiv'd Custom, and is what it may be said, every-body does, and therefore every Servant looks for; and whereas in common Charity one would expect that this should influence the generality of Servants for the better, and help to reclaim them, on the contrary, it is indeed, *the Ruin of them all.*

Nor is this Advance of Servants Wages any Wealth to them, but as above, their Morals being destroy'd, this overplus is generally laid out, either in Luxury or Vanity, that is to say, in *Strong-Drink* by the Men-Servants, and in *gay things* by the Women-Servants; and take all that little Frugality which is to be found among them, and set it against the horrible encrease of Pride and Debauchery, that is, *Drink*, (for I must be allow'd to call Drunkenness Debauchery) I say take all that little Frugality that is left, I believe it will be granted,

1. That the Poor are poorer than when Labour was cheaper.
2. Servants lay up less, *take them one with another*, than they did when they were hir'd at half the Wages.

So that upon the whole, neither the Labourer without-Doors, or the menial Labourer within-Doors, are one jott the better in their Behaviour, or the richer in their Pockets for all the advance of Pay which they receive, which yet in the whole Kingdom, amounts to an immense Sum by the Year.

To begin with the labouring Poor, they are indeed the Grievance of the Nation, and there seems an absolute necessity to bring them, by severe regulations, to some State of immediate Subordination; their Case is briefly summ'd up in two Heads.

1. Under *a stop of Trade*, and a general want of Work, then they are clamorous and mutinous, run from their Families, load the Parishes with their Wives and Children, who they leave perishing and starving, and themselves grow ripe for all manner of Mischief, whether publick Insurrection, or private plunder and robbery, and seeing they have not Work enough, they will not work at all, and that brings them to wander, starve, beg, steal, and be Hang'd.

2. *In a Glut of Trade* they grow saucy, lazy idle, and debauch'd; when they may have Work, and may get Money enough to live well, and lay up for a Time of less Business; then instead of Diligence and Good-Husbandry which might be expected from honest Men, on the contrary they will Work but two or three Days in the Week, or till they get Money enough to keep them the rest of the Week, and all the other part of their Time they lie in the Alehouse to spend it.

The present Juncture of Time, while I am writing this Letter, furnishes me with flagrant Examples of this kind; there is now, and has been, for near two Year past, a prodigious Run of Trade for all sorts of the Woollen-Manufactures, of which *England* makes so much.

This Demand for Goods makes a propotion'd Encrease of Work, and an Encrease of Work, of course produces an Encrease of Wages: This the Poor in *France* wou'd rejoice at, and any People indeed, that were in their Sences would take it for a Blessing from Heaven, and it would prompt their Diligence, and make them work the harder, that they might take the honest Advantage of it, and as we say, *make Hay while the Sun shines*.

That the Encrease of Trade and Wages is real, and the Fact true, you may take it thus in a few Words, *viz.* The rate for spinning, weaving, and all other Manufacturing-Work, I mean in *WOOL*, is so risen, that the Poor all over *England*, can now earn or gain near twice as much in a Day, and in some Places, more than twice as much as they could get for the same Work two or three Years ago: Particularly in *Essex*, *Suffolk*, and *Norfolk*, *Eastward*; and in *Wiltshire*, *Somerset*, and *Devon*, *West*; the Poor Women now get 12d to 15d a Day for spinning, the Men more in proportion, and are full of Work; whereas before, they cou'd not get half so much, and very often not find Employment neither.

And what now is the Consequence of this? not Diligence, not Thankfulness, *I assure you*; less is it enriching the Poor, or furnishing themselves with Conveniences, Cloaths, and Necessaries; *least of all* is it attended with a provident laying-up for a time of Scarcity; when Work may be wanting and Wages abate again; as 'tis very likely may be the Case hereafter: *No*, *No*, just the contrary; This Prosperity introduces Sloth, Idleness, Drunkenness, and all manner of Wickedness; instead of making *Hay while the Sun shines*, they slight their Work, and bully their Employers; perhaps they will work two or three Days, or it may be a Week, till they find a few Shillings gingle and chink in their Pockets; but then, as if they cou'd not bear that kind of Musick, away they go to the Alehouse, and 'tis impossible to bring them to work again, while they have a Farthing of it left.

The Manufacturers are distress'd for Hands; they have Workmen, but they had as good have none, for they will not Work; the Masters beg and intreat, and with Money in Hand, as we say, they Pray and Pay too, but 'tis all one, no Work can be done as long as there's a Farthing of Money in their Pockets.

If we go out of the Manufacturing Towns into the County-Villages, there they feel the same thing another way; the Farmers Wives can get no Dairy-Maids, their Husbands no Plowmen, and what's the matter? truly the Wenches answer, they won't go to Service at 12d or 18d a Week, while they can get 7s to 8s a Week at spinning; the Men answer they won't drudge at the Plow and Cart, hedging and ditching, threshing and stubbing, and perhaps get 6l. a Year, and course Diet, when they can sit still and dry within Doors, and get 9 or 10s a Week at Woolcombing, or at carding, and such Work about the Woollen Manufacture.

Now it is true, the Argument on their side would be very just, and some way unanswerable, were the end really to work, and so to get as much as they could by a Diligent Application to the Business, and then by a frugal, honest virtuous Life, laying up what they got, for their Use in harder times.

But instead of this, we find these Wenches and Fellows run to the Manufacturing-Towns; there perhaps, they Spin and Work, and when they have got a little Money in their Pockets before-hand, then they turn Vagrant and Idle, spend the little they have got in revelling, drinking, and by consequence something worse, till the Magistrates have been call'd upon to rout them out, to secure the Parishes from the charge of their Debaucheries.

From these wicked Haunts, they spread themselves about the Villages, where they draw in other young People, (till then sober and diligent), into the like Wickedness; till we have seen six or seven of them in a House with big-Bellies, to the Shame and Affliction of their poor Parents, and the Scandal of the whole Country.

As soon as they can drop their Burden, they fly, for fear of the House of Correction, and away they go to *London* to get Services.

London, like the Ocean, that receives the muddy and dirty Brooks, as well as the clear and rapid Rivers, swallows up all the scum and filth of the Country, and here they need not fear of getting Places; what Servants are likely to come out of such Nurseries is not hard to suggest, nor is it any breach of Charity, to suppose that this helps to fill the Town with a generation of Whores and Thieves, and makes our Maid-Servants recommend themselves as they do: Hence nothing is more Natural than the common Jest we put upon the Country-Girls, when we see them come up to *London* in the Carriers Waggons, and on the Pack-Horses, *viz.* to ask them *if they have been Church'd before they came from home*; nor is there any thing unreasonable in the Question, as things go now in the Country, when Work is so plenty and Wages so high; for who wou'd come away to *London* to go to Service, if things were all well at home?

This is one of the Grievances which we want a Law to restrain, and which if not taken in Time, and restrain'd, will quickly make Servants Wages as dear in the Country as they are now in the City; and the poor Farmers must give 6l. and 8l. a Year Wages for Dairy-Maid as the Ladies here do for their Chamber-Maids, and a proportion for Plowmen, and Carters; of which I shall say more hereafter.

It is true we have Laws here for regulating of Servants, and among the rest, a Justice of Peace may oblige young People who are idle, and live, as 'tis call'd, at their own Hands, to go to Service, and may, if they refuse it, send them to the House of Correction; but this is a Concern which the Law takes for Parents, whose Circumstances being but mean, and their Children lying heavy upon them, are willing to be maintain'd in Idleness and Sloth, and refuse either to Work for themselves, or go out to Service; in such a Case, the Magistrate may oblige them to go out, as above.

But if the single Person so challeng'd by the Justice, answers that she work'd and maintains herself, and is able to maintain herself without being a Charge to her Parents, or the Parish, I do not find the Magistrate can compel such a one to go to Service.

In the next Place, as this Insolence of *the labouring Poor* is, in spight of *double Pay*, so it is with this particular Aggravation, that at the same Time that their Wages has been rais'd, the Price of Provisions has been cheaper than it has been for many Years before; particularly Bread-Corn has been so low that none can complain, except the poor Farmers, who cannot pay their Rents, by reason of the Cheapness of Corn; and I am Witness to this, that when Bread, about 16 or 17 Years ago, was sold for double the Price that it is now, the Wages for spinning and Manufacturing, was not much above half the Price that it is now, so that they gain'd less, and spent more, and yet were able to subsist, even then.

This makes good the ordinary Remark here, *viz.* that the poor are always poor; it is very plain, when Wages were cheap, or low, and Provisions high and dear, the Poor were not poorer then they are now; *and now* Wages are higher, and Provisions so much lower than it was then, yet the Poor are not richer now than they were then; but this Riddle is easily expounded, by saying, 1. The Poor are, (as above) idle, proud, and saucy, and when Wages are good, they won't work, *any more than from Hand to Mouth*; or if they do work, they spend it in Riot and Luxury; so that it Turns to no Account to them.

While this, then, is the Temper of the *labouring Poor*, what are we to expect from them, but that, as above, they will be mutinous when they want Employment, and idle and saucy when they have it? Would the poor Maid-Servants who choose rather to spin, while they can gain 9s per Week by their Labour, than go to service at 12d a Week to the Farmers Houses, as before; I say, would they sit close to their work, live near and close, as labouring and poor People ought to do, and by their Frugality, lay up six or seven Shillings *per* Week, none could object or blame them for their Choice; but while, on the contrary, they either play half their Time, and neglect the Work they have; or if they do work, spend it all in Drink and Debauchery, as is too much the Case, this height of Wages is by it made a publick grievance; the Poor are ruin'd, even by that which is their Blessing, or would be so, were it rightly made use of; I mean plenty of Work, and good Pay; nay the very plenty of Provisions which was always receiv'd by reasonable People, and especially by Christians, as the Gift and Mercy of Heaven, is curs'd to them, and becomes their Ruin; for while they have Bread, they won't work, and when they do not work, 'tis easie to judge what else they do, and how they employ their Time.

Again, as soon as Trade receives a check, and there is a little discouragement upon the Clothiers and Manufacturers, so that Work is a little stop'd, and the Masters and Employers can give no more Wool out to spin, or perhaps but a little, and that in consequence of this, the Price abates too; what follows? why, then they grow clamorous, noisy, and, as I said before, mutinous and saucy another way, and in the mean time they disperse, run away, leave their Families, and especially the numerous throng of Bastards, which, (as I hinted,) the Wickedness of their Working-Life had produc'd upon the Parishes, and wander about in Beggary and Distress.

In consequence of this, it has been observ'd, that in our great populous Manufacturing Towns, whenever a run of Trade has happen'd, and after it the Poor disperse again, there is generally an Encrease of Bastards, greater than in any of the precedent Years, and I could give such particular Examples of this in the *Western* and *Northern* Counties, as would be surprising.

Thus Gods Blessing, and the Bounty of Providence, is abused by these sorts of People not to encrease and encourage their Diligence, their frugality, and thriftiness, to lay up in a time of plenty of Work, for a time of scarcity and deadness of Trade; but on the contrary, to support them in their extravagant Follies and Wickedness, prompt their Vices, and fill them with Pride and Insolence, both against God and Man.

And so far are they from improving the Advantages of a Glut of Business, that as soon as it stops, even the very first Week, perhaps the first Day, they are reduced to their Original Poverty and Distress; for having not laid up a Shilling, but just working from Hand to Mouth; as soon as the Workmaster stops, the Workman or Workwoman starves, and it must be confess'd such as these deserve no Pity, seeing their wastefulness, and the Expence both of their Money and their Time, was in the very Teeth of that merciful Providence, and double Pay, and that they had reduc'd themselves by their Sloth to want when they might have been, *as we call it*, before-hand in the World.

Passage 4.5
(*from* Jonathan Swift, *A Proposal for Giving Badges to Beggars*, 1737)

IT hath been a general Complaint, that the Poor-House, especially since the new Constitution by Act of Parliament, hath been of no Benefit to this City, for Ease of which it was wholly intended. I had the Honour to be a Member of it many Years before it was new modelled by the Legislature; not from any personal Regard, but meerly as one of the two Deans, who are of Course put into most Commissions that relate to the City; and I have likewise the Honour to have been left out of several Commissions upon the Score of Party, in which my Predecessors, Time out of Mind, have always been Members.

THE first Commission was made up of about fifty Persons, which were the Lord Mayor, Aldermen, and Sheriffs, and some few other Citizens: The Judges, and two Arch-Bishops, the two Deans of the City, and one or two more Gentlemen. And I must confess my Opinion, that the dissolving the old Commission, and establishing a new one of near three Times the Number, have been the great Cause of rendering so good a Design not only useless, but a Grievance instead of a Benefit to the City. In the present Commission all the City-Clergy are included, besides a great Number of 'Squires, not only those who reside in *Dublin*, and the Neighbourhood, but several who live at a great Distance, and cannot possibly have the least Concern for the Advantage of the City.

At the few General Meetings that I have attended since the new Establishment, I observed very little was done except one or two Acts of extream Justice, which I then thought might as well have been spared: And I have found the Court of Assistants usually taken up in little Brangles about Coachmen, or adjusting Accounts of Meal and Small-Beer; which, however necessary, might sometimes have given Place to Matters of much greater Moment, I mean some Schemes recommended to the General Board, for answering the chief Ends in erecting and establishing such a Poor-House, and endowing it with so considerable a Revenue: And the principal End I take to have been that of maintaining the Poor and Orphans of the City, where the Parishes are not able to do it; and clearing the Streets from all Strollers, Foreigners, and sturdy Beggars, with which, to the universal Complaint and Admiration, *Dublin* is more infested since the Establishment of the Poor-House, than it was ever known to be since its first Erection.

As the whole Fund for supporting this Hospital is raised only from the Inhabitants of the City; so there can be hardly any Thing more absurd than to see it misemployed in maintaining Foreign Beggars and Bastards, or Orphans, whose Country Landlords never contributed one Shilling towards their Support. I would engage, that half this Revenue, if employed with common Care, and no very great Degree of common Honesty, would maintain all the real Objects of Charity in this City, except a small Number of Original Poor in every Parish, who might without being burthensome to the Parishioners find a tolerable Support.

I HAVE for some Years past applied my self to several Lord Mayors, and to the late Arch-Bishop of *Dublin*, for a Remedy to this Evil of Foreign Beggars; and they all appeared ready to receive a very plain Proposal, I mean, that of badging the Original Poor of every Parish, who begged in the Streets; that, the said Beggars should be confined to their own Parishes; that, they should wear their Badges well sown upon one of their Shoulders, always visible, on Pain of being whipt and turned out of Town; or whatever legal Punishment may be thought proper and effectual. But, by the wrong Way of thinking in some Clergymen, and the Indifference of others, this Method was perpetually defeated to their own continual disquiet, which they do not ill deserve; and if the Grievance affected only them, it would be of less Consequence; because the Remedy is in their own Power. But, all Street-walkers, and Shop-keepers, bear an equal Share in this hourly Vexation.

I NEVER heard more than one Objection against this Expedient of badging the Poor, and confining their Walks to their several Parishes. The Object was this: What shall we do with the Foreign Beggars? Must they be left to starve? I answered, No; but they must be driven or whipt out of Town; and let the next Country Parish do as they please, or rather after the Practice of *England*, send them from one Parish to another, until they reach their own Homes. By the old Laws of *England* still in Force, and I presume by those of *Ireland*, every Parish is bound to maintain its own Poor; and the Matter is of no such Consequence in this Point as some would make it, whether a Country Parish be rich or poor. In the remoter and poorer Parishes of Kingdom, all Necessaries for Life proper for poor People are comparatively cheaper; I mean Butter-milk, Oatmeal, Potatoes, and other Vegetables; and every Farmer or Cottager, who is not himself a Beggar, can sometimes spare a Sup or a Morsel, not worth the fourth Part of a Farthing, to an indigent Neighbour of his own Parish, who is disabled from Work. A Beggar Native of the Parish is known to the 'Squire, to the Church Minister, to the Popish Priest, or the Conventicle Teachers, as well as to every Farmer: He hath generally some Relations able to live, and contribute something to his Maintenance. None of which Advantages can be reasonably expected on a Removal to Places where he is altogether unknown. If he be not quite maimed, he and his Trull, and Litter of Brats (if he hath any) may get half their Support by doing some Kind of Work in their Power, and thereby be less burthensome to the People. In short, all Necessaries of Life grow in the Country, and not in Cities, and are cheaper where they grow; nor is it equal that Beggars should put us to the Charge of giving them Victuals, and the Carriage too.

BUT, when the Spirit of wandring takes him, attended by his Female, and their Equipage of Children, he becomes a Nuisance to the whole Country: He and his Female are Thieves, and teach the Trade of Stealing to their Brood at four Years old; and if his infirmities be counterfeit, it is dangerous for a single Person unarmed to meet him on the Road. He wanders from one County to another, but still with a View to this Town, whither he arrives at last, and enjoys all the

Priviledges of a *Dublin* Beggar.

I DO not wonder that the Country 'Squires should be very willing to send up their Colonies; but why the City should be content to receive them, is beyond my Imagination.

If the City were obliged by their Charter to maintain a thousand Beggars, they could do it cheaper by eighty per Cent a hundred Miles off, than in this Town, or any of its Suburbs.

THERE is no Village in *Connaught*, that in Proportion shares so deeply in the Daily encreasing Miseries of *Ireland*, as its Capital City; to which Miseries there hardly remained any Addition, except the perpetual Swarms of Foreign Beggars, who might be banished in a Month without Expence, and with very little Trouble.

As I am personally acquainted with a great Number of Street Beggars, I find some weak Attempts have been made in one or two Parishes to promote the wearing of Badges; and my first Question to those who ask an Alms is, *Where is your Badge?* I have in several Years met with about a Dozen who were ready to produce them, some out of their Pockets, others from under their Coat, and two or three on their Shoulders, only covered with a Sort of Capes which they could lift up or let down upon Occasion. They are too lazy to work; they are not afraid to steal, nor ashamed to beg, and yet are too proud to be seen with a Badge, as many of them have confessed to me, and not a few in very injurious Terms, particularly the Females. They all look upon such an Obligation as a high Indignity done to their Office. I appeal to all indifferent People whether such Wretches deserve to be relieved. As to my self, I must confess, this absurd Insolence hath so affected me, that for several Years past, I have not disposed of one single Farthing to a Street Beggar, nor intend to do so until I see a better Regulation; and I have endeavoured to persuade all my Brother-walkers to follow my Example, which most of them assure me they do. For, if Beggary be not able to beat out Pride, it cannot deserve Charity. However, as to Persons in Coaches and Chairs, they bear but little of the Persecution we suffer, and are willing to leave it intirely upon us.

To say the Truth, there is not a more undeserving vicious Race of human Kind than the Bulk of those who are reduced to Beggary, even in this beggarly Country. For, as a great Part of our publick Miseries is originally owing to our own Faults (but, what those Faults are I am grown by Experience too wary to mention) so I am confident, that among the meaner People, nineteen in twenty of those who are reduced to a starving Condition, did not become so by what Lawyers call the Work of GOD, either upon their Bodies or Goods; but meerly from their own Idleness, attended with all Manner of Vices, particularly Drunkenness, Thievery, and Cheating.

WHOEVER inquires, as I have frequently done, from those who have asked me an Alms, what was their former Course of Life, will find them to have been Servants in good Families, broken Tradesmen, Labourers, Cottagers, and what they call decayed Housekeepers; but (to use their own Cant) reduced by Losses and Crosses, by which nothing can be understood but Idleness and Vice.

Passage 4.6

(*from* William Temple, *A Vindication of Commerce and the Arts*, 1758)
(A reply to Mr Bell's *Dissertation* (1756) on the question 'what causes contribute to render a nation populous?')

Our learned author remarks, *that a general application to agriculture, &c. that is a general industry, must evidently produce a vast plenty of all the necessaries of life, so that every single person will* be able fully to supply his wants *with the utmost ease.*

1. The author of these remarks apprehends that the learned writer of the Dissertation had no clear, determinate, precise, and distinct ideas of a general application, or industry. If he had, we must confess ourselves so dull as not to be able to perceive it; and so ignorant and stupid as not to be able to understand or comprehend his meaning. If he mean by a general industry, that all in a society shall work, it will be necessary immediately, that all the lands and property of the kingdom should be equally divided. This would be a pretty scheme truly, but is as impracticable as *Plato*'s republick.

2. Besides there is a manifest repugnancy and contradiction in what our author proposes. By a general industry, is commonly understood, every man's labouring in his particular craft as much time as his health, spirits and strength will permit. And yet he proposes and declares, that by this industry every man shall be able fully to supply his wants *with the utmost ease*. This is a palpable contradiction in terms.

3. If he had said, 'in case every one in the community laboured equally, and all imaginary wants were abolished, then each individual might procure all the simple and coarse necessaries of life in plenty, by labouring a small part of his time', there would have been some sense in it; but to talk of the practice of general industry in a country, and yet at the same time propose *the acquisition* of *all the necessaries of life with the utmost ease*, is rank nonsense. It is likewise absurd and nonsense, to

talk of banishing all imaginary wants out of a community, and yet at the same time propose the universal practice of industry. When all these wants are expelled from society, what are the people to be employed about? It is proposed to prohibit the practice of commerce, so no foreign consumption could engage and employ their industry. Truly when this fine scheme and these political *Lycurgic* institutions are reduced to practice, you will have little or nothing to do, but to follow the example of the disciples of the *Spartan* legislator, that is, to sing, dance, fiddle, wrestle, run, eat black broth, live in huts, and wear sheep-skins, and in the issue, be extinguished or made slaves of by your invading neighbours. But there can be no place for the practice of general industry.

4. The institutions of *Lycurgus* were far from being favourable to populosity, though he enjoined an equal division of the lands. In the time of *Agis* king of *Sparta*, we find there were but seven hundred *Spartan* families left out of thirty-nine thousand, among whom their great founder or legislator had divided the lands, and not above a hundred of these possessed estates. So little favourable was his system to populosity. War destroyed the original *Spartans*, they were too proud and vain to admit of naturalizations, disdained strangers, puffed up with a conceit of themselves; and thus in the issue, spilled their blood to defend a state for the posterity of their slaves to inherit.

5. But if property be equally divided, how is each individual to be made perform his share of the general fund of labour necessary to support the community in the simple way proposed? Where one man is idle or impotent, and another is industrious and vigorous, and the first has an inclination to alienate his property, and the other to purchase it; what is to be done in this case? How is this to be prevented? Here is an end of your political institutions at once.

6. If general industry and oeconomy, if prudence and frugality, could be enforced among our labourers, they might all, as things stand at present, be furnished not only with all manner of necessaries, but also with superfluities, and the means of gratifying their fantastical and imaginary wants. But if this conduct cannot be enforced as things stand at present; what reason have we to expect it when property has been put on a level? In short, our author's scheme tends to destroy all industry and to lessen labour instead of increasing it.

7. The best spur to industry is necessity. The mass of labourers work only to relieve the present want, and are such votaries to indolence, ease and voluptuousness, that they sacrifice all considerations to the pleasures of the present moment, regardless of sickness and old age. Nay some declare it a crime to provide for either and rely on the parish.

Mr *Locke* observes, that they live only from hand to mouth. To this purpose Sir *William Temple* remarks, *All men prefer ease to labour, and will not take pains if they can be idle*: That is, unless by practice and habit their disposition be altered. The author of *the causes of the decline of our foreign trade*, Sir *Josiah Child* and others observe, 'that in cheap times of provision our poor do not work half their time; that they are paid extravagant wages at all times,' &c. If this be the case, as most certainly it is, what other reason but the want of industry and oeconomy can be assigned, why all the labourers in the kingdom have not a full supply of all their wants? And that too at all times; in both good and bad seasons? But our author's scheme is impracticable, as well as absurd and contradictory.

8. Nothing but necessity can enforce industry. We must take human nature as it is: But what is necessary to make one family industrious would starve another. And what wages would be sufficient to supply a family with all the necessaries of life after a common harvest, and with many of the luxuries after a plentiful, would not afford him a living support after a bad one. There is no making provision for numerous families, sickness, old age, frosts, floods, rains, wars, want of employment, fires, deaths and other distressing accidents, but by oeconomy. But not one in a thousand is possessed of this oeconomy, but live as Mr *Locke* observes *in diem*, from hand to mouth.

9. It has been observed that those nations have excelled most in industry and commerce, which have laboured under the greatest disadvantages from soil and scantiness of territory; and that their necessities from those inconveniences have whetted their invention and spurred their industry. As for example, *Phoenicia*, *Athens*, *Tyre*, *Carthage*, *Venice*, *Marseilles*, and *Holland*. Why may not then wants created by the arts of the politician, if judiciously introduced, produce the same effects as those arising from nature? But it requires great dexterity and finesse in governors to conduct such matters so as to attain the end desired; and whenever it is carried into execution, its progress must be gentle, and its approaches almost imperceptible, and especially in a popular state. It is as unnatural to expect men should labour, when they have no real nor imaginary wants, as it would be to expect matter to act contrary to the laws of gravitation and attraction. The greater the weight to be moved, the less the velocity in mechanicks, when the moving power is feeble. It is the same in morals and politicks as in physicks.

10. As this is the general disposition of human nature, no wages, not if the present were trebled, would keep the bulk of labourers, or at least a great part of them from want; because they never provide against the

times of calamity specified above, which they might all do, if they were as industrious as our author proposes they should be, and banished the imaginary wants he explodes. For this reason his chimerical scheme would be of no use, if it could be reduced to practice, so far as to level all the property of the kingdom; alienations would soon be made, and the old system of things restored or revived.

Passage 4.7

(*from* Samuel Johnson, *A Review of 'A Free Inquiry into the Nature and Origin of Evil'*, 1757)

(Johnson devotes much of his review of Soame Jenyns's *Free Inquiry* to an attack on the doctrines of philosophical optimism, as they are expounded by Jenyns and by Pope in the *Essay on Man*. In this passage he treats Jenyns's argument as a prose summary of Pope's poem.)

We are next entertained with *Pope*'s alleviations of those evils which we are doomed to suffer.

> Poverty, or the want of riches, is generally compensated by having more hopes and fewer fears, by a greater share of health, and a more exquisite relish of the smallest enjoyments, than those who possess them are usually bless'd with. The want of taste and genius, with all the pleasures that arise from them, are commonly recompensed by a more useful kind of common sense, together with a wonderful delight, as well as success, in the busy pursuits of a scrambling world. The sufferings of the sick are greatly relieved by many trifling gratifications imperceptible to others, and sometimes almost repaid by the inconceivable transports occasioned by the return of health and vigour. Folly cannot be very grievous, because imperceptible; and I doubt not but there is some truth in that rant of a mad poet, that there is a pleasure in being mad, which none but madmen know. Ignorance, or the want of knowledge and literature, the appointed lot of all born to poverty, and the drudgeries of life, is the only opiate capable of infusing that insensibility which can enable them to endure the miseries of the one, and the fatigues of the other. It is a cordial administered by the gracious hand of providence; of which they ought never to be deprived by an ill-judged and improper education. It is the basis of all subordination, the support of society, and the privilege of individuals: and I have ever thought it a most remarkable instance of the divine wisdom, that whereas in all animals, whose

individuals rise little above the rest of their species, knowledge is instinctive; in man, whose individuals are so widely different, it is acquired by education; by which means the prince and the labourer, the philosopher and the peasant, are in some measure fitted for their respective situations.

Much of these positions is perhaps true, and the whole paragraph might well pass without censure, were not objections necessary to the establishment of knowledge. *Poverty* is very gently paraphrased by *want of riches*. In that sense almost every man may in his own opinion be poor. But there is another poverty which is *want of competence*, of all that can soften the miseries of life, of all that can diversify attention, or delight imagination. There is yet another poverty which is want *of necessaries*, a species of poverty which no care of the publick, no charity of particulars, can preserve many from feeling openly, and many secretly.

That hope and fear are inseparably or very frequently connected with poverty, and riches, my surveys of life have not informed me. The milder degrees of poverty are sometimes supported by hope, but the more severe often sink in motionless despondence. Life must be seen before it can be known. This author and *Pope* perhaps never saw the miseries which they imagine thus easy to be born. The poor indeed are insensible of many little vexations which sometimes imbitter the possessions and pollute the enjoyments of the rich. They are not pained by casual incivility, or mortified by the mutilation of a compliment; but this happiness is like that of a malefactor who ceases to feel the cords that bind him when the pincers are tearing his flesh.

That want of taste for one enjoyment is supplied by the pleasures of some other, may be fairly allowed. But the compensations of sickness I have never found near to equivalence, and the transports of recovery only prove the intenseness of the pain.

With folly no man is willing to confess himself very intimately acquainted, and therefore its pains and pleasures are kept secret. But what the author says of its happiness seems applicable only to fatuity, or gross dulness, for that inferiority of understanding which makes one man without any other reason the slave, or tool, or property of another, which makes him sometimes useless, and sometimes ridiculous, is often felt with very quick sensibility. On the happiness of madmen, as the case is not very frequent, it is not necessary to raise a disquisition, but I cannot forbear to observe, that I never yet knew disorders of mind encrease felicity: every madman is either arrogant and irascible, or gloomy and suspicious, or possessed by some passion or notion destructive to his quiet. He has always discontent in his look, and malignity in his bosom. And, if we had the power of choice, he would soon repent who should resign his reason to secure his peace.

Concerning the portion of ignorance necessary to make the condition of the lower classes of mankind safe to the public and tolerable to themselves, both morals and policy exact a nicer enquiry than will be very soon or very easily made. There is undoubtedly a degree of knowledge which will direct a man to refer all to providence, and to acquiesce in the condition which omniscient goodness has determined to allot him; to consider this world as a phantom that must soon glide from before his eyes, and the distresses and vexations that encompass him, as dust scattered in his path, as a blast that chills him for a moment, and passes off for ever.

Such wisdom, arising from the comparison of a part with the whole of our existence, those that want it most cannot possibly obtain from philosophy, nor unless the method of education, and the general tenour of life are changed, will very easily receive it from religion. The bulk of mankind is not likely to be very wise or very good: and I know not whether there are not many states of life, in which all knowledge less than the highest wisdom, will produce discontent and danger. I believe it may be sometimes found, that a *little learning* is to a poor man a *dangerous thing*. But such is the condition of humanity, that we easily see, or quickly feel the wrong, but cannot always distinguish the right. Whatever knowledge is superfluous, in irremediable poverty, is hurtful, but the difficulty is to determine when poverty is irremediable, and at what point superfluity begins. Gross ignorance every man has found equally dangerous with perverted knowledge. Men left wholly to their appetites and their instincts, with little sense of moral or religious obligation, and with very faint distinctions of right and wrong, can never be safely employed, or confidently trusted: they can be honest only by obstinacy, and diligent only by compulsion or caprice. Some instruction, therefore, is necessary, and much perhaps may be dangerous.

Though it should be granted that those who are *born to poverty and drudgery* should not be *deprived* by an *improper education* of the opiate of *ignorance*; even this concession will not be of much use to direct our practice, unless it be determined who are those that are *born to poverty*. To entail irreversible poverty upon generation after generation only because the ancestor happened to be poor, is in itself cruel, if not unjust, and is wholly contrary to the maxims of a commercial nation, which always suppose and promote a rotation of property, and offer every individual a chance of mending his condition by his diligence.

Those who communicate literature to the son of a poor man, consider him as one not born to poverty, but to the necessity of deriving a better fortune from himself. In this attempt, as in others, many fail, and many succeed. Those that fail will feel their misery more acutely; but since poverty is now confessed to be such a calamity as cannot be born without the opiate of insensibility, I hope the happiness of those whom education enables to escape from it, may turn the ballance against that exacerbation which the others suffer.

Passage 4.8
(Samuel Johnson, *The Idler*, No. 4, 6 May 1758)

Πάυτας γὰρ φιλέεσκε.
Homer[2]

Charity, or tenderness for the poor, which is now justly considered, by a great part of mankind, as inseparable from piety, and in which almost all the goodness of the present age consists, is, I think, known only to those who enjoy, either immediately or by transmission, the light of revelation.

Those antient nations who have given us the wisest models of government, and the brightest examples of patriotism, whose institutions have been transcribed by all succeeding legislators, and whose history is studied by every candidate for political or military reputation, have yet left behind them no mention of alms-houses or hospitals, of places where age might repose, or sickness be relieved.

The Roman emperors, indeed, gave large donatives to the citizens and soldiers, but these distributions were always reckoned rather popular than virtuous: nothing more was intended than an ostentation of liberality, nor was any recompence expected, but suffrages and acclamations.

Their beneficence was merely occasional; he that ceased to need the favour of the people, ceased likewise to court it; and therefore, no man thought it either necessary or wise to make any standing provision for the needy, to look forward to the wants of posterity, or to secure successions of charity, for successions of distress.

Compassion is by some reasoners, on whom the name of philosophers has been too easily conferred, resolved into an affection merely selfish, an involuntary perception of pain at the involuntary sight of a being like ourselves languishing in misery. But this sensation, if ever it be felt at all from the brute instinct of uninstructed nature, will only produce effects desultory and transient; it will never settle into a principle of action, or extend relief to calamities unseen, in generations not yet in being.

The devotion of life or fortune to the succour of the poor, is a height of virtue, to which humanity has never risen by its own power. The charity of the Mahometans is a precept which their teacher evidently transplanted from the doctrines of Christianity; and the care with which some of the Oriental sects attend, as is said, to the necessities of the diseased and indigent, may be added to the other arguments, which prove Zoroaster to have borrowed his institutions from the law of Moses.

The present age, though not likely to shine hereafter, among the most splendid periods of history, has yet given examples of charity, which may be very properly recommended to imitation. The equal distribution of wealth, which long commerce has produced, does not enable any single hand to raise edifices of piety like fortified cities, to appropriate manors to religious uses, or deal out such large and lasting beneficence as was scattered over the land in antient times, by those who possessed counties or provinces. But no sooner is a new species of misery brought to view, and a design of relieving it professed, than every hand is open to contribute something, every tongue is busied in sollicitation, and every art of pleasure is employed for a time in the interest of virtue.

The most apparent and pressing miseries incident to man, have now their peculiar houses of reception and relief, and there are few among us raised however little above the danger of poverty, who may not justly claim, what is implored by the Mahometans in their most ardent benedictions, the prayers of the poor.

Among those actions which the mind can most securely review with unabated pleasure, is that of having contributed to an hospital for the sick. Of some kinds of charity the consequences are dubious; some evils which beneficence has been busy to remedy, are not certainly known to be very grievous to the sufferer, or detrimental to the community; but no man can question whether wounds and sickness are not really painful; whether it be not worthy of a good man's care to restore those to ease and usefulness, from whose labour infants and women expect their bread, and who, by a casual hurt, or lingering disease, lye pining in want and anguish, burthensome to others, and weary of themselves.

Yet as the hospitals of the present time subsist only by gifts bestowed at pleasure, without any solid fund of support, there is danger lest the blaze of charity, which now burns with so much heat and splendor, should die away for want of lasting fuel; lest fashion should suddenly withdraw her smile, and inconstancy transfer the publick attention to something which may appear more eligible, because it will be new.

Whatever is left in the hands of chance must be subject to vicissitude; and when any establishment is found to be useful, it ought to be the next care to make it permanent.

But man is a transitory being, and his designs must partake of the imperfections of their author. To confer duration is not always in our power. We must snatch the present moment, and employ it well, without too much sollicitude for the future, and content ourselves with reflecting that our part is performed. He that waits for an opportunity to do much at once, may breathe out his life in idle wishes, and regret, in the last hour, his useless intentions, and barren zeal.

The most active promoters of the present schemes of charity cannot be cleared from some instances of misconduct, which may awaken contempt or censure, and hasten that neglect which is likely to come too soon of itself. The open competitions between different hospitals, and the animosity with which their patrons oppose one another, may prejudice weak minds against them all: for it will not be easily believed, that any man can, for good reasons, wish to exclude another from doing good. The spirit of charity can only be continued by a reconciliation of these ridiculous feuds; and therefore, instead of contentions, who shall be the only benefactors to the needy, let there be no other struggle than who shall be the first.

Passage 4.9

(*from* Samuel Johnson, *The False Alarm*, 1770)

(This pamphlet is a response to agitation for parliamentary reform led by John Wilkes, several times elected and expelled from parliament as member for Middlesex.)

The progress of a petition is well known. An ejected place-man goes down to his county or his borough, tells his friends of his inability to serve them, and his constituents of the corruption of the government. His friends readily understand that he who can get nothing, will have nothing to give. They agree to proclaim a meeting, meat and drink are plentifully provided, a crowd is easily brought together, and those who think that they know the reason of their meeting, undertake to tell those who know it not. Ale and clamour unite their powers, the crowd, condensed and heated, begins to ferment with the leven of sedition. All see a thousand evils, though they cannot show them, and grow impatient for a remedy, though they know not what.

A speech is then made by the Cicero of the day, he says much, and suppresses more, and credit is equally given to what he tells, and what he conceals. The petition is read and universally approved. Those who are sober enough to write add their names, and the rest would sign it if they could.

Every man goes home and tells his neighbour of the glories of the day; how he was consulted and what he advised; how he was invited into the great room, where his lordship called him by his name; how he was caressed by Sir Francis, Sir Joseph, or Sir George; how he eat turtle and venison, and drank unanimity to the three brothers.

The poor loiterer, whose shop had confined him, or whose wife had locked him up, hears the tale of luxury with envy, and at last enquires what was their petition. Of the petition nothing is remembered by the narrator, but that it spoke much of fears and apprehensions, and something very alarming, and that he is sure it is against the government; the other is convinced that it must be right, and wishes he had been there, for he loves wine and venison, and is resolved as long as he lives to be against the government.

The petition is then handed from town to town, and from house to house, and wherever it comes the inhabitants flock together, that they may see that which must be sent to the King. Names are easily collected. One man signs because he hates the papists; another because he has vowed destruction to the turnpikes; one because it will vex the parson; another because he owes his landlord nothing; one because he is rich; another because he is poor; one to shew that he is not afraid, and another to shew that he can write.

The passage, however, is not always smooth. Those who collect contributions to sedition, sometimes apply to a man of higher rank and more enlightened mind, who instead of lending them his name, calmly reproves them for being seducers of the people.

You who are here, says he, complaining of venality, are yourselves the agents of those, who having estimated themselves at too high a price, are only angry that they are not bought. You are appealing from the Parliament to the rabble, and inviting those, who scarcely, in the most common affairs, distinguish right from wrong, to judge of a question complicated with law written and unwritten, with the general principles of government, and the particular customs of the House of Commons; you are shewing them a grievance, so distant that they cannot see it, and so light that they cannot feel it; for how, but by unnecessary intelligence and artificial provocation, should the farmers and shopkeepers of

Yorkshire and Cumberland know or care how Middlesex is represented. Instead of wandering thus round the county to exasperate the rage of party, and darken the suspicions of ignorance, it is the duty of men like you, who have leisure for enquiry, to lead back the people to their honest labour; to tell them, that submission is the duty of the ignorant, and content the virtue of the poor; that they have no skill in the art of government, nor any interest in the dissentions of the great; and when you meet with any, as some there are, whose understandings are capable of conviction, it will become you to allay this foaming ebullition, by shewing them that they have as much happiness as the condition of life will easily receive, and that a government, of which an erroneous or unjust representation of Middlesex is the greatest crime that interest can discover, or malice can upbraid, is a government approaching nearer to perfection, than any that experience has known, or history related.

The drudges of sedition wish to change their ground, they hear him with sullen silence, feel conviction without repentance, and are confounded but not abashed; they go forward to another door, and find a kinder reception from a man enraged against the government, because he has just been paying the tax upon his windows.

That a petition for a dissolution of the Parliament will at all times have its favourers, may be easily imagined. The people indeed do not expect that one House of Commons will be much honester or much wiser than another; they do not suppose that the taxes will be lightened; or though they have been so often taught to hope it, that soap and candles will be cheaper; they expect no redress of grievances, for of no grievances but taxes do they complain; they wish not the extension of liberty, for they do not feel any restraint; about the security of privilege or property they are totally careless, for they see no property invaded, nor know, till they are told, that any privilege has suffered violation.

Least of all do they expect, that any future Parliament will lessen its own powers, or communicate to the people that authority which it has once obtained.

Yet a new Parliament is sufficiently desirable. The year of election is a year of jollity; and what is still more delightful, a year of equality. The glutton now eats the delicacies for which he longed when he could not purchase them, and the drunkard has the pleasure of wine without the cost. The drone lives a while without work, and the shopkeeper, in the flow of money, raises his price. The mechanic that trembled at the presence of Sir Joseph, now bids him come again for an answer; and the poacher, whose gun has been seized, now finds an opportunity to reclaim it. Even the honest man is not displeased to see himself important, and willingly resumes in two years that power which he had resigned for seven. Few love their friends so well as not to desire superiority by unexpensive benefaction.

Passage 4.10
(Oliver Goldsmith, *The Revolution in Low Life*, 1762)

Sir,
I spent part of the last summer in a little village, distant about fifty miles from town, consisting of near an hundred houses. It lay entirely out of the road of commerce, and was inhabited by a race of men who followed the primeval profession of agriculture for several generations. Though strangers to opulence, they were unacquainted with distress; few of them were known either to acquire a fortune or to die in indigence. By a long intercourse and frequent intermarriages they were all become in a manner one family; and, when the work of the day was done, spent the night agreeably in visits at each other's houses. Upon those occasions the poor traveller and stranger were always welcome; and they kept up the stated days of festivity with the strictest observance. They were merry at Christmas and mournful in Lent, got drunk on St George's-day, and religiously cracked nuts on Michaelmas-eve.

Upon my first arrival I felt a secret pleasure in observing this happy community. The chearfulness of the old, and the blooming beauty of the young, was no disagreeable change to one like me, whose whole life had been spent in cities. But my satisfaction was soon repressed, when I understood that they were shortly to leave this abode of felicity, of which they and their ancestors had been in possession time immemorial, and that they had received orders to seek for a new habitation. I was informed that a Merchant of immense fortune in London, who had lately purchased the estate on which they lived, intended to lay the whole out in a seat of pleasure for himself. I staid 'till the day on which they were compelled to remove, and own I never felt so sincere a concern before.

I was grieved to see a generous, virtuous race of men, who should be considered as the strength and the ornament of their country, torn from their little habitations, and driven out to meet poverty and hardship among strangers. No longer to earn and enjoy the fruits of their labour, they were now going to toil as hirelings under some rigid Master, to flatter the opulent for a precarious meal, and to leave their children the inheritance of want and slavery. The modest matron followed her husband in tears, and often looked back at the little mansion where she had passed her life in innocence, and to which she was never more to return; while the beautiful daughter parted for ever from her Lover, who was now become too poor to maintain her as his wife. All the connexions of kindred were now irreparably broken; their neat gardens and well cultivated fields were left to desolation.

Strata jacent passim, hominumque boumque labores.[3]

Such was their misery, and I could wish that this were the only instance of such migrations of late. But I am informed that nothing is at present more common than such revolutions. In almost every part of the kingdom the laborious husbandman has been reduced, and the lands are now either occupied by some general undertaker, or turned into enclosures destined for the purposes of amusement or luxury. Whereever the traveller turns, while he sees one part of the inhabitants of the country becoming immensely rich, he sees the other growing miserably poor, and the happy equality of condition now entirely removed.

Let others felicitate their country upon the encrease of foreign commerce and the extension of our foreign conquests; but for my part, this new introduction of wealth gives me but very little satisfaction. Foreign commerce, as it can be managed only by a few, tends proportionably to enrich only a few; neither moderate fortunes nor moderate abilities can carry it on; thus it tends rather to the accumulation of immense wealth in the hands of some, than to a diffusion of it among all; it is calculated rather to make individuals rich, than to make the aggregate happy.

Wherever we turn we shall find those governments that have pursued foreign commerce with too much assiduity at length becoming Aristocratical; and the immense property, thus necessarily acquired by some, has swallowed up the liberties of all. Venice, Genoa, and Holland, are little better at present than retreats for tyrants and prisons for slaves. The Great, indeed, boast of their liberties there, and they have liberty. The poor boast of liberty too; but, alas, they groan under the most rigorous oppression.

A country, thus parcelled out among the rich alone, is of all others the most miserable. The Great, in themselves, perhaps, are not so bad as they are generally represented; but I have almost ever found the dependents and favourites of the Great, strangers to every sentiment of honour and generosity. Wretches, who, by giving up their own dignity to those above them, insolently exact the same tribute from those below. A country, therefore, where the inhabitants are thus divided into the very rich and very poor, is, indeed, of all others the most helpless; without courage and without strength; neither enjoying peace within itself, and, after a time, unable to resist foreign invasion.

I shall conclude this paper with a picture of Italy just before its conquest, by Theodoric the Ostrogoth. 'The whole country was at that time [says the Historian] one garden of pleasure; the seats of the great men of Rome covered the face of the whole kingdom; and even their villas were supplied with provisions not of their own growth, but produced in distant countries, where they were more industrious. But in proportion as Italy was then beautiful, and its possessors rich, it was also weak and defenceless. The rough peasant and hardy husbandman had been long obliged to seek for liberty and subsistence in Britain or Gaul; and, by leaving their native country, brought with them all the strength of the nation. There was none now to resist an invading army, but the slaves of the nobility or the effeminate citizens of Rome, the one without motive, the other without strength to make any opposition. They were easily, therefore, overcome, by a people more savage indeed, but far more brave than they.'

Passage 4.11

(*from* Arthur Young, *A Six Weeks' Tour through the Southern Counties of England and Wales*, 1769)

(This passage follows a table of the medium average wages for agricultural labourers in each of the southern counties.)

These mediums, according to the distance from the capital, are as follow:

	s	d
Twenty miles around *London*, mean price,	10	9
From 20 to 60, – – –	7	8
From 60 to 110, – – –	6	4
From 110 to 170, – – –	6	3

General medium, 7s 9d per week.

One remark I should make, which is, that throughout the whole Tour, the labourers earn in the year more than the above sums, for I every where found that much work was done by the piece. Now it is well known they always earn more in that manner than at daily wages; which in the year makes a very considerable difference; within the extent of my experience and information, this difference amounts to a full fourth, the proportion taken of all sorts of work; for if you turn over the preceding sheets, you will find that the prices of the piece-work are, in general, out of proportion to the daily prices; they are so much higher: and this is the case, not with any particular county or place, but universally. No labourers will take work by the piece, without a certainty of earning more than the common pay, in return for working so much harder for themselves than they do for their masters.

In my own opinion, this circumstance will more than raise the general medium 7s 9d to 8s.

You see, Sir, by these tables, that the influence of the capital, in raising the price of labour, is prodigious; the difference between the extremes, being no less than 4s 6d or near three-fourths of the lowest country price. Nor can any the least reason be given for this. At *London* the bread is eat as cheap as any where, and meat only 1d per lb dearer than the cheapest part of the country; the price of provisions, therefore, has nothing to do with labour. The vast populousness of *London* and its neighbourhood, ought to lower the price of labour; and did not the debauched life of its inhabitants occasion them to be more idle than in the country, it would have that effect: but the very maxims and principles upon which life is founded in great cities, are the most powerful of all enemies to common industry.

But it is not only on a general view, that a want of proportion between labour and provisions is found; for it is the same at particular places; where provisions are the cheapest, it will not be found that labour is the same.

Upon comparing the prices of both, they will be found so various, that chance alone seems to guide them: this random variation, however, has nothing to do with the rise of prices, the nearer you approach *London*; as it is regular, and has an evident and powerful cause.

Politicians are so clear in their opinion, that low prices of labour are of the utmost importance to all trading states; that I must be allowed to express my amazement, at the legislature's suffering the capital to increase in the prodigious manner it has done of late. If *London*, as it is calculated, contains one sixth part of the nation; one sixth part of the nation's labour is thereby raised near *three-fourths* of its price; and another vast rise, is to the distance of near 100 miles; and this amounts to *a third*. All this is upon a supposition, that the influence of the capital does not reach 175 miles; which there is no reason to believe the case; but as that was the furthest point of the Tour, and of course labour the cheapest, it is taken as the uninfluenced mean: was it extended to a much greater distance, this influence of *London* would appear yet stronger. If a low price of labour is a public *benefit*, sure the size of *London* is a public *evil*! – I wish these inquiries were regularly extended, even to the Highlands of *Scotland* and the western isles; such a journey would afford plenty of matter for enlarging upon these subjects. – I shall now pass on to manufacturers. Of their earnings I shall give you a little sketch:

	s	d
Lavenham, says and calimancoes, earn *per* week, on a medium, the year round, – – –	5	9
Sudbury, burying-crape, &c. – – –	7	6
Hedingham, bays and says, – – –	7	0
Braintree, says and druggets, – – –	6	0
Witney, piece-goods and blankets, – –	11	0
Gloucester, pins, – – –	11	0
Wilton, carpets, – – –	11	0
Salisbury, flannels and linseys, – – –	8	0
Rumsey, ratinets, – – –	9	0
Wool-combers every where on an average, –	13	0
Medium earnings in the East of *England*; from *Lavenham* to *Braintree* inclusive, – –	6	6
In the West, at *Witney* and *Gloucester*, – –	11	0
In the South, *Wilton*, *Salisbury*, and *Rumsey*, –	9	4
Medium of labourers pay in the East, about the above manufacturing towns and neighbourhoods, taken from the [earlier] table . . . – – –	8	0
Ditto, around those in the West, – –	5	10
Ditto, those in the South, – – –	6	0
	s	d
General medium of manufacturers, – –	8	5
Ditto, of labourers, – – –	7	9
The former superior by – – –	0	8

NB The *Woodstock* manufacturers earn infinitely more than any; but I leave them out, because their number is very small, and their work a matter of mere elegance.

You observe that I have contrasted the earnings of labourers and manufacturers in the East, West, and South of *England*. I did this for a reason which I shall now explain.

In the West of *England*, the late riots on account of the high prices of provisions, ran higher and were more violent than in any part of the kingdom. As I passed through these parts, I made many inquiries concerning the rioters, and found that they in general consisted of manufacturers;

– that the labourers among them were instigated by the manufacturers, who were not only infinitely the most numerous, but were those who *began*.

I was not at all surprized at this information; which, from its generality, I have great reason to believe true. In the South of *England* likewise, about the above named manufacturing towns, was much rioting; and also by manufacturers, few labourers among them. In the East too, was a riot, particularly at *Long Melford*, &c. between *Sudbury* and *Lavenham*; this was composed of labourers, remarkably so; for they gathered like a snow-ball, at almost every farm-yard they came to.

Now, Sir, remark the comparisons above drawn up, between the manufacturers and labourers pay; – there you will find, that in the West and South of *England*, the manufacturers earn nine and eleven shillings; the labourers five and six shillings. The former were those who rioted.

In the East the manufacturers earn 6s 6d the labourers 8s. The latter were those who rioted.

Very far is it from my thoughts, to assert or hint, that our poor are too well paid – I am sensible that there is much wretchedness amongst some of them, which ought to be alleviated; but I must at the same time assert, riots and public disturbances form no just rules to judge by. If the above state of the case, candidly drawn up, from the best information I could get, does not at least prove this; I am sure it proves nothing.

It was always my opinion, and experience confirms it; that sober and industrious workmen, of any sort, *never* riot. In all occupations, there will be idle, drunken, unsettled, and disorderly persons; a few of these getting together, and talking over the *dearness of provisions*, (which presently becomes a cant term among them) inflame each other, and all of their own stamp; they know a riot is their best diversion; to stroll in a party about the country, eating and drinking at free cost, and having no work to do but mischief, suits such geniuses to a hair: and one riot is no sooner kicked up, than the news occasions many others. But what are the effects of all this? – Why the price of provisions is the topic bandied about, from one side of the kingdom to another; with abundance of rhetorical flourishes, on the distresses of the poor rioters, until, at last, the reality of their complaints is taken for granted; they are pitied in proportion to the degree of their plundering and burning; and our statesmen are clamoured into measures. – But let me avoid sliding into the mysterious region of politicks. I mean to deal in facts alone; happy when I can discover them pure and unalloyed with prejudice.

Whatever may be your opinion of this point, *the Price of Provisions*, let me request that you would not give any credit to the pleas of rioters.

You may have good reasons for thinking either way; but let not these lawless plunderers, who are universally the very scum, and riff raff of their neighbourhood, have the least effect upon your opinions. The more such fellows earn, the more succeeding time and money they have for the ale-house and disorderly meetings; and of course more in their power to do mischief.

Labour in some parts of the kingdom is certainly too low; in the West of *England*, for instance, to have it at several places so low as 5 or 6s the year round, bears no proportion to the prices of necessaries. If anything could justify riots, it was the low earnings of these labourers, and not those of the manufacturers, who could earn twice as much. I am, by no means, a competent judge of what ought to be the price of labour; but it is clear enough to me, that this price is as much too low, as that about the capital is too high.

It is worthy of remarks, that the general medium of manufacturers, is 8d a week more than labourers; and that without taking in the very great earnings of woolcombers.

Notes

1. Ovid, *Amores*, 2, 14, 35-8: No Armenian tigress would foul her den with such actions: No lioness would destroy her own cubs. Yet tender young girls do this – though not with impunity: often the uterine murderess dies herself.

2. *Iliad*: VI, 15: He that was born to care for people.

3. Virgil, *Eclogues*, vii, 54, and *Georgics*, i, 118: They lie strewn about, the labours of men and oxen.

5 CRIME

The discussions of crime and the law in these passages concentrate on three areas: the moral causes of crime, particularly among the poor; the role of the magistrate in society; and the nature and ends of punishment. As in the last section the passages reflect on a range of larger social and economic issues in the course of their arguments.

Passages 5.2 and 5.3 present the magistrate as an ideally exemplary figure in society. In passage 5.2 Shaftesbury describes him as a paternal figure whose main task is to encourage 'Virtue' in the population. In passage 5.3 Berkeley insists that his prime task is to instil the principles of Christianity into the population as the basis of their respect for the authorities of civil life. Defoe's attack on the corruption of magistrates and on the hypocrisy of 'punishing Vices in the Poor, which are daily practis'd by the Rich' (passage 5.1) forms an interesting commentary on these arguments, and strikes an unusual note in the anthology in its championship of the 'Poor Man' against the 'Master'.

The last three passages in the section discuss the effectiveness of various forms of punishment. The extracts from Fielding's *Enquiry* involve wide-ranging discussions of social policy, which have been examined in the introduction. Fielding's demands for rigorous exemplary punishments, particularly in passage 5.4c, are typical of much of the judicial and legal writing of the period. In contrast, in *The Rambler*, No. 114 (passage 5.5), Johnson appears as an early advocate of more lenient punishment, urging a 'scheme of invigorating the laws by relaxation', based partly on humane and partly on utilitarian considerations. The final reading, from Goldsmith, (passage 5.6), presents an intriguing argument, celebrating both the severity of the laws of England and the degree to which they can be by-passed in their operation.

Passage 5.1

(Daniel Defoe, *The Review*, Vol. 1, No. 85, 26 December 1704)

The Digression of the last two *Reviews*, had ended with them, had not some new Advocates appear'd to Vindicate our Workhouses, as useful Steps to our *Reformation of Manners*, by being Houses of Correction, and Punishment to Stroulers, Rogues, Whores, and all sorts of Vagrants.

I would be very forward to yield up any Point in their Favour, and shall, I hope, never be guilty of saying any thing to Dishonour, or Discourage the Needful Work of *Reformation of Manners*.

But it has been long in vain, that I have been an Impertinent Fellow in Preaching this Doctrine, *viz.*

For shame your Reformation Clubs *give o'er,*
And Jest with Men, and Jest with Heaven no more:
But if you would Avenging Heaven appease,
Avert his Plagues, and heal the Vile Disease:
Impending Ruine avoid, and calm the Fates,
Ye Hyppocrites, Reform your Magistrates.

Reform. of Man, a Satyr, p. 42

The punishing Vices in the Poor, which are daily practis'd by the Rich, seems to me to be, setting our Constitution with the wrong end upward, and making Men Criminals because they want Money.

'Tis now 8 Years since I first had the Misfortune to Anger my Masters the Magistrates, by Writing a little Book, call'd, *The Poor Men's Plea*, against all the Proclamations, or Acts of Parliament for *Reformation*; wherein the Honest Poor Man protests against being set in the Stocks by a Drunken Justice; or Fin'd for Swearing, by a Magistrate, with a *G–d D—n him, let the Dog pay for it?* Nay, and tho' an Honest, Learned, and Judicious Clergyman, was pleased to do that Book more Honour than its Author deserv'd, by taking it into the Pulpit with him, 'tis plain he has been Censur'd for the Sermon, and is hated to this Day, by all the Leading Men of the Parish of St J——, not far from the City of *London*.

And yet I must still take the Liberty, against the Rule of Authors, to Quote my self, and say to our Gentlemen of Justice and Correction.

Our Modes of Vice from high Examples came,
And 'tis Example only, must reclaim.
You'll eas'ly Check the Vices of the Town,
When e'er you please but to Suppress your own:

From hence, I confess, I have long ago left off Complaining of the Prophaneness and Immoralities of our People, and the Lewdness, Drunkenness, and Ill Language of our Streets; and if ever I meddle with our Vices, I place it chiefly on those who practice it in the very Chair and Bench of Authority; where they have (Heavens regard their Impudence) not stuck to punish with one Hand the Crimes they commit with the other.

For this I am ill treated by the Guilty, or their Friends, as a Reproacher of Magistrates, a Reviler of the Rulers of the People, and a

Medler with what is not my Business; and a certain Noble Person descended so much below the Honour of his Quality, as well as Office, as to tell me, in Defence of these things, That *if I saw a Man Lie with another Man's Wife, in the middle of the Street, I had no Right to publish the Scandal, nor unless I was a Magistrate, to meddle with the Matter*: Had his Lordship told me, *If I saw my Neighbour's House on Fire, I had no Right to* cry out, *because it would raise a Tumult*, I might have given Credit to it, but to the other, I can never agree.

Every Man who is subject to the Law, and punishable by it, has a Right in the Execution of the Law upon all Offenders equally with himself; and if one is punish'd for a Crime, and another goes free, the first Man is Injur'd, because he has not Equal Justice with his Neighbours. Again, I have a Right of Complaint, when any Offender is not brought to Justice, because it is an Encouragement to the Offence; and I may one time or other find the Effect of it.

But to avoid these Reasons, the Reproach to Justice, the Scandal to the Nation, the Encouragement to Vice, by Example is what we are all concern'd in; and I am, and ever shall be concern'd to hear us talk of Reformation, when those who should Reform us, practice all the Crimes they ought to punish.

What a noise has a poor Author about him, if he tells a Story of a Drunken Justice: – All the Drunken Justices in the Town, *and Lord, how many are they!* Think themselves concern'd, if a poor Author tells of a Magistrate Bound-over to the Peace for Fighting, throwing Brickbats, and the like, and Fin'd for Swearing; all the Fighting, Swearing, Justices, that stand Bound-over to the Peace, of whom our Records can easily tell the Number, are abusing me for calling it to mind: What have I to do, *say they*, with Swearing Mayors, Drunken Aldermen, and Justices, keeping the Peace? Why, that's true, Gentlemen, but then pray don't Talk of Reformation; Societies that can't bear a Sermon, because 'twas Preach'd in *Plain English*. Talk no more of well Govern'd Cities with Aldermen, and Great Folks in 'em, amongst whom are Crimes Black as the Robes they wear; whose Feasts are Debauches and Drunkenness; whose Houses are fill'd with all manner of Excesses; their Heads with Wine, in their Hands is Bribery and Oppression, and their Mouths are full of Cursings, and Blasphemy.

Shall fear of the powerful Injury of Man, stop the Just Exclamation of my Pen, at the flagrant Abuses of the Nations Laws; may these Writers be for ever D———d to Silence, who seeing the Laws broke, Good Manners invaded, Justice Abus'd, the Innocent Punish'd, and the Guilty sit in the Chair of Authority, are afraid to let the World know who is the Villain, that the Honest Man may be Distinguish'd.

I am charg'd with promoting Scandal, say some of my Friends, and Well-wishers, I boldly affirm, I never charg'd Person, Party, Members, or Body of high or low Quality, or Degree, with one Fact either obliquely or directly, which I was not able to bring untainted undeniable Testimony to the Truth of, and by God's Grace I never will: If I am Impos'd upon in any particular Relation, I'll do effectual Justice to any Injur'd Person; of which, I shall soon give the World a satisfactory Example.

From hence I say also, our *Scan. Club* Stories, tho' they have some Mirth in 'em, have all their Morals; and this serious sad Reflection goes with most of them, That as to Vices of every kind, *the Lord have Mercy upon the Magistrates and Clergy of this Nation*.

On this score, fewer Houses of Correction would serve; if none of the Poor are to be punish'd till the Magistrates, and Rich People are Reform'd; *Bridewell*, and *New-Prison* was large enough before; and the Usefulness of another House of Correction, in *Bishopsgate-Street*, remains to be prov'd.

Passage 5.2

(*from* Anthony Ashley Cooper, Earl of Shaftesbury, 'An Inquiry concerning Virtue, or Merit', Book 1, Part 3, Section 3, *Characteristicks*, 1711)

Thus in *a civil* State or Publick, we see that a virtuous Administration, and an equal and just Distribution of Rewards and Punishments, is of the highest service; not only by restraining the Vitious, and forcing them to act usefully to Society; but by making Virtue to be apparently the Interest of every-one, so as to remove all Prejudices against it, create a fair reception for it, and lead Men into that path which afterwards they cannot easily quit. For thus a People rais'd from Barbarity or despotick Rule, civiliz'd by Laws, and made virtuous by the long Course of a lawful and just Administration; if they chance to fall suddenly under any Misgovernment of unjust and arbitrary Power, they will on this account be the rather animated to exert a stronger Virtue, in opposition to such Violence and Corruption. And even where, by long and continu'd Arts of a prevailing Tyranny, such a People are at last totally oppress'd, the scatter'd Seeds of Virtue will for a long time remain alive, even to a second Generation; e'er the utmost Force of misapply'd Rewards and Punishments can bring them to the abject and compliant State of long-accustom'd Slaves.

But tho a right Distribution of Justice in a Government be so essential a cause of Virtue, we must observe in this Case, that it is *Example* which chiefly influences Mankind, and forms the Character and Disposition of a People. For a virtuous Administration is in a manner necessarily accompany'd with Virtue in the Magistrate. Otherwise it cou'd be of little effect; and of no long duration. But where it is sincere and well-establish'd, there Virtue and the Laws must necessarily be respected and belov'd. So that as to Punishments and Rewards, their Efficacy is not so much from the Fear or Expectation which they raise, as from a natural Esteem of *Virtue*, and Detestation of *Villany*, which is awaken'd and excited by these publick Expressions of the Approbation and hatred of Mankind in each Case. For in the publick Executions of the greatest Villains, we see generally that the Infamy and Odiousness of their Crime, and the Shame of it before Mankind, contribute more to their Misery than all besides; and that it is not the immediate Pain, or Death it-self, which raises so much Horrour either in the Sufferers or Spectators, as that ignominious kind of Death which is inflicted for publick Crimes, and Violations of Justice and Humanity.

And as the Case of Reward and Punishment stands thus in the Publick, so, in the same manner, as to *private Familys*. For Slaves and mercenary Servants, restrain'd and made orderly by Punishment, and the Severity of their Master, are not on this account made good or honest. Yet the same Master of the Family using proper Rewards and gentle Punishments towards his Children, teaches them Goodness, and by this help instructs them in a Virtue, which afterwards they practise upon other grounds, and without thinking of a Penalty or Bribe. And this is what we call *a Liberal Education* and *a Liberal Service*: the contrary Service and Obedience, whether towards God or Man, being *illiberal*, and unworthy of any Honour or Commendation.

Passage 5.3

(*from* George Berkeley, *A Discourse Addressed to Magistrates and Men in Authority*, 1732)

There is no Magistrate so ignorant as not to know that Power, physical Power, resides in the People; but Authority is from Opinion, which Authority is necessary to restrain and direct the People's Power, and therefore Religion is the great Stay and Support of a State. Every Religion that inculcates Virtue, and discourageth Vice, is so far of publick Benefit. The Christian Religion doth not only do this, but further makes every legal Constitution sacred by commanding our Submission thereto. *Let every Soul be subject to the higher Powers*, saith St PAUL, *for the Powers that be, are ordained of God*. And in Effect for several Years past, while the Reverence for our Church and Religion, hath been decaying and wearing off from the Minds of Men, it may be observed, that Loyalty hath in Proportion lost Ground; and now the very Word seems quite forgotten. Submission for Conscience, as well as for Wrath, was once reckoned an useful Lesson; but now, with other good Lessons is laid aside as an obsolete Prejudice.

THAT Prince or Magistrate, however great or powerful, who thinks his own Authority sufficient to make him respected and obeyed, lies under a woful Mistake, and never fails to feel it sooner or later. Obedience to all civil Power is rooted in the religious Fear of God: It is propagated, preserved, and nourished by Religion. This makes Men obey, not with Eye-Service, but in Sincerity of Heart. Human Regards may restrain Men from open and penal Offences; but the Fear of God is a Restraint from all Degrees of all Crimes however circumstanced. Take away this Stay and Prop of Duty, this Root of civil Authority; and all that grew from it shall soon languish. The Authority, the very Being of the Magistrate, will prove a poor and precarious Thing.

An inward Sense of the supreme Majesty of the King of Kings, is the only Thing that can beget and preserve a true Respect for subordinate Majesty in all the Degrees of Power, the first Link of Authority being fixed at the Throne of God. But in these our Days, that *Majestas imperii*, that Sacredness of Character, which rooted in a religious Principle, was the great Guard and Security of the State, is through Want thereof become the publick Scorn. And indeed, what Hold can the Prince or Magistrate have on the Conscience of those who have no Conscience? How can he build on the Principles of such as have no Principles? Or how can he hope for Respect where God himself is neglected?

It is manifest, that no Prince upon Earth can hope to govern well, or even to live easy and secure, much less respected by his People, if he do not contribute by his Example and Authority, to keep up in their Minds an awful Sense of Religion. As for a moral Sense, and moral Fitness, or eternal Relations, how insufficient those Things are for establishing general and just Notions of Morality, or for keeping Men within due Bounds, is so evident from Fact and Experience, that I need not now enter into a particular Disquisition about them.

It must be owned, that the Claws of Rapine and Violence, may in some Degree be pared and blunted by the outward Polity of a State. But should we not rather try, if possible, to pull them quite out? The Evil

Effects of Wickedness may be often redressed by publick Justice. But would it not be better to heal the Source; and by an inward Principle extirpate Wickedness from the Heart, rather than depend altogether on human Laws for preventing or redressing the bad Effects thereof? 'I might (said the *Chinese* Doctor *Confucius*) hear and decide Controversies as well as another: But what I would have is, that Men should be brought to abstain from Controversies, out of an inward Love and Regard for each other.'

Too many in this Age of free Remarks, and Projects, are delighted with Republican Schemes, and imagine they might remedy whatever was amiss, and render a People great and happy, merely by a new Plan or Form of Government. This dangerous Way of thinking and talking, is grown familiar, through the foolish Freedom of the Times. But alas! Those Men do not seem to have touched either the true Cause or Cure of Publick Evils: Be the Plan ever so excellent, or the Architects ever so able, yet no Man in his Wits would undertake to build a Palace with mere Mud or Dirt of the Streets. There must be fit Materials; and without a religious Principle, Men can never be fit Materials for any Society, much less for a Republique. Religion is the Centre which unites, and the Cement which connects the several Parts or Members of the political Body. Such it hath been held by all wise Men, from the remotest Times, down to our ingenious Contemporaries, who, if they are in the Right, it must be admitted that all the rest of the World have been in the Wrong.

From the Knowledge of its being absolutely necessary to the good Government of a State, that the Hearts and Minds of the People be inwardly imbued with good Principles, *Plato* tells us, that '*Jupiter*, to preserve the Race of Men from perishing, sent *Mercury*, with Orders to introduce Modesty and Justice among them, as the firmest Ties of humane Society; and without which, it could not subsist.' And elsewhere the same Author giveth it plainly as his Sense, that 'Concerning those great Duties which Men's Appetites and Passions render difficult, it should seem rather the Work of God to provide, than of humane Legislators, if it were possible to hope for a System of Laws framed and promulgated by God himself.' You see how agreeable the *Mosaic* and Christian Institutions are to be Wishes of the wisest Heathen.

Moses, indeed, doth not insist on a future State, the common Basis of all political Institutions. Nor do other Lawgivers make a particular mention of all Things necessary, but suppose some Things as generally known or believed. The Belief of a future State (which it is manifest the Jews were possessed of, long before the coming of Christ) seems to have obtained among the *Hebrews* from primæval Tradition; which might render it unnecessary for *Moses* to insist on that Article. But the *Sadducees* and *Epicureans* had, in Progress of Time, gone so far towards rooting out this ancient and original Sentiment, that it was in Danger of being lost, had it not been taught and promulgated in a new Light by our blessed Saviour.

But many among us, who would pass for Asserters of Truth and Liberty, are accustomed to rail at this, and all other established Opinions, as Prejudices which People are taught whether they will or no, and before they are able to distinguish whether they are right or wrong. These Lovers of Truth would do well to consider, that in political, moral, and religious Matters, the Opinions of the Vulgar, whether they go in Coaches, or walk on Foot, are for the most Part Prejudices; and are so like to be, whatever Side of the Question they embrace; whether they follow the old Maxims of the Religion of their Country, or the modern Instructions of their new Masters. I have already observed, that a Point being useful, and inculcated betimes, can be no Argument of its Falshood, even although it should be a Prejudice; far otherwise, Utility and Truth are not to be divided; the general Good of Mankind, being the Rule or Measure of moral Truth.

I shall now add, that it is to be apprehended, many of those who are the most forward to banish Prejudices, would be the first to feel the Want of them. It is even pitiful to think, what would become of certain modern Declaimers on that Article, were Prejudice really set aside, and were all Men to be weighted in the exact Scale of Merit, and considered in Proportion only to their intrinsic Worth. Some Prejudices are grounded in Truth, Reason, and Nature. Such are the Respects which are paid to Knowledge, Learning, Age, Honesty, and Courage in all civilized Countries. Others are purely the Effect of particular Constitutions, such as the Respects, Rights, and Preheminencies ascribed to some Men by their Fellow-Subjects, on Account of their Birth and Quality; which in the great empires of *Turky* and *China*, pass for nothing; and will pass for nothing elsewhere, as soon as Men have got rid of their Prejudices, and learned to despise the Constitutions of their Country. It may behove those who are concerned, to reflect on this betimes.

God, comprehending within himself, the Beginning, End, and Middle of all Things and Times, exerts his Energy throughout the whole Creation. He never ceaseth to influence by Instinct, by the Light of Nature, by his declared Will. And it is the Duty of Magistrates and Law-givers, to cultivate and encourage those divine Impressions in the Minds of all Men under their Care. We are not to think, it is the Work of God, and therefore not to be seconded by humane Care. Far otherwise, for that very Reason it claims our utmost Care and Diligence, it being the indispensable Duty of all good Men, throughout the whole Course of their Lives, to co-operate with the Designs of Providence. In Religion, as in Nature, God doth somewhat, and somewhat is to be done on the Part of Man. He causeth the Earth to bring forth Materials for Food and Raiment; but humane Industry must improve, cultivate, prepare, and properly apply both the one and the other; or Mankind may perish with Cold and Hunger. And according to this same Analogy, the Principles of Piety and Religion, the Things that belong to our Salvation, although originally and primarily the Work of God, yet require the Protection of humane Government, as well as the Furtherance and Aid of all wise and good Men.

And if Religion in all Governments be necessary, yet it seemeth to be so more especially in Monarchies: Forasmuch as the frugal Manners, and more equal Fortunes in Republiques, do not so much inflame Men's Appetites, or afford such Power or Temptation to Mischief, as the high Estate and great Wealth of Nobles under a King. Therefore, although the Magistrate, (as was already observed) hath for his peculiar Object, the temporal Well-being of the State; yet this will by no Means exempt him from a due Concern for the Religion of his Country.

What was the Sense of our Ancestors on this Point, appears throughout the whole Constitution of these Kingdoms; and in order to justify this Constitution, and the Wisdom of those who framed it, I shall crave Leave to make Use of some unsuspected Testimonies ancient and modern, which will shew, that the publick Care of a national Religion, hath been always a most principal Point in the Esteem of wise Men, however run down by the prevailing Licence of our Times.

Passage 5.4a

(*from* Henry Fielding, Preface, *An Enquiry into the Causes of the Late Increase in Robbers*, 1751)

If the Constitution, as I have above asserted, be the Result of the Disposition of the several Parts beforementioned, it follows, that this Disposition can never be altered, without producing a proportional Change in the Constitution. 'If the Soul, says *Simmias* in *Plato*, be a Harmony resulting from the Disposition of the corporeal Parts, it follows, that when this Disposition is confounded, and the Body is torn by Diseases or other Evils, the Soul immediately (whatever be her Divinity) must perish.' This will be apparent, if we cast our Eyes a Moment towards the animal Oeconomy; and it is no less true in the political.

The Customs, Manners, and Habits of the People, do, as I have said, form one Part of the Political Constitution; if these are altered therefore, this must be changed likewise; and here, as in the Natural Body, the Disorder of any Part will, in its Consequence, affect the whole.

One known Division of the People in this Nation is into the Nobility, the Gentry, and the Commonalty. What Alterations have happened among the two former of these, I shall not at present enquire; but that the last, in their Customs, Manners, and Habits, are greatly changed from what they were, I think to make appear.

If we look into the earliest Ages, we shall find the Condition of this Third Part to have been very low and mean. The highest Order of this Rank, before the Conquest, were those Tenants in Socage, who held their Lands by the Service of the Plough; who, as *Lyttleton* tells us, 'were to come with their Plough for certain Days in the Year, to plow and sow the Demesne of the Lords'; as the Villians, saith the same Author, 'were to carry and recarry the Dung of his Lord, spread it upon his Land, and to perform such like Services'.

This latter was rightly accounted a slavish Tenure. The Villains were indeed considered in Law as a Kind of Chattle belonging to their Masters: for though these had not the Power of Life and Death over them, nor even of maiming them with Impunity, yet these Villains had not even the Capacity of purchasing Lands or Goods; but the Lord, on such Purchase, might enter into the one, and seize the other for his own Use. And as for the Land which they held in Villenage, tho' Lord *Coke* says, it was not only held at the Will of the Lord, but according to the Custom of the Manor; yet, in antient Times, if the Lord ejected them, they were manifestly without Remedy.

And as to the former, tho' they were accounted Freemen, yet were they obliged to swear Fealty to their Lord; and tho' Mr *Rapin* be mistaken, when he says they could not alienate their Land, (for before the Statute of *Magna Charta, Chap*. 32, they could have given or sold the whole, but without any Alteration of the Tenure) yet was the Estate of these but very mean. 'Tho' they are called Freemen,' says Lord *Coke*, 'yet they ploughed, harrowed, reaped; and mowed, &c. for the Lord'; and *Bracton, Disuntur Socmanni eo quod deputati sunt tantummodo ad culturam*.

Besides such as were bound by their Tenures to the Service of Agriculture, the Number of Freemen below the Degree of Gentry, and who got their Livelihood in the Mercantile or Mechanical Way, was very inconsiderable. As to the Servants, they were chiefly bound by Tenure, and those of the lower Sort differed very little from Slaves.

That this Estate of the Commonalty is greatly changed, is apparent; and to this Alteration many Causes in subsequent Ages have contributed.

First, The Oath of Fealty, or Fidelity, which of old Time was administered with great Ceremony, became afterwards to be omitted; and though this Fealty still remained incident to every Socage Tenure, yet the Omission of the Form was not without its Consequences; for, as Lord *Coke* says, speaking of Homage, *Prudent Antiquity did, for the more Solemnity and better Memory and Observation of that which is to be done, express Substances under Ceremonies*.

2ndly, Whereas in the antient Tenures the principal Reservation was of personal Services from the inferior Tenants, the Rent being generally trifling, such as Hens, Capons, Roses, Spurs, Hawks, &c. afterwards the Avarice or Necessity of the Lords incited them to convert these for the most part into Money, which tended greatly to weaken the Power of the Lord, and to raise the Freedom and Independency of the Tenant.

3rdly, The dismembering Manors by Leases for Years, as it flowed from the same Sources, so it produced the same Effects. These were probably very rare before the Reign of *Edward I* at which Time the Statute of *Glocester* secured the Estate of this Tenant.

4thly, The Estate of the Villain or Copyholder seems clearly, as I have said, to have originally been holden only at the Will of the Lord; but the Law was afterwards altered, and in the Reign of *Edward* IV some of the best Judges were of Opinion, that if the Copyholder was unlawfully ejected by his Lord, he should have an Action of Trespass against him at the Common Law.

From this Time the Estate of the Copyholder (which, as *Briton* tells us, was formerly a base Tenure) began to grow into Repute, and, though still distinguished in some Privileges from a Freehold, became the Possession of many opulent and powerful Persons.

By these and such like Means the Commonalty, by Degrees, shook off their Vassalage, and became more and more independent on their Superiors. Even Servants, in Process of Time, acquired a State of Freedom and Independency, unknown to this Rank in any other Nation; and which, as the Law now stands, is inconsistent with a servile Condition.

But nothing hath wrought such an Alteration in this Order of People, as the Introduction of Trade. This hath indeed given a new Face to the whole Nation, hath in a great Measure subverted the former State of Affairs, and hath almost totally changed the Manners, Customs, and Habits of the People, more especially of the lower Sort. The Narrowness of their Fortune is changed into Wealth; the Simplicity of their Manners into Craft; their Frugality into Luxury; their Humility into Pride, and their Subjection into Equality.

The Philosopher, perhaps, will think this a bad Exchange, and may be inclined to cry out with the Poet,[1]

– Saevior armis
Luxuria incubuit. –
Nullum crimen abest, facinusque libidinis, ex quo
Paupertas Romana perit.

Again,

Prima peregrinos obscoena pecunia mores
Intulit, & turpi fregerunt saecula luxu
Divitiae molles –

But the Politician finds many Emoluments to compensate all the moral Evils introduced by Trade, by which the Grandeur and Power of the Nation is carried to a Pitch that it could never otherwise have reached; Arts and Sciences are improved, and human Life is embellished with every Ornament, and furnished with every Comfort which it is capable of tasting.

In all these Assertions he is right; but surely he forgets himself a little, when he joins the Philosopher in lamenting the Introduction of Luxury as a casual Evil; for as Riches are the *certain* Consequence of Trade, so is Luxury the no less *certain* Consequence of Riches: Nay, Trade and Luxury do indeed support each other; and this latter, in its Turn, becomes as useful to Trade, as Trade had been before to the Support of Luxury.

To prevent this Consequence therefore of a flourishing Commerce is totally to change the Nature of Things, and to separate the Effect from the Cause. A Matter as impossible in the Political Body as in the Natural. Vices and Diseases, with like Physical Necessity, arise from certain Habits in both; and to restrain and palliate the evil Consequences, is all that lies within the Reach of Art. How far it is the Business of the Politician to interfere in the Case of Luxury, we have attempted to shew in the following Treatise.

Now, to conceive that so great a Change as this in the People should produce no Change in the Constitution, is to discover, I think, as great Ignorance as would appear in the Physician, who should assert, that the whole State of the Blood may be entirely altered from poor to rich, from cool to inflamed, without producing any Alteration in the Constitution of the Man.

To put this in the clearest Light: There appear to me to be Four Sorts of Political Power; that of Bodily Strength, that of the Mind, the Power of the Purse, and the Power of the Sword. Under the Second of these Divisions may be ranged all the Art of the Legislator and Politician, all the Power of Laws and Government. These do constitute the Civil Power; and a State may then be said to be in good Order, when all the other Powers are subservient to this; when they own its superior Excellence and Energy, pay it a ready Obedience, and all unite in Support of its Rule.

But so far are these Powers from paying such voluntary Submission, that they are all extremely apt to rebel, and to assert their own Superiority; but none is more rebellious in its Nature, or more difficult to be governed, than that of the Purse or Money. Self-opinion, Arrogance, Insolence, and Impatience of Rule, are its almost inseparable Companions.

Now if these Assertions are true, what an immense Accession of this Power hath accrued to the Commonalty by the Increase of Trade? for tho' the other Orders have acquired an Addition by the same Means, yet this is not in the same Proportion, as every Reader, who will revolve the Proposition but a Moment in his own Mind, must be satisfied.

And what may we hence conclude? Is that Civil Power, which was adapted to the Government of this Order of People in that State in which they were at the Conquest, capable of ruling them in their present Situation? Hath this Civil Power kept equal Pace with them in the Increase of its Force, or hath it not rather, by the Remissness of the Magistrate, lost much of its antient Energy? Where is now that Power of the Sheriff, which could formerly awaken and arm a whole County in an Instant? Where is that *Posse Comitatus*, which attended at his Beck? What is become of the Constitutions of *Alfred*, which the Reader will find set forth at large in the following Treatise? What of the antient Conservators of the Peace? Have the Justices, on whom this whole Power devolves, an Authority sufficient for the Purpose? In some Counties, perhaps, you may find an overgrown Tyrant, who lords it over his Neighbours and Tenants with despotic Sway, and who is as regardless of the Law as he is ignorant of it; but as to the Magistrate of a less Fortune, and more Knowledge, every riotous independent Butcher or Baker, with two or three thousand Pounds in his Pocket, laughs at his Power, and every Pettyfogger makes him tremble.

It is a common and popular Complaint, that the Justices of Peace have already too much Power. Indeed a very little is too much, if it be abused; but, in truth, this Complaint proceeds from a Mistake of Business for Power: The Business of the Justice is indeed multiplied by a great Number of Statutes; but I know not of any (the Riot Act perhaps excepted) which hath at all enlarged his Power. And what the Force of that Act is, and how able the Magistrate is, by means of the Civil Power alone, to execute it in any popular Commotion, I have myself experienced. But when a Mob of Chairmen or Servants, or a Gang of Thieves and Sharpers, are almost too big for the Civil Authority to suppress, what must be the Case in a seditious Tumult, or general Riot of the People?

From what hath been said, I may, I think, conclude, that the Constitution of this Country is altered from its antient State.

2ndly, That the Power of the Commonalty hath received an immense Addition; and that the Civil Power having not increased, but decreased, in the same Proportion, is not able to govern them.

What may and must be the Consequences of this, as well as what Remedy can be applied to it, I leave to the Consideration of others: I have proceeded far enough already on the Subject, to draw sufficient Ill-will on myself, from unmeaning or ill-meaning People, who either do not foresee the mischievous Tendency of a total Relaxation of Government, or who have some private wicked Purpose to effect from public Confusion.

In plain Truth, the principal Design of this whole Work, is to rouse the CIVIL Power from its present lethargic State. A Design which alike opposes those wild Notions of Liberty that are inconsistent with all Government, and those pernicious Schemes of Government, which are destructive of true Liberty. However contrary indeed these Principles may seem to each other, they have both the same common Interest; or, rather, the former are the wretched Tools of the latter: for Anarchy is almost sure to end in some Kind of Tyranny.

Dr *Middleton*, in his Life of *Cicero*, hath a fine Observation to my present Purpose, with which I will conclude this Preface.

'From the Railleries of the *Romans*,' [says he] on the *Barbarity and Misery of our Island*, one cannot help reflecting on the surprising Fate and Revolutions of Kingdoms: how *Rome*, once the Mistress of the World, the Seat of Arts, Empire and Glory, now lies sunk in Sloth, Ignorance and Poverty; enslaved to the most cruel, as well as to the most contemptible of Tyrants, *Superstition and Religious Imposture*: while this remote Country, anciently the Jest and Contempt of the *polite Romans*, is become the happy Seat of Liberty, Plenty and Letters; flourishing in all the Arts and Refinements of Civil Life; yet running perhaps the same Course, which *Rome* itself had run before it; from virtuous Industry to Wealth; from Wealth to Luxury; from Luxury to an Impatience of Discipline and Corruption of Morals; till by a total

Degeneracy and loss of Virtue, being grown ripe for Destruction, it falls a Prey at last to some hardy Oppressor, and, with the Loss of Liberty, losing every Thing else, that is valuable, sinks gradually again into its original Barbarism.'

Passage 5.4b
(*from* Fielding, 'Of too frequent and expensive Diversions among the Lower Kind of People', *Enquiry*, 1751)

First then, I think, that the vast Torrent of Luxury which of late Years hath poured itself into this Nation, hath greatly contributed to produce, among many others, the Mischief I here complain of. I aim not here to satirize the Great, among whom Luxury is probably rather a moral than a political Evil. But Vices no more than Diseases will stop with them; for bad Habits are as infectious by Example, as the Plague itself by Contact. In free Countries, at least, it is a Branch of Liberty claimed by the People to be as wicked and as profligate as their Superiors. Thus while the Nobleman will emulate the Grandeur of a Prince; and the Gentleman will aspire to the proper State of the Nobleman; the Tradesman steps from behind his Counter into the vacant Place of the Gentleman. Nor doth the Confusion end here: It reaches the very Dregs of the People, who aspiring still to a Degree beyond that which belongs to them, and not being able by the Fruits of honest Labour to support the State which they affect, they disdain the Wages to which their Industry would intitle them; and abandoning themselves to Idleness, the more simple and poor-spirited betake themselves to a Stage of Starving and Beggary, while those of more Art and Courage become Thieves, Sharpers and Robbers.

Could Luxury be confined to the Palaces of the Great, the Society would not perhaps be much affected with it; at least, the Mischiefs which I am now intending to obviate can never be the Consequence. For tho', perhaps, there is not more of real Virtue in the higher State, yet the Sense of Honour is there more general and prevalent. But there is a much stronger Reason. The Means bear no probable Proportion to the End. For the Loss of Thousands, or of a great Estate, is not to be relieved or supplied by any Means of common Theft or Robbery – With regard to such Evils therefore the Legislature might be justified in leaving the Punishment, as well as the pernicious Consequence, to end in the Misery, Distress, and sometimes utter Ruin of a private Family. But when this Vice descends downward to the Tradesman, the Mechanic, and the Labourer, it is certain to engender many political Mischiefs, and among the rest it is most evidently the Parent of Theft and Robbery, to which not only the Motive of Want but of Shame conduces; For there is no greater Degree of Shame than the Tradesman generally feels at the first Inability to make his regular Payments; nor is there any Difficulty which he would not undergo to avoid it. Here then the Highway promises, and hath, I doubt not, often given Relief. Nay I remember very lately a Highwayman who confessed several Robberies before me, his Motive to which, he assured me, (and so it appeared) was to pay a Bill that was shortly to become due. In this Case therefore the Publick becomes interested, and consequently the Legislature is obliged to interpose.

To give a final Blow to Luxury by any general Prohibition, if it would be adviseable, is by no Means possible. To say the Truth, bad Habits in the Body Politic, especially if of any Duration, are seldom to be wholly eradicated. Palliatives alone are to be applied; and these too in a free Constitution must be of the gentlest Kind, and as much as possible adapted to the Taste and Genius of the People.

The gentlest Method which I know, and at the same Time perhaps one of the most effectual, of stopping the Progress of Vice, is by removing the Temptation. Now the two great Motives to Luxury, in the Mind of Man, are Vanity and Voluptuousness. The former of these operates but little in this Regard with the lower Order of People. I do not mean that they have less of this Passion than their Betters; but the apparent Impossibility of gratifying it this Way deters them, and diverts at least this Passion into another Channel; for we find it puts them rather on vying with each other in the Reputation of Wealth, than in the outward Appearance of Show and Grandeur. Voluptuousness or the Love of Pleasure is that alone which leads them into Luxury. Here then the Temptation is with all possible Care to be withdrawn from them.

Now what greater Temptation can there be to Voluptuousness, than a Place where every Sense and Appetite of which it is compounded, are fed and delighted; where the Eyes are feasted with Show, and the Ears with Musick, and where Gluttony and Drunkenness are allured by every Kind of Dainty; nay where the finest Women are exposed to View, and where the meanest Person who can dress himself clean, may in some Degree mix with his Betters, and thus perhaps satisfy his Vanity as well as his Love of Pleasure?

It may possibly be said that these Diversions are cheap: I answer, that is one Objection I have to them: Was the Price as high as that of a Ridotto, or an Opera, it would, like these Diversions, be confined to the higher People only; besides the Cheapness is really a Delusion. Unthinking Men are often deceived into Expence, as I once knew an honest Gentleman who carried his Wife and two Daughters to a Masquerade, being told that he could have four Tickets for four Guineas; but found afterwards, that in Dresses, Masques, Chairs, &c. the Night's Entertainment cost him almost Twelve. I am convinced that many thousands of honest Tradesmen have found their Expences exceed their Computation in a much greater Proportion. And the Sum of seven or eight Shillings (which is a very moderate Allowance for the Entertainment of the smallest Family) repeated once or twice a Week through a Summer, will make too large a Deduction from the reasonable Profits of any low Mechanic.

Besides the actual Expence in attending these Places of Pleasure, the Loss of Time and Neglect of Business are Consequences which the inferior Tradesman can by no Means support. To be born for no other Purpose than to consume the Fruits of the Earth is the Privilege (if it may be really called a Privilege) of very few. The greater Part of Mankind must sweat hard to produce them, or Society will no longer answer the Purpose for which it was ordained. *Six Days shalt thou labour*, was the positive Command of God in his own Republick. A Severity, however, which the divine Wisdom was pleased somewhat to relax; and appointed certain Times of Rest and Recreation for his People. Such were the Feast of the unleavened Bread, the Feast of the Weeks, and the Feast of the Tabernacles. On which Occasions it is written, *Thou shall rejoice before the Lord thy God, thou and thy Son and thy Daughter, and thy Servant, and thy Maid, and the Levite that is within thy Gates, and the Stranger, and the Fatherless, and the Widow . . .*

* * *

But while I am recommending some Restraint of this Branch of Luxury, which surely appears to be necessary, I would be understood to aim at the Retrenchment only, not at the Extirpation of Diversion; nay, and in this Restraint, I confine myself entirely to the lower Order of People. Pleasure always hath been, and always will be, the principal Business of Persons of Fashion and Fortune, and more especially of the Ladies, for whom I have infinitely too great an Honour and Respect to rob them of any their least Amusement. Let them have their Plays, Operas, and Oratorios, their Masquerades and Ridottos; their Assemblies, Drums, Routs, Riots and Hurricanes; their *Ranelagh* and *Vauxhall*; their *Bath*, *Tunbridge*, *Bristol*, *Scarborough*, and *Cheltenham*; and let them have their Beaus and Danglers to attend them at all these; it is the only Use for which such Beaus are fit; and I have seen in the Course of my Life, that it is the only one to which by sensible Women they are applied.

In Diversion, as in many other Particulars, the upper Part of Life is distinguished from the Lower. Let the Great therefore answer for the Employment of their Time, to themselves, or to their spiritual Governors. The Society will receive some temporal Advantage from their Luxury. The more Toys which Children of all Ages consume, the brisker will be the Circulation of Money, and the greater the Increase of Trade.

The Business of the Politician is only to prevent the Contagion from spreading to the useful Part of Mankind, the ΕΠΙΠΟΝΟΝ ΠΕΦΥΟΣ ΓΕΝΟΣ;[2] and this is the Business of Persons of Fashion and Fortune too, in order that the Labour and Industry of the rest may administer to their Pleasures, and furnish them with the Means of Luxury. To the upper Part of Mankind Time is an Enemy, and (as they themselves often confess) their chief Labour is to kill it; whereas, with the others, Time and Money are almost synonymous; and as they have very little of each to spare, it becomes the Legislature, as much as possible, to suppress all Temptations whereby they may be induced too profusely to squander either the one or the other; since all such Profusion must be repaired at the Cost of the Public.

Such Places of Pleasure, therefore, as are totally set apart for the Use of the Great World, I meddle not with. And though *Ranelagh* and *Vaux-hall*, by reason of their Price, are not entirely appropriated to the People of Fashion, yet they are seldom frequented by any below the middle Rank; and a strict Regard to Decency is preserved in them both. But surely two such Places are sufficient to contain all those who have any Title to spend their Time in this idle, though otherwise innocent Way. Nor should such a Fashion be allowed to spread into every Village round *London*, and by degrees all over the Kingdom; by which means, not only Idleness, but all Kinds of Immorality, will be encouraged.

I cannot dismiss this Head, without mentioning a notorious Nuisance which hath lately arisen in this Town; I mean, those Balls where Men and Women of loose Reputation meet in disguised Habits. As to the Masquerade in the *Hay-market*, I have nothing to say; I really think it a silly rather than a vicious Entertainment: But the Case is very different with these inferiour Masquerades; for these are indeed no other than the Temples of Drunkenness, Leudness, and all Kind of Debauchery.

Passage 5.4c
(Fielding, 'Of the Encouragement given to Robbers by Frequent Pardons', *Enquiry*, 1751)

I come now to the sixth Encouragement to Felons, from the Hopes of a Pardon, at least with the Condition of Transportation.

This I am aware, is too tender a Subject to speak to. To pardon all Crimes where the Prosecution is in his Name, is an undoubted Prerogative of the King. I may add, it is his most amiable Prerogative, and that which as *Livy* observes, renders Kingly Government most dear to the People: For in a Republic there is no such Power. I may add farther, that it seems to our excellent Sovereign to be the most favourite Part of his Prerogative, as it is the only one which hath been carried to its utmost Extent in the present Reign.

Here therefore I beg to direct myself only to those Persons who are within the Reach of his Majesty's sacred Ear. Such Persons will, I hope, weigh well what I have said already on the Subject of false Compassion, all which is applicable on the present Occasion: And since our King (as was with less Truth said of another) *is of all Men the truest Image of his Maker in Mercy*, I hope too much Good-nature will transport no Nobleman so far as it once did a Clergyman in *Scotland*, who in the Fervour of his Benevolence prayed to God that he would graciously be pleased to pardon the poor Devil.

To speak out fairly and honestly, tho' Mercy may appear more amiable in a Magistrate, Severity is a more wholesome Virtue; nay Severity to an Individual may, perhaps, be in the End the greatest Mercy, not only to the Public in general, for the Reason given above; but to many Individuals for the Reasons to be presently assigned.

To consider a human Being in the Dread of a sudden and violent Death; to consider that his Life or Death depended on your Will; to reject the Arguments which a good Mind will officiously advance to itself; that violent Temptation, Necessity, Youth, Inadvertency have hurried him to the Commission of a Crime which hath been attended with no Inhumanity; to resist the Importunities, Cries, and Tears of a tender Wife, and affectionate Children, who, though innocent, are to be reduced to Misery and Ruin by a strict adherence to Justice. These altogether form an Object which whoever can look upon without Emotion, must have a very bad Mind; and whoever by the Force of Reason can conquer that Emotion must have a very strong one.

And what can Reason suggest on this Occasion? First, that by saving this Individual, I shall bring many others into the same dreadful

Situation. That the Passions of the Man are to give Way to the Principles of the Magistrate. Those may lament the Criminal, but these must condemn him. It was nobly said by *Bias* to one who admired at his shedding Tears whilst he past Sentence of Death, 'Nature exacts my Tenderness, but the Law my Rigour'. The elder *Brutus*, is a worthy Pattern of this Maxim; an Example, says *Machiavel*, most worthy of being transmitted to Posterity. And *Dionysius Halicarnasseus* calls it a *great and wonderful Action, of which the Romans were proud in the most extraordinary Degree*. Whoever derives it therefore from the Want of humane and paternal Affections is unjust; no Instances of his Inhumanity are recorded. 'But the Severity, says *Machiavel*, was not only profitable but necessary'; and why? Because a single Pardon granted *ex mera Gratia & Favore*, is a Link broken in the Chain of Justice, and takes away the Concatenation and Strength of the whole. The Danger and Certainty of Destruction are very different Objects, and strike the Mind with different Degrees of Force. It is of the very Nature of Hope to be sanguine, and it will derive more Encouragement from one Pardon, than Diffidence from twenty Executions.

It is finely observed by *Thucydides*, 'that though civil Societies have allotted the Punishment of Death to many Crimes, and to some of the inferior Sort, yet Hope inspires Men to face the Danger; and no Man ever came to a dreadful End, who had not a lively Expectation of surviving his wicked Machinations.' – Nothing certainly can more contribute to the raising his Hope than repeated Examples of ill grounded Clemency: For as *Seneca* says, *Ex Clementia omnes idem sperant*.

Now what is the principal End of all Punishment: Is it not as Lord *Hale* expresses it, 'to deter Men from the Breach of Laws, so that they may not offend, and so not suffer at all? And is not the inflicting of Punishment more for Example, and to prevent Evil, than to punish?' And therefore, says he, presently afterwards, 'Death itself is necessary to be annexed to Laws in many Cases by the Prudence of Law-givers, though possibly beyond the single Merit of the Offence simply considered.' No Man indeed of common Humanity or common Sense can think the Life of a Man and a few Shillings to be of an equal Consideration, or that the Law in punishing Theft with Death proceeds (as perhaps a private Person sometimes may) with any View to Vengeance. The Terror of the Example is the only Thing proposed, and one Man is sacrificed to the Preservation of Thousands.

If therefore the Terror of this Example is removed (as it certainly is by frequent Pardons) the Design of the Law is rendered totally ineffectual; the Lives of the Persons executed are thrown away, and sacrificed rather to the Vengeance than to the Good of the Public, which receives no other Advantage than by getting rid of a Thief, whose Place will immediately be supplied by another. Here then we may cry out with the Poet:[3]

– Sævior Ense
Parcendi Rabies –

This I am confident may be asserted, that Pardons have brought many more Men to the Gallows than they have saved from it. So true is that Sentiment of *Machiavel*, that Examples of Justice are more merciful than the unbounded Exercise of Pity.

Passage 5.5
(Samuel Johnson, *The Rambler*, No. 114, 20 April 1751)

Audi,
Nulla unquam de morte hominis cunctatio longa est.
Juvenal, VI.220-21

When man's life is in debate,
The judge can ne'er too long debate.
Dryden.

Power and superiority are so flattering and delightful, that, fraught with temptation and exposed to danger as they are, scarcely any virtue is so cautious, or any prudence so timorous, as to decline them. Even those that have most reverence for the laws of right, are pleased with shewing that not fear, but choice, regulates their behaviour; and would be thought to comply, rather than obey. We love to overlook the boundaries which we do not wish to pass; and, as the Roman satirist remarks, he that has no design to take the life of another, is yet glad to have it in his hands.

From the same principle, tending yet more to degeneracy and corruption, proceeds the desire of investing lawful authority with terror, and governing by force rather than persuasion. Pride is unwilling to believe the necessity of assigning any other reason than her own will; and would rather maintain the most equitable claims by violence and penalties, than descend from the dignity of command to dispute and expostulation.

It may, I think, be suspected, that this political arrogance has sometimes found its way into legislative assemblies, and mingled with deliberations upon property and life. A slight perusal of the laws by which the measures of vindictive and coercive justice are established, will discover so many disproportions between crimes and punishments, such capricious distinctions of guilt, and such confusion of remissness and severity, as can scarcely be believed to have been produced by publick wisdom, sincerely and calmly studious of publick happiness.

The learned, the judicious, the pious Boerhaave relates, that he never saw a criminal dragged to execution without asking himself, 'Who knows whether this man is not less culpable than me?' On the days when the prisons of this city are emptied into the grave, let every spectator of the dreadful procession put the same question to his own heart. Few among those that croud in thousands to the legal massacre, and look with carelessness, perhaps with triumph, on the utmost exacerbation of human misery, would then be able to return without horror and dejection. For, who can congratulate himself upon a life passed without some act more mischievous to the peace or prosperity of others, than the theft of a piece of money?

It has been always the practice, when any particular species of robbery becomes prevalent and common, to endeavour its suppression by capital denunciations. Thus, one generation of malefactors is commonly cut off, and their successors are frighted into new expedients; the art of thievery is augmented with greater variety of fraud, and subtilized to higher degrees of dexterity, and more occult methods of conveyance. The law then renews the pursuit in the heat of anger, and overtakes the offender again with death. By this practice, capital inflictions are multiplied, and crimes very different in their degrees of enormity are equally subjected to the severest punishment that man has the power of exercising upon man.

The lawgiver is undoubtedly allowed to estimate the malignity of an offence, not merely by the loss or pain which single acts may produce, but by the general alarm and anxiety arising from the fear of mischief, and insecurity of possession: he therefore exercises the right which societies are supposed to have over the lives of those that compose them, not simply to punish a transgression, but to maintain order, and preserve quiet; he enforces those laws with severity that are most in danger of violation, as the commander of a garrison doubles the guard on that side which is threatened by the enemy.

This method has been long tried, but tried with so little success, that rapine and violence are hourly encreasing; yet few seem willing to despair of its efficacy, and of those who employ their speculations upon the present corruption of the people, some propose the introduction of more horrid, lingering and terrifick punishments; some are inclined to accelerate the executions; some to discourage pardons; and all seem to think that lenity has given confidence to wickedness, and that we can only be rescued from the talons of robbery by inflexible rigour, and sanguinary justice.

Yet since the right of setting an uncertain and arbitrary value upon life has been disputed, and since experience of past times gives us little reason to hope that any reformation will be effected by a periodical havock of our fellow-beings, perhaps it will not be useless to consider what consequences might arise from relaxations of the law, and a more rational and equitable adaptation of penalties to offences.

Death is, as one of the ancients observes, *τὸ τῶν φοβερῶν φοβερώτατον*, 'of dreadful things the most dreadful', an evil, beyond which nothing can be threatened by sublunary power, or feared from human enmity or vengeance. This terror should, therefore, be reserved as the last resort of authority, as the strongest and most operative of prohibitory sanctions, and placed before the trasure of life, to guard from invasion what cannot be restored. To equal robbery with murder is to reduce murder to robbery, to confound in common minds the gradations of iniquity, and incite the commission of a greater crime to prevent the detection of a less. If only murder were punished with death, very few robbers would stain their hands in blood; but when, by the last act of cruelty no new danger is incurred, and greater security may be obtained, upon what principle shall we bid them forbear?

It may be urged, that the sentence is often mitigated to simple robbery; but surely this is to confess, that our laws are unreasonable in our own opinion; and, indeed, it may be observed, that all but murderers have, at their last hour, the common sensations of mankind pleading in their favour.

From this conviction of the inequality of the punishment to the offence proceeds the frequent solicitation of pardons. They who would rejoice at the correction of a thief, are yet shocked at the thought of destroying him. His crime shrinks to nothing, compared with his misery; and severity defeats itself by exciting pity.

The gibbet, indeed, certainly disables those who die upon it from infesting the community; but their death seems not to contribute more to the reformation of their associates than any other method of separation. A thief seldom passes much of his time in recollection or anticipation, but from robbery hastens to riot, and from riot to robbery; nor, when the grave closes upon his companion, has any other care than to find another.

The frequency of capital punishments therefore rarely hinders the commission of a crime, but naturally and commonly prevents its detection, and is, if we proceed only upon prudential principles, chiefly for that reason to be avoided. Whatever may be urged by casuists or politicians, the greater part of mankind, as they can never think that to pick the pocket and to pierce the heart is equally criminal, will scarcely believe that two malefactors so different in guilt can be justly doomed to the same punishment; nor is the necessity of submitting the conscience to human laws so plainly evinced, so clearly stated, or so generally allowed, but that the pious, the tender, and the just, will always scruple to concur with the community in an act which their private judgment cannot approve.

He who knows not how often rigorous laws produce total impunity, and how many crimes are concealed and forgotten for fear of hurrying the offender to that state in which there is no repentance, has conversed very little with mankind. And whatever epithets of reproach or contempt this compassion may incur from those who confound cruelty with firmness, I know not whether any wise man would wish it less powerful, or less extensive.

If those whom the wisdom of our laws has condemned to die, had been detected in their rudiments of robbery, they might by proper discipline and useful labour, have been disentangled from their habits, they might have escaped all the temptations to subsequent crimes, and passed their days in reparation and penitence; and detected they might all have been, had the prosecutors been certain, that their lives would have been spared. I believe, every thief will confess, that he has been more than once seized and dismissed; and that he has sometimes ventured upon capital crimes, because he knew, that those whom he injured would rather connive at his escape, than cloud their minds with the horrors of his death.

All laws against wickedness are ineffectual, unless some will inform, and some will prosecute; but till we mitigate the penalties for mere violations of property, information will always be hated, and prosecution dreaded. The heart of a good man cannot but recoil at the thought of punishing a slight injury with death; especially when he remembers, that the thief might have procured safety by another crime, from which he was restrained only by his remaining virtue.

The obligations to assist the exercise of publick justice are indeed strong; but they will certainly be overpowered by tenderness for life. What is punished with severity contrary to our ideas of adequate retribution, will be seldom discovered; and multitudes will be suffered to advance from crime to crime, till they deserve death, because if they had been sooner prosecuted, they would have suffered death before they deserved it.

This scheme of invigorating the laws by relaxation, and extirpating wickedness by lenity, is so remote from common practice, that I might reasonably fear to expose it to the publick, could it be supported only by my own observations: I shall, therefore, by ascribing it to its author, Sir Thomas More, endeavour to procure it that attention, which I wish always paid to prudence, to justice, and to mercy.

Passage 5.6
(*from* Oliver Goldsmith, 'Letter L', *The Citizen of the World*, 1762)

From Lien Chi Altangi, to Fum Hoam, first president of the Ceremonial Academy at Pekin, in China
Ask any Englishman what nation in the world enjoys most freedom, and he immediately answers, his own. Ask him in what that freedom principally consists, and he is instantly silent. This happy pre-eminence does not arise from the people's enjoying a larger share in legislation than elsewhere; for in this particular several states in Europe excel them; nor does it arise from a greater exemption from taxes, for few countries pay more; it does not proceed from their being restrained by fewer laws, for no people are burthened with so many; nor does it particularly consist in the security of their property, for property is pretty well secured in every polite state of Europe.

How then are the English more free (for more free they certainly are) than the people of any other country, or under any other form of government whatever? Their freedom consists in their enjoying all the advantages of democracy with this superior prerogative borrowed from monarchy, *that the severity of their laws may be relaxed without endangering the constitution*.

In a monarchical state, in which the constitution is strongest, the laws may be relaxed without danger; for though the people should be unanimous in the breach of any one in particular, yet still there is an *effective* power superior to the people, capable of enforcing obedience, whenever it may be proper to inculcate the law either towards the support or welfare of the community.

But in all those governments, where laws derive their sanction from the *people alone*, transgressions cannot be overlooked without bringing the constitution into danger. They who transgress the law in such a case, are those who prescribe it, by which means it loses not only its influence but its sanction. In every republic the laws must be strong, because the constitution is feeble: they must resemble an Asiatic husband who is justly jealous, because he knows himself impotent. Thus in Holland, Switzerland, and Genoa, new laws are not frequently enacted, but the old ones are observed with unremitting severity. In such republics therefore the people are slaves to laws of their own making, little less than in unmix'd monarchies where they are slaves to the will of one subject to frailties like themselves.

In England, from a variety of happy accidents, their constitution is just strong enough, or if you will, monarchical enough, to permit a relaxation of the severity of laws, and yet those laws still remain sufficiently strong to govern the people. This is the most perfect state of civil liberty, of which we can form any idea; here we see a greater number of laws than in any other country, while the people at the same time obey only such as are *immediately* conducive to the interests of society; several are unnoticed, many unknown; some kept to be revived and enforced upon proper occasions, others left to grow obsolete, even without the necessity of abrogation

Scarce an Englishman who does not almost every day of his life, offend with impunity against some express law, and for which in a certain conjuncture of circumstances he would not receive punishment. Gaming houses, preaching at prohibited places, assembled crowds, nocturnal amusements, public shews, and an hundred other instances are forbid and frequented. These prohibitions are useful; though it be prudent in their magistrates, and happy for their people, that they are not enforced, and none but the venal or mercenary attempt to enforce them.

The law in this case, like an indulgent parent, still keeps the rod, though the child is seldom corrected. Were those pardoned offences to rise into enormity, were they likely to obstruct the happiness of society, or endanger the state, it is then that justice would resume her terrors, and punish those faults she had so often overlooked with indulgence. It is to this ductility of the laws that an Englishman owes the freedom he enjoys superior to others in a more popular government; every step therefore the constitution takes towards a Democratic form, every dimunition of the regal authority is, in fact a diminution of the subject's freedom; but every attempt to render the government more popular, not only impairs natural liberty, but even will at last, dissolve the political constitution.

Every popular government seems calculated to last only for a time, it grows rigid with age, new laws are multiplying, and the old continue in force, the subjects are oppressed, burthen'd with a multiplicity of legal injunctions, there are none from whom to expect redress, and nothing but a strong convulsion in the state can vindicate them into former liberty; thus the people of Rome, a few great ones excepted, found more real freedom under their Emperors tho' tyrants, than they had experienced in the old age of the common wealth, in which their laws were become numerous and painful, in which new laws were every day enacting and the old ones executed with rigour. They even refused to be reinstated in their former prerogatives, upon an offer made them to this purpose; for they actually found Emperors the only means of softening the rigours of their constitution.

The constitution of England, is at present possessed of the strength of its native oak, and the flexibility of the bending tamarisk, but should the people at any time with a mistaken zeal, pant after an imaginary freedom, and fancy that abridging monarchy was encreasing their privileges, they would be very much mistaken, since every jewel plucked from the crown of majesty would only be made use of as a bribe to corruption; it might enrich the few who shared it among them, but would in fact impoverish the public.

As the Roman senators by slow and imperceptible degrees became masters of the people, yet still flattered them with a shew of freedom, while themselves only were free; so is it possible for a body of men while they stand up for privileges, to grow into an exuberance of power themselves, and the public become actually dependent, while some of its individuals only govern.

If then, my friend, there should in this country, ever be on the throne a King who, thro' good nature or age, should give up the smallest part of his prerogative to the people, if there should come a minister of merit and popularity. – But I have room for no more.

Adieu.

Notes

1. Juvenal, *Satires*, 6, 292-300: Luxury, more deadly than any foe, has laid her hand upon us . . . Since the day when Roman poverty perished, no deed of crime or lust has been wanting to us . . . Filthy lucre first brought in amongst us foreign ways; wealth ennervated and corrupted the ages with foul indulgences.
2. Plato: The race that is laborious by nature.
3. Claudian: The madness of sparing is more savage than the sword.

SELECT BIBLIOGRAPHY

Historical Studies

Dickinson, H.T., *Liberty and Property: Political Ideology in Eighteenth Century Britain* (London, 1977)

Furniss, E.S., *The Position of the Labourer in a System of Nationalism* (New York, 1925)

George, M.D., *London Life in the Eighteenth Century* (London, 1925)

—— *England in Transition: Life and Work in the Eighteenth Century* (London, 1931)

Hay, D. and others, *Albion's Fatal Tree: Crime and Society in Eighteenth Century England* (London, 1973)

Hill, C., *The Century of Revolution* (London, 1961)

—— *Reformation to Industrial Revolution* (Harmondsworth, 1977)

Hirschman, A.O., *The Passions and the Interests: Political Arguments for Capitalism before its Triumph* (Princeton, 1977)

Jarrett, D., *England in the Age of Hogarth* (London, 1974)

Johnson, E.A.J., *Predecessors of Adam Smith: the Growth of British Economic Thought* (London, 1937)

Kramnick, I., *Bolingbroke and his Circle: the Politics of Nostalgia in the Age of Walpole* (Cambridge, Mass., 1968)

Letwin, J., *The Origins of Scientific Economics: English Economic Thought, 1660-1776* (London, 1963)

Macpherson, C.B., *The Political Theory of Possessive Individualism* (Oxford, 1962)

Mingay, G.E., *English Landed Society in the Eighteenth Century* (London, 1963)

Plumb, J.A., *England in the Eighteenth Century* (Harmondsworth, 1950)

Pocock, J.G.A., *The Machiavellian Moment: Florentine Republican Thought and the Atlantic Tradition* (Princeton, 1975)

Polanyi, K., *The Great Transformation* (Boston, 1944)

Vereker, C., *Eighteenth Century Optimism* (Liverpool, 1967)

Viner, J., *The Role of Providence in the Social Order* (Philadelphia, 1972)

Zirker, M.R., *Fielding's Social Pamphlets* (Berkeley, 1966)

Literary Studies

Barrell, J. *An Equal Wide Survey* (London, 1983)

Bloom, E.A. and Bloom, L.D., *Joseph Addison's Sociable Animal* (Providence, Rhode Island, 1971)

Erskine-Hill, H., *The Social Milieu of Alexander Pope* (New Haven, Conn., 1975)

Feingold, R., *Nature and Society: Later Eighteenth Century Uses of Pastoral and Georgic* (New Brunswick, NJ, 1978)

Forsgren, A., *John Gay, Poet 'of a Lower Order'*, 2 vols. (Uppsala, 1971)

Fussell, P., *The Rhetorical World of Augustan Humanism* (Oxford, 1965)

Price, M., *To the Palace of Wisdom* (Carbondale, Ill., 1964)

Sekora, J., *Luxury: the Concept in Western Thought, Eden to Smollett* (Baltimore, Md., 1977)
Williams, R., *The Country and the City* (London, 1975)
—— *Keywords* (Glasgow, 1976)

SUBJECT INDEX